Art as Language

ALSO BY G. L. HAGBERG

Meaning and Interpretation: Wittgenstein, Henry James, and Literary Knowledge

Art as Language

WITTGENSTEIN, MEANING, AND AESTHETIC THEORY

G. L. Hagberg

CORNELL UNIVERSITY PRESS

ITHACA AND LONDON

First published 1995 by Cornell University Press.
First printing, Cornell Paperbacks, 1998.

Library of Congress Cataloging-in-Publication Data

Hagberg, Garry, 1952–
   Art as language : Wittgenstein, meaning, and aesthetic theory /
G. L. Hagberg.
     p. cm.
   Includes bibliographical references and index.
   ISBN 0–8014–3040–2 (cloth : alk. paper)
   ISBN 0–8014–8531–2 (pbk. : alk. paper)
    1. Wittgenstein, Ludwig, 1889–1951. 2. Aesthetics, Modern—20th
century. I. Title
  B3376.W564H25 1995
  111'.85'092—dc20
                                                94–46202

Printed in the United States of America

Cornell University Press strives to utilize environmentally responsible suppliers and materials to the fullest extent possiible in the publishing of its books. Such materials include vegetable-based, low-VOC inks and acid-free papers that are also either recycled, totally chlorine-free, or partly composed of nonwood fibers.

Cloth printing   10 9 8 7 6 5 4 3 2 1

Paperback printing   10 9 8 7 6 5 4 3 2 1

For my mother

CONTENTS

ACKNOWLEDGMENTS

Many parts of this work have benefited from publication in journals or collections and many parts have benefited by presentation to various audiences. I am very grateful to what is at this point a rather large number of editors, readers, conference and colloquium organizers, commentators, respondents and participants, and other somewhat less classifiable *philosophes* for bringing about this pleasantly diversified state of affairs. I regret that it is impossible to name them all here. All the parts have been revised, some strenuously, some slightly. Details of publication and presentation are given below; I thank the editors and publishers for permission to reprint and even more so for their willingness to expose some of this work initially in their pages.

Chapter 1 saw light initially in *The British Journal of Aesthetics* 24, no. 4 (1984): 325–40, Oxford University Press, ed. T. J. Diffey. Chapter 2 was published in *Philosophical Investigations* 9, no. 4 (1986): 257–73, Blackwell, Oxford, ed. D. Z. Phillips. Chapter 3 appeared in *The Journal of Comparative Literature and Aesthetics*, Orissa, India, ed. A. C. Sukla. An early version was presented to the Eastern Division meeting of the American Society for Aesthetics, where William Grimes contributed an incisive commentary. Chapter 4 was published in *The Journal of Aesthetic Education* 22, no. 3 (1988): 63–75, University of Illinois Press, ed. Ralph Smith. An early version was presented to the Graduate Aesthetics Seminar at the University of Oregon, where Robert Herbert helped with finely focused questions; Catherine Wilson very generously contributed to its revisions and reformulations. The final part of this chapter was published in *Philosophy* 61 (1986): 513–17, Cambridge University Press, ed. Renford Bambrough, and was presented to the Tenth International Congress in Aesthetics in Montreal. Chapter 5 saw print in *The Journal of Aesthetics and Art Criticism* 46, no. 2 (1987): 249–58, ed. John Fisher, and was presented to the Pacific Division meetings of the American Society for Aesthetics; here both Roger Shiner and Jay Bachrach were most helpful. Chapter 6 was presented to a meeting of Cambridge aestheticians at Darwin College; it is published here for the first time. The first parts of Chapter 7 were published in *Visual Theory: Painting and Interpretation*, ed. Norman Bryson, Michael Ann Holly, and Keith Moxey (New York: HarperCollins, 1991), pp. 221–30. This piece has its roots in a 1987 NEH Institute on Theory and Interpretation in the Visual Arts; many participants aided this work, but I am indebted particularly to Arthur Danto for conversation then that greatly helped shape the position I take in this chapter, as well as for his kind encouragement since that time. An early version was presented to the Graduate Philosophy Seminar at Cambridge University, where an extensive discussion of it with Robert Stern was very helpful. The final part of this chapter was presented to the Seminar on Wittgenstein: Reason and Disagreement, held at Cambridge, where discussion with Renford Bambrough on the rationality of doubt proved most fruitful; it is published here for the first time. An earlier version of Chapter 8 was presented to the Cambridge Moral Sciences Club, where Hugh Mellor generously provided acute and constructive comments as well as chairing the session; it too appears in print here for the first time.

My debts extend well beyond the already wide range I have indicated. During the initial drafting some time ago of the first parts of this book I was helped in further ways by William Davie, Robert Herbert, Roger Shiner, and particularly Catherine Wilson. More recently, I have benefited a great deal from the support and advice of John Gilmour, Peter Kivy, Michael Krausz, Alex Neill, Richard Shusterman, and, particularly with regard to the final chapters, Renford Bambrough. And it is a pleasure to be able to acknowledge a great debt of long standing to Henry Alexander, whose philosophical example and encouragement have meant much more over the years than can be expressed in this context. An anonymous reader for the Press provided a full, careful, and, indeed, charitable set of comments on the penultimate version; I profited much from the scrutiny, and I send my heartfelt thanks to this mysterious presence. Also, Terence McKiernan-White's meticulous copyediting invariably tightened the connection between what was said and what was meant, and I am grateful for his fine work and discernment. Last, Roger Haydon at Cornell University Press has done his usual superb job of seeing this work along its way from idea to object; those who have enjoyed the benefit of his editorship will know what I mean.

Because the work brought together here spans a decade, I owe a good deal to various institutions as well: The National Endowment for the Humanities, The Pennsylvania State University Capital College Research Council, the Office of the Dean for Research and Graduate Studies and the Humanities Division at Penn State Harrisburg, and Bard College, which provided an Asher B. Edelman Fellowship in support of this project as well as a most stimulating environment for work in aesthetics. Carol Brener (to whom I am also indebted for numerous stylistic suggestions), Renée Horley, Kathleen Jacob, Marie Ratchford, and Jan Russ graciously prepared numerous manuscripts and I remain extremely grateful to them.

GARRY HAGBERG

Annandale-on-Hudson, New York

Introduction

This book attempts to assess the significance of one particular kind of work in the philosophy of language, specifically that of Ludwig Wittgenstein, both for some widely influential systematic aesthetic theories and for some less formalized but nevertheless powerfully influential ways of thinking about artistic meaning.

I begin with chapters on three pre-Wittgensteinian theorists: Susanne Langer,[1] R. G. Collingwood, and Curt Ducasse, now less discussed but nevertheless the perfect exemplar of a familiar type of linguistically based aesthetic theory. Many of the questions we now face throughout the larger field of analytical aesthetics[2] were given shape by these authors in the first half of the century. A theoretical retrospective will highlight those questions in their fundamental formulations, which have shaped our expectations concerning the answers to aesthetic questions and thus our sense of what does and does not constitute aesthetic progress. Indeed, in the post-Wittgensteinian climate, it is now widely understood that any particular conception of linguistic meaning to which one subscribes can shape one's beliefs in related fields of philosophy such as the philosophy

1. As we shall see, the description "pre-Wittgensteinian" does not fit Langer with complete accuracy; her aesthetic theory was built on the atomistic foundations of Wittgenstein's *Tractatus Logico-Philosophicus*. Thus what is intended here, to be precise, is "pre-late-Wittgensteinian."

2. The larger field of analytical aesthetics is very large indeed; interpretative questions possessing the same form as those within technical philosophy arise in visual arts criticism and theory, music criticism and musicology, architectural theory, film aesthetics, performance art, literary theory, and so forth.

of mind, metaphysics and the philosophy of perception, and of course aesthetics.

To take a preliminary example of this shaping power: if one conceives of language in mentalistic terms, whereby meaning is a mental phenomenon only contingently associated with a particular physical sign or specific utterance, one is then led, through the fundamentally influential analogy between language and art, to a number of further assumptions concerning artistic meaning. One such assumption would define the meaning of an artwork as an entity originating in the mind of the artist, a mental object whose existence we infer through the physical work itself. Another assumption, proceeding from the behavioristic conception of language which gives priority to the material over the mental, results in a competing conception of artistic meaning: the artist discovers the work's meaning in the materials of the medium rather than by infusing the materials with significance through the embodiment of an artistic intention. Such views hold immediate significance for criticism as well. On the latter view criticism would seem to function best in isolation from any imputed or stated intention of the artist, as was the case with New Criticism, whereas on the former view criticism would be elucidated in terms of intentional retrieval. Again, this is only a preliminary example; in what follows I try to explore a large number of such relations between aesthetic conception and linguistic preconception.

The first chapter, "Art and the Unsayable," considers a theory of art that is constructed explicitly on linguistic foundations, specifically Wittgenstein's early atomistic philosophy of language. The particular problems discussed include whether artistic meaning lies beyond the sayable and thus cannot be captured in language, and how form in art functions as a determinant of its emotional or expressive content beyond the reach of language. Chapter 2, "Art as Thought," examines the problem of the nature and identity of the work of art, and in particular how the idealist conception of the work of art—that is, as an object created in the imagination—explicitly rests on a theory of linguistic expression. This discussion leads to an assessment of the aesthetic significance of Wittgenstein's criticism of that linguistic theory. The third chapter, "The

Language of Feeling," examines critically the view that, whereas language functions to communicate cognitive meaning, art functions to communicate emotive meaning. I discuss the Lockeian conception of linguistic meaning that underlies this way of construing aesthetic experience, and examine Wittgenstein's critique of that conception. Returning from the linguistic to the aesthetic, the chapter closes with a discussion of some of the ways in which artworks can in fact excite ideas and stimulate emotions and the ways in which meaning is in fact experienced.

Whereas the first chapters of the book center on theories of artistic expression and their linguistically shaped foundations, Chapters 4, 5, and 6 center on the nature and significance of artistic intention, again employing the method of looking into the analogous issues of the nature of linguistic intention and its significance for the understanding of speech. Chapter 4, "Artistic Intention and Mental Image," attempts to unearth some unquestioned assumptions housed within the historical debates over the critical relevance of intention. A prevalent, but, as I argue, too narrow and overly simple conception of intention holds that the material work of art is an embodiment of a prior immaterial mental image, and that the proper function of criticism is to come to an understanding of the artist's initial envisagement through a critical examination of the later material work, or to see behind the work or text for its significance.[3] The linguistic parallel to this aesthetic position requires an investigation into the seemingly obvious but ultimately indefensible suggestion that verbal intention equals silent soliloquy. A subunit of this chapter, "Music and Imagination," continues this investigation with special reference to music, the art that most naturally invites the aesthetic variant of linguistic mentalism. Specifically, some theorists have concluded that, as a musical work cannot be identical with any particular performance of that work, it must be in essence an imaginary object or a mental

---

3. If this view were no longer prevalent, I could have discussed the envisagement–embodiment dichotomy in aesthetic intention as part of the theoretical retrospective mentioned above. This conceptual template is still in wide currency, however, particularly in architectural circles, where the vast majority of work remains unbuilt, or indeed, envisaged but disembodied.

ideal toward which particular performances aspire. The musical work, on this view, assumes the status of a general type rather than a specific instance, or token, of that type, and the general type is regarded as a fully articulated mental or imaginary object. An examination of detailed cases in music, however, shows that the concept of imagination cannot intelligibly occupy the theoretical position assigned it by the aesthetic idealist.

In Chapter 5, entitled "Against Creation as Translation," I discuss the conceptual parallels and dissimilarities between the problems of artistic creation and linguistic translation. Here I argue that the art-language analogy can be powerfully misleading. It implies that the creative act in art can be elucidated using a conceptual model derived from the linguistic case, where it is alleged that a translation from one language to another retains the same mental content but changes the outward sign to which the inner meaning is attached. More generally, this chapter investigates the foundations of the belief that the meaning of an artwork can be captured in another genre, for example, that the content of a poem can be expressed in music or in painting. The final section of this chapter looks into the experience of searching, in writing, to find the right expression, which seems—but only seems—to support a translation model or mental-content-into-physical-embodiment model of intentional meaning.

The linguistic core of the aesthetic views examined in the last section of Chapter 5—that the meaning of an utterance is detachable from its particular outward expression—is investigated in Chapter 6, "The Silence of Aesthetic Solipsism," which ventures into what are often regarded as the darkest recesses of Wittgenstein's philosophy of language, specifically the issue of linguistic privacy. Here, after drawing out explicitly the parallel between the foregoing expressionist and intentionalist conceptions of artistic meaning (where words are allegedly imbued with meaning through inner mental associations between pure thought and outward signs or symbols), the clarifying and demystifying results from Wittgenstein's labors deep within the philosophy of language are brought back to the understanding of the expressive qualities of art. Artistic expression is widely held to be a material embodiment of a prior inner emotional state, and to be the direct artistic analogue to linguistic meaning. In Chapter 6 I argue that this view is itself vulnerable to the private language argument—a relation between linguistic and aesthetic philosophy that is often vaguely sensed but too rarely, I think, articulated. Throughout these middle three chapters, many of the points of intersection between Wittgenstein's philosophy of mind and his philosophy of language are located on the larger terrain of aesthetics.

The way in which aesthetic questions are powerfully shaped by underlying conceptions in mental and linguistic philosophy is also an important theme of my final two chapters, where I reconsider three of the most prominent views developed in post-Wittgensteinian years, which together constitute a strong return to aesthetic theory.[4] In each case I identify both the benefits offered by these theoretical construals of aesthetic experience and the construals of the aesthetic objects with which we engage in that experience. I also identify the issues in Wittgenstein's philosophy which these theories have overlooked and which might prove helpful. In Chapter 7, "The Aesthetics of Indiscernibles," I examine Arthur Danto's method of indistinguishable counterparts, wherein the difference between art and non-art is elucidated in terms, to put it platonically, of that which is available to the intellect but not to the senses. This examination progresses into some proximate issues raised by Wittgenstein on the interrelations between description and perception. There follows a reconsideration of the related, or indeed engendered, institutional theory developed by George Dickie. Of greatest interest here is not the explicit content of the theory itself but, rather, the presuppositions embedded within that aesthetic movement's conceptual foundations. In this context some of Wittgenstein's remarks on the nature of certainty, and on the limits of doubt and the refusal of doubt to submit to the will, become directly relevant to a critical reexamination of the questions faced by institutional theorists.

---

4. For a superb overview of the antitheoretical stance that immediately preceded this return, see Mary Mothersill, *Beauty Restored* (Oxford: Oxford University Press, 1984), pp. 33–73.

In Chapter 8, "Art and Cultural Emergence," I reconsider the ontological questions in art that Joseph Margolis asks and answers, leading to an examination of the ineradicable dualism implicit in certain conceptions of aesthetic entities and, beyond this, to a preliminary consideration of the similarities both between our perception of artworks and persons and between artworks and human beings themselves.

In this Introduction, I have summarized the chapters in a way that brings out their affinities: the first three chapters concern the perception of artistic meaning by the viewer, listener, or reader; the second three chapters concern the mind of the creator of the object whose meaning is perceived; and the final two chapters concern the nature of that object in and of itself. I hope it is also clear from the summaries that the chapters share many common concerns that cut across any general organization. A partial list of the issues treated in the following study would include: the reflection of an emotional state in an art object and the relation of form to feeling; the arguments for and against aesthetic idealism; the dualistic conception of artistic meaning and the excitation of ideas by an object; the relevance of articulated imaginative objects for our understanding of artistic intention and, in musical cases, the complicated relations of sound to thought; the conceptions of meaning generated by applying a model of linguistic translation to aesthetic creation and by searching for a nuanced verbal expression we, somewhat oddly, know we have not yet found; the attempt to conceive of art as a private language and the implications for meaning that such a conception would carry; the relations between perception and description and the shaping influence of earlier philosophy of language on recent aesthetic theory; the doubt concerning artistic definition that is prerequisite to the institutional theory yet unavailable to it in genuine, contextually rooted form; the mind-matter dualism inherent in recent aesthetic ontology; and the parallels between perceiving works of art and seeing human beings. These issues obviously are interrelated in countless and conceptually helpful ways, intersecting in unpredictable places on the larger aesthetic landscape.

Clearly there are in the following pages many formulations and reformulations of dualistic conceptions of aesthetic experience, of artworks, of artistic creation, and of interpretation. I believe that mind-matter dualism has been and, more controversially, continues to be the most powerful shaping influence on aesthetic thought, and that its philosophical unravelling requires attention to detail; the chapters thus engage this fundamental issue in various ways. I have tried in what follows to remain mindful of the fact that Wittgenstein's famous remark concerned a *constant* battle against the bewitchment of our intelligence. The work included here is primarily of a critical-analytical nature. There is obviously much more to be said about Wittgenstein's positive conception of linguistic meaning and its significance for art.[5] The fundamental objective here has been to consider the sources of our problems, to reconsider what these problems in their formulations and structurings presume, and to investigate the significance of Wittgenstein's philosophy for these problems and presumptions. It is true that the theoretical answers to these aesthetic problems have enormously increased in subtlety and sophistication, but the formulations and structurings of the problems themselves have still not, to my mind, received the attention they need.

I do not find general assertions or arguments claiming that art is or is not a language compelling or even minimally satisfying. Assertions are objectionable for obvious reasons (or lack thereof); arguments, when they are stated in a phrase, because they suggest that the connections, parallels, analogies, structural disanalogies, asymmetries, and so forth, are fundamentally simple, implying that a general pronouncement one way or the other will suffice. I tend toward the belief, consistent with Wittgenstein's later philosophy, that these issues are irreducibly complex, and that artistic meaning can no more be succinctly encapsulated or reduced to definitional formulas than can linguistic meaning. Of course, complexity does not preclude conceptual clarity; on the contrary, complexity promotes it. My philosophical aspiration in this book has been to afford, at least occasionally, something approximating a clear view of that complexity.

5. I have pursued this subject in *Meaning and Interpretation: Wittgenstein, Henry James, and Literary Knowledge* (Ithaca: Cornell University Press, 1994).

I   Art and the Unsayable

Perhaps the very last conviction about art we would be willing to give up is that art possesses meaning. Yet when called on to say anything concerning the precise nature of this meaning, one is very often prone to fall mute, not only because of the threat of impending conceptual confusion, but also because of a sense that meaning in art somehow lies beyond the sayable. Standing transfixed before Giorgione's *Tempest* or Rothko's *Green and Maroon*, or on hearing Stravinsky's *Rite of Spring*, we find our conviction that art has meaning deepened. Yet at the same time, with a little reflection, one begins to feel the presence of an impenetrable barrier between aesthetic seeing and saying. In this chapter, in the interest of clarifying and understanding this doctrine of unsayability which enjoys a sort of perennial popularity, I reconsider Susanne Langer's theory of art. It is my hope that this will yield a deeper understanding of a very general conception of artistic meaning by which we are led to look behind or through the work of art for its meaning; this view is by no means limited to those who explicitly endorse Langer's conclusions.

In the first section I consider what it means to say, "Art is the creation of forms symbolic of human feeling."[1] In the second part I will turn to a discussion of the perception of artistic form, for to perceive this is, on this theory, to see the unsayable. In these sections my interest is primarily in the exposition and clarification of a theory that, in spite of its ultimate shortcomings, is not always

---

1. Susanne Langer, *Feeling and Form* (London: Routledge & Kegan Paul, 1953), p. 49.

appreciated for its richness and complexity. In the final section I turn to what I take to be rather serious problems that appear through the attempt to clarify the crucial relationship between the feeling expressed in a work and the form it exhibits.

LANGER'S TRACTARIAN AESTHETICS

Langer claims that art picks up where language leaves off. This would seem at a glance to suggest a radical disanalogy between art and language. In fact, however, it is a claim that stems directly from the thoroughgoing assimilation of art to language, or rather an assimilation to a particular view of language. This view is the Picture Theory of meaning developed in Wittgenstein's *Tractatus*,[2] and it is Langer's adoption of this model of language as a model for art, along with the other components of her theory derived from this adoption, that I want presently to explore.

Traditional theories of expression are unsatisfactory for Langer because she finds them confused about the particular role the emotions play in the experience of art. Rudolf Carnap, for example, committed this error in an encapsulated form when he said, "The aim of a lyrical poem in which occur the words 'sunshine' and 'clouds,' is not to inform us of certain meteorological facts, but to express certain feelings of the poet and to excite similar feelings in us."[3] Langer characterizes this error as a failure to distinguish

---

2. Ludwig Wittgenstein, *Tractatus Logico-Philosophicus* (1922), trans. D. F. Pears and B. F. McGuinness (Atlantic Highlands: Humanities Press, 1974). The influence of the *Tractatus* is central to all of Langer's work and is implicit on almost every page. One place, however, where it is made explicit is in the following quotation: "The logical theory on which this whole study of symbols is based is essentially that which was set forth by Wittgenstein, some twenty years ago, in his *Tractatus Logico-Philosophicus*: 'One name stands for one thing, and another for another thing, and they are connected together. And so the whole, like a living picture, presents the atomic fact.' (4.0311) 'At the first glance the proposition—say as it stands printed on paper—does not seem to be a picture of the reality of which it treats. But neither does the musical score appear at first sight to be a picture of a musical piece; nor does our phonetic spelling (letters) seem to be a picture of our spoken language. . . .' (4.011)." Susanne Langer, *Philosophy in a New Key* (Cambridge: Harvard University Press, 1978), p. 79.

3. Quoted in Langer, *Philosophy in a New Key*, p. 84.

between self-expression and an expressive act in the "logical" sense.[4] A percussionist in a rage may strike out at all the instruments and, in the midst of the clatter, smash the largest mallet into the bass drum. This is the sort of expressive act that is performed with "inner momentary compulsion" and is thus not an expressive act in the artistic sense. If this same percussionist strikes the same drum in exactly the same way in, say, the *1812 Overture*, an artistic act has been performed without inner momentary compulsion, and so "it is no longer *self-expressive*; it is expressive in the logical sense" (152). The beating of the drum is no longer what Langer calls a sign of an inner event such as anger or frustration; it is now a *symbol* of an inner experience. The artistically expressive drum-beating has been improperly understood as a gesture performed in order not only to vent but also to *excite* an emotion, whereas on Langer's theory it is more properly understood as a gesture that *denotes* an emotion or inner experience. To put her words back in context, she says: "But as soon as an expressive act is performed without inner momentary compulsion it is no longer *self-expressive*; it is expressive in the logical sense. It is not a sign of the emotion it conveys, but a symbol of it; instead of completing the natural history of a feeling, it denotes the feeling, and may merely bring it to mind, even for the actor. When an action acquires such a meaning it becomes a gesture" (152). These gestures, then, are "expressive forms, true symbols. Their aspect becomes fixed, they can be deliberately used to communicate the *idea* of the feelings that begot their prototype," (152). Thus from this perspective Carnap's claim, like those of the expression theorists Langer is dissatisfied with, appears false. A physical gesture in dance or a drumbeat in music is not self-expressive for Langer, but logically expressive; not performed for excitation, but for denotation, not—in short—a sign, but a symbol. A dance gesture or a drumbeat can carry meaning on its back, and this meaning she identifies as the idea of a feel-

---

4. Langer, *Philosophy in a New Key*, p. 152. See also p. 83: "According to our logicians, those structures are to be treated as 'expressions' in a different sense, namely as 'expressions' of emotions, feelings, desires. They are not symbols for thought, but symptoms of the inner life, like tears and laughter, crooning, or profanity." See also pp. 218–20.

ing. Artistic activity is essentially, she says, symbolic activity.[5] Let us look more closely at her notion of a symbol.

In the *Tractatus* Wittgenstein began with the famous statement that the world is all that is the case, and what is the case amounts to the sum total of particular states of affairs.[6] These states of affairs, in the external world, are the objects, together with the logical relations that hold between those objects, that are mirrored in language. It is in virtue of this mirroring or picturing of the facts that language possesses meaning, but Langer considers it of special importance that these pictures of states of affairs in the form of propositions are not pictures in a simple photographic sense but rather pictures in a logical sense. In *Tractatus* 2.2 Wittgenstein said, "A picture has logico-pictorial form in common with what it depicts." Similarly, Langer claims that the art symbol bears its resemblance to the inner feeling through a morphological similarity. Wittgenstein gave an account of the meaning of propositions in terms of their logical picturing, or formal similarity to objects and relations in the *external* world,[7] whereas Langer is offering an

5. One example of gestures that carry meaning is a game of charades, in which a player tries to communicate to the audience an idea of some feeling. When the player succeeds, the guesser cries out, "I've got it! It's *jealousy!*" Here, of course, the guesser has the idea, and has acquired it through the reading of gestures. This case, however, goes much further in following a piece of advice of Wittgenstein's than it does in giving content to Langer's theory. Although I certainly do not want here to accuse Langer of "talking bosh," the comparison between an imaginable case in practice and Langer's theory is interesting. Wittgenstein advises, "If someone talks bosh, imagine a case in which it is not bosh. The moment you imagine it, you see at once it is not like that in our case." Ludwig Wittgenstein, *Lectures and Conversations on Aesthetics, Psychology, and Religious Belief*, ed. Cyril Barrett (Oxford: Basil Blackwell, 1966), p. 34.

6. I am not, of course, here trying to provide anything approximating a full exegesis of Wittgenstein's atomistic theory of meaning; it is my intention, rather, to bring out the central components of that view upon which Langer constructs her theory of meaning and communication in art.

7. Wittgenstein was unable to say what precise relation held between the atomistic constituents of the proposition and the state of affairs mirrored by that proposition. As will be seen below, Langer, finding herself unable to answer this, claims that the point is so obvious that we need not take "discursive" account of it. See P. M. S. Hacker, *Insight and Illusion* (Oxford: Oxford University Press, 1972), p. 48; Ludwig Wittgenstein, *Notebooks, 1914–1916* ed. G. H. von Wright and G. E. M. Anscombe, trans. G. E. M. Anscombe (Oxford: Basil Blackwell, 1961), pp. 129–30; and Langer, *Philosophy in a New Key*, p. 82.

account of meaning in art in terms of formal similarity to the *internal* world, the world of inner feeling. This, then, is the precise sense in which art allegedly takes up where language leaves off. Wittgenstein ended the *Tractatus* with the equally famous and even more cryptic remark that whereof we cannot speak, there must we pass over in silence. Langer, however, begins her account of the meaning of art at this point, the point just beyond the reach of language. Whereof we cannot speak, there we must compose, paint, write, sculpt, and so forth.

This brings us to our central question: How, having employed the theory of meaning in the *Tractatus* as the model of meaning in art, can Langer proceed with meanings, if not of words, then of works, beyond the sayable into the unsayable? Here she introduces the distinction between "discursive" and nondiscursive or "presentational" symbols (pp. 79–102). It was, she suggests, the failure to distinguish between these two types of symbols that led Wittgenstein to the error enshrined in the concluding statement of the *Tractatus*.

A discursive symbol is simply a word with a meaning; it is through these symbols that we are able to communicate with each other in everyday discourse. Thus she says that in "language, which is the most amazing symbol system humanity has invented, separate words are assigned to separately conceived items in experience on a basis of simple, one-to-one correlation." Later in that discussion she adds, "A word or mark used arbitrarily to denote or connote something may be called an associative symbol, for its meaning depends entirely on association."[8]

The early Wittgensteinian influence on Langer's thought is further manifested in her historical account of the evolution of language.[9] Understandably overlooking the stage-setting involved,[10]

8. Langer, *Feeling and Form*, p. 30.

9. I should note that, in addition to the strictly Wittgensteinian model, Langer also depends on a Lockeian component in her account of language. In successful communication the speaker, by uttering the word, fires in the mind of a listener the same representation or picture of a given state of affairs that is present in the speaker's mind. See John Locke, *An Essay Concerning Human Understanding* (1690; reprint, New York: Dover, 1959), bk. 3, chap. 2, sec. 8, p. 13.

10. Ludwig Wittgenstein, *Philosophical Investigations*, 3d ed., trans. G. E. M. Anscombe (New York: Macmillan, 1958), sec. 257.

she claims that, in the early phase of language, simple sounds were given meaning by the "clear prominence in the [speaker's] mind" of the object or referent. A listener "grasps a conception of it [the thing referred to] by means of a sound."[11] From this relatively primitive stage of atomistic words with referents, language proceeded to an inclusion of relational symbols. The state of affairs in the world includes, say, a cat and a mat, which stand in a certain relation to each other. This relation is then captured by the symbol "on," and the state of affairs is logically pictured in the sentence.[12] The material furniture of the world itself encourages, in a way that feelings do not, this kind of representation in language; the physical objects to which these symbols refer, and the relations in which they stand to each other, mirrored by relational symbols, provide the solid raw material upon which to build a symbol system—the system that, Langer tells us, we call "language." These symbols, by virtue of their external referents, are discursive.

Now, what of the nondiscursive, or presentational symbols? According to Langer, Wittgenstein, like Russell and Carnap before him, had failed to give the inner life of feeling a proper place in his ontology, and this failure had led to the wholesale exclusion of the inner life in his account of meaning. It is a mistake, she claims, to pass over the inner realm of possible referents just because of their ineffable nature. The vagueness of felt life in comparison with hard external objects has led to the belief "that feeling is a formless affair . . . with no structure of its own. Yet subjective experience has a structure; it is not only met from moment to moment, but can be conceptually known, reflected on, imagined and symbolically expressed in detail and to a great depth. . . . [Art]works are expressive forms, and what they express is the nature of human feeling."[13] Presentational symbols, then, have no discursive referent; they do not mirror a state of affairs in the external world. But they do somehow symbolize inner states of affairs; they mirror

11. Langer, *Philosophy in a New Key*, p. 134.
12. Ibid., p. 135.
13. Susanne Langer, *Problems of Art* (New York: Charles Scribner's Sons, 1957), pp. 7–8.

inner objects of the private world of feeling. Thus nondiscursive symbols have

> a different office, namely to articulate knowledge that cannot be rendered discursively because it concerns experiences that are not *formally* amenable to the discursive projection. Such experiences are the rhythms of life, organic, emotional, and mental . . . , which are not simply periodic, but endlessly complex, and sensitive to every sort of influence. All together they compose the dynamic pattern . . . that only nondiscursive symbolic forms can present, and that is the point and purpose of artistic construction.[14]

To comprehend better this aspect of Langer's theory, we might picture the inner life being connected to a delicately tuned instrument that functions as an emotional seismograph, inscribing the movements of the inner life on a paper roll. The presentational symbol, the work of art, symbolizes that movement by possessing a form like that of the line; the work reflects the inner state of affairs through a formal correspondence. But again, the discursive symbol, we are told, is a *logical* picture of a state of affairs, and it is through the logical-formal similarity of relations, with the external objects referred to by association, that it can operate as a symbol. The presentational symbol is similarly a symbol of an episode of emotional experience in virtue of a logical-formal parallel.

> The tonal structures we call "music" bear a close logical similarity to the forms of human feeling—forms of growth and of attenuation, flowing and stowing, conflict and resolution, speed, arrest, terrific excitement, calm, or subtle activation and dreamy lapses—not joy and sorrow perhaps, but the poignancy of either and both—the greatness and brevity and eternal passing of everything vitally felt. Such is the pattern, or logical form, of sentience; and the pattern of music is that same form worked out in pure, measured sound and silence. Music is a tonal analogue of emotive life.

14. Langer, *Feeling and Form*, pp. 240–41.

Such formal analogy, or congruence of logical structures, is the prime requisite for the relation between a symbol and whatever it is to mean. The symbol and the object symbolized must have some common logical form.[15] *like the Tractatus, she asserts but 1 picture*

Expressive meaning in art, then, is given an explanation which implicitly resides within the traditional dualistic categories of the outward symbolization of inward feeling. Artists, or at least the successful ones, all share a common function: They "give the subjective events an objective symbol"; of their work, Langer adds, "the reason that it can symbolize things of the inner life is that it has the same kinds of relations and elements."[16] Elements and their relations—atomistic particulars in a given state of affairs— provided the material out of which meaning was made in Wittgenstein's early analysis of language, and they are, as we have seen, the materials in terms of which Langer gives an account of meaning in her analysis of art. We are now in a position, however, to see as well the crucial difference between these analytical programs. Langer claims that discursive symbols—sentences—are constructed out of analyzable particulars—words—which assemble in various ways to mirror the particular structure or state of affairs in the world. By contrast, the inner life, she insists somewhat confusingly, affords no similar division into atomistic particulars, and thus the presentational symbols of art are whole indivisible units. There is a correspondence between the structural form of the feeling and the structural form of the created artwork, but these forms are not, Langer insists, amenable to analysis or reduction. This puts the general distinction between presentational and discursive symbols into clearer focus, and shows as well the surface disanalogy between art and language essential to Langer's theory; that is, it shows why, despite their fundamental likeness, art and language do not collapse into each other to become identical. The line of demarcation between the two thus corresponds to the limit of the sayable.

15. Ibid., p. 27.
16. *Problems of Art*, p. 9.

We began with the suggestion that art takes up where language leaves off. This claim is very different from those of the other expression theorists, such as Collingwood and Ducasse, who claim, for admirably detailed reasons, that art *is* a language.[17] Langer says that "music is not a language, because it has no vocabulary,"[18] yet that it is fundamentally similar to language through its symbolic or referential function. In fact, she suggests, in the general development of her symbol-theory of art in *Feeling and Form*, that we replace talk of the "meaning" of music with talk of "the vital import" of music.[19] This article of linguistic legislation is designed to preserve the search for the thing to which the work of art refers as a symbol but at the same time to prevent us from making the mistake of searching for the literal meaning of it—of trying, in short, to articulate the unsayable. Roger Fry and Clive Bell found themselves unable to define "significant form" and yet were quite certain that this did in fact constitute the essence of art.[20] Langer says that, rather than seeing this as a shortcoming, they should have revelled in this fact. The meaning or vital import cannot be translated into literal linguistic form; the real subject matter of art, the inner felt life, does not so translate. One can see here the deeper reasons for her agreement with Bell that the subject matter or the program of a work is irrelevant to its real meaning or vital import. Her theory of artistic meaning thus excludes any references to objects or places, e.g., bowls of fruit or the light of Venice, in the analysis of artistic meaning.

This error of looking for the meaning in literal or discursive terms is, according to Langer, illustrated by the case of Eduard Hanslick's claim that in music, form and content are one, and that the meaning of a phrase *is* the pure musical material and nothing more.[21] The

---

17. R. G. Collingwood, *The Principles of Art* (Oxford: Oxford University Press, 1938); C. J. Ducasse, *The Philosophy of Art* (New York: Dover, 1966).

18. Langer, *Feeling and Form*, p. 31.

19. Ibid., p. 32.

20. See Clive Bell, *Art* (New York: Capricorn, 1958), chap. 1.

21. Langer discusses this in *Philosophy in a New Key*, pp. 237–45. See particularly her discussion of the passages she quotes from Hanslick: "The theme of a musical composition is its essential content" (p. 237); and "In the art of music there is no content opposed to form, because music has no form over and above its content" (p. 237, n. 67).

meaning is in fact something else, Langer says, but what it is, echo-
ing the *Tractatus* in this respect as well, cannot be said but rather
only shown. Thus she claims that the "analogy between music and
language breaks down if we carry it beyond the mere semantic function in general."[22] It is in precisely this way that art and language are
for Langer at the deepest level alike but in a less fundamental way
disanalogous. "Music articulates forms which language cannot set
forth."[23] For Langer, art is the language of the unsayable. I will
return to the question of whether it is possible intelligibly to lessen
the tension of this paradoxical phrase, or even to resolve it.

THE MIRRORING OF EMOTION

Logical atomism and formalism are not the only influences on
Langer's theory of art. When we consider what she says about the
aesthetic experience, it becomes clear that she relies upon a version
of the theory of disinterested aesthetic perception. The need to add
this component to her general theory is felt as soon as we ask how
the symbols of feeling are perceived or recognized by the appreciator of an artwork.

We have already seen that it is the presence of virtual form which
determines aesthetic merit for Langer, and this feature accounts as
well for the essentialist uniformity of the concept of art. Virtual
form, she claims, is the property that all artworks share; indeed,
only through the presence of virtual form *are* they works of art (i.e.,
this quality is definitionally as well as expressively significant).
Not surprisingly, then, a special mode of perception is required to
see this value-laden and defining feature, a mode referred to as
"presentational perception." This mode can be characterized most
succinctly as a form of abstraction. The work is divorced "from its
usual causal and practical surroundings," and it is this divorce
which accounts for what Langer calls the "unreality" of art.[24] What
is of interest in a work of art is, in the way it was for Kant and

---

22. Ibid., p. 232.
23. Ibid., p. 233.
24. See Langer, *Feeling and Form*, pp. 50–63.

Schopenhauer, out of this world: it lies beyond the physical. Thus it is only through this special perceptual channel that the virtual form is visible. The artwork has been defined as a symbol, and "a symbol," she says, "is any device whereby we are enabled to make an abstraction."[25] Let us consider what Langer offers by way of assistance in the attempt to give content to the notion of aesthetic abstraction.

A circus, we are told, is not a work of art, precisely because it lacks virtual form; it lacks "a conception of feeling, something to express."[26] Similarly, food cannot attain the status of art, because its appreciation must remain at the level of sensory pleasure, which is a less rarefied form of perception that virtual form eludes. The implication is that any appreciation of a work of art for its sensuous qualities alone, excluding the abstraction of the virtual form, is not *aesthetic* appreciation at all. These are cases in which what we want to understand—the perceptual act of abstraction—is absent. What, then, are some cases in which it is present? "A shell," says Langer, "cannot be *composed* of concave and convex; [it can] only [be] described that way after the fact."[27] This description presupposes formal abstraction. The shell is indispensably present but the form that it embodies can be seen in the mind's eye, independently from the idea of a shell, as a geometric shape characterized by convexity and concavity. She also offers the examples of lampshades, hands, and waterfalls. Lampshades exhibit particular forms, which we abstract in the instant we see them. This perceptual act, she explains, underwrites our ability to ask for the same shade in a smaller size or different color. She reminds us that we do not mean, in asking for a smaller shade, the very same shade but rather the same form in another instantiation. We employ the same special perceptual mode when we recognize that our two hands, although presented to us with a symmetrical reversed-plan design, are the same. The idea of the virtual form is perhaps made clearer by Langer's illustration of the waterfall, which seems to hang suspended in air. In fact, of course, the overall shape made by

25. Ibid., Preface, p. xi.
26. Ibid., p. 365.
27. Ibid., p. 369.

the moving water remains constant, while the content of that form, the water, rushes downward. If we were to concentrate only on the water itself, she seems to be suggesting, thereby excluding the aesthetic mode of perception and preventing the abstraction of the overall shape or form, we would see only . . . what? Raging water following no predictable path? Similarly, we would see only the seashell, and not its convex and concave forms, and unlike G. E. Moore, we would say, "Here is one hand, and here is . . . something else." Although I will turn to these questions again, clearly the perceptual addition and subtraction one would expect, from Langer's account, to be able to carry out are not easily accomplished.

Langer holds as well that maps and graphs function in essentially the same way as works of art, and that we recognize their meaning in the same way as we do in art. Both are "articulate forms," and their "characteristic symbolic function is *logical expression.*"[28] Maps and graphs give us a view at a glance of, say, the locations and geographical shapes of countries or the course over time of a monetary exchange rate. "Created *Gestalten*"—by this she means unanalyzable symbols similar to maps and graphs—"that give us logical insight into feeling, vitality, and emotional life, are works of art."[29]

Now, we know what the relation is between geographic or economic facts and the maps and graphs that present them. The question we want to ask within aesthetics, however, concerns the relation between the meaning of the artwork and its abstractable essence: what, in short, is the exact relation between feeling and form? As we shall see more clearly, Langer's answer, although perhaps less than one would hope for, is all that one could really expect, given the limitations inherent in her notion of presentational symbols and, in fact, in her acquired model of language itself. What sort of positive account does her theory afford?

Music, for example, "is not self expression, but *formulation and representation* of emotions, moods, mental tensions and resolu-

28. Ibid., p. 31.
29. Ibid., p. 129.

tions—a 'logical picture' of sentient, responsive life."[30] Langer recognizes that for music to function as a symbol, it must have formal
characteristics in common with the thing symbolized. The symbol
must exhibit the same "logical form as that possessed by the object
symbolized."[31] So, even if the idea of *logical* form remains a bit
puzzling, we know that the similarity between symbol and object
is morphological. Wolfgang Köhler, another central influence on
Langer, developed a theory around what he took to be a fundamental similarity between the dynamics of the inner life and the
dynamics of music; words like "crescendo," "diminuendo,"
"accelerando," and "ritardando" can be aptly applied to each.[32]
Langer notes that these terms apply as well to "the description of
overt behavior, [which is] the reflection of inner life in physical
attitudes and gestures." She also notes that the "expressive gestic-
ulations of the conductor" (226) reflect the expressive form of the
music. To review, then, we are given (1) formal properties in physical behavior or movement that symbolize through a commonality
of form, (2) feelings of the inner life, and (3) a realm of the formal
properties of art—"vital forms" (227)—which like physical behavior have a formal resemblance to the events or entities of the inner
life, and also thereby symbolize them. All of these—behavior, feelings, and art—may exhibit "patterns of motion and rest, of tension
and release, of agreement and disagreement, preparation, fulfill-
ment, excitation, sudden change, etc." (228). Any particular pattern
will have the same expressive meaning in each of the three realms:
melancholy will take the same form physically, emotionally, or
graphically. At one point Langer concludes that the "requirement
of a connotative relationship between music and subjective experience, a . . . similarity of logical form, is certainly satisfied" (228).
We are, however, told—and this is where the disappointment mentioned above is felt—that one should not try to say anything about
the exact nature of this formal similarity. One should not try to
explain it because, here returning to the *Tractatus* influence, one
cannot explain it. The artwork is a symbol of the inner life whose

30. Langer, *Philosophy in a New Key*, p. 222.
31. Ibid., p. 225.
32. See ibid., pp. 226–37 for Langer's discussion of this.

very nature defies the linguistic projection that language is thought to involve (35). Thus at this juncture a defender of the doctrine of unsayability must plead self-evidence: "Once the work is seen purely as a form, its symbolic character—its logical resemblance to the dynamic forms of life—is self-evident. We need not even take discursive account of it."[33]

At this point one may begin to suspect that the unsayability doctrine has gone out of control. The suspicion derives from this fact: It is one thing to be limited in what we can say about the expressive or emotional content of particular works of art, and it is quite another thing to be limited in what we can say to explain the *theory* designed to show how those works possess meaning. What can be discursively captured may have limits, but this fact—if it is a fact—in no way justifies the ultimately obscurantist and very different claim that the "logical resemblance" between work and feeling, a resemblance that must be understood if the theory is to prove illuminating, need not itself be explained. On the *Tractatus* model of language, we determine the truth of a proposition by holding it up against the facts it reflects; in short, we compare words with the world.[34] In the next section I examine the parallel relation in art; holding the external work of art up to the inner world of emotion, or in other words, comparing the form and the feeling.

33. *Problems of Art*, p. 42.

34. It should be stated, however, that the word-to-world comparison in the *Tractatus* that Langer employs as a conceptual model is not by any means itself transparent or unproblematic; thus the problem in Langer's theory at this stage can be seen as the aesthetic manifestation of Wittgenstein's early linguistic problems. If, indeed, as Wittgenstein came to see in his criticism of his own early work, nothing can be meaningfully said about the relationship between language and the world, or about the isomorphism between proposition and fact, then the propositions of the *Tractatus* that address that isomorphic relation must themselves be meaningless. (It can be argued that Wittgenstein sensed this problem well before he investigated and clarified it; the very image of the ladder which must be climbed and then kicked away anticipates metaphorically what he was later to elucidate fully.) Wittgenstein's recognition of the incoherence of the position that such relations can be shown but not said (i.e., that the Picture Theory of meaning if correct cannot be meaningfully stated, and thus that it not only is not but in fact could not be true), led him ultimately to abandon this entire word-world construction of the very problem of meaning. Langer, staying within this construction of the problem in aesthetic guise, i.e., form-feeling relations, is thus understandably led into, as we shall see below, insuperable difficulties.

FEELING IN FORM

From the preceding discussion we know that there is, in Langer's view, a special perceptual mode which, if not identical with aesthetic experience, is at least necessary for that experience. We also know that, in some still rather ill-defined way of seeing or hearing, this perceptual mode involves disinterestedness and abstraction, and furthermore that it is this mode which gives us access to the unsayable.

Given that the direct and positive characterization of this variety of perception is a troublesome enterprise, it would seem a reasonable strategy to look for cases where it initially is *not* present and then try to see what difference would be made by its addition. At this point, however, we already want to know how, to take one case, the perception of a waterfall could be described while totally excluding considerations of form. By form it becomes clear that Langer means, of course, the shape or contour of a thing. Because the waterfall is composed of rushing water, so are we to conclude, as she seems to suggest, that rushing water is in fact present or given in experience, and that the form or shape made by the cascading water is what she calls a virtual image, a sort of perceptual illusion? We could with propriety speak of such an illusion if the content were intelligibly separable from the form, but here it is not at all clear that this is the case, precisely because it is not clear how to describe the simple perception of content alone. We cannot suppose that the perception of rushing water, with no determinate direction or shape or contour, would be the simple perception on which the virtual image (the arched constant form of the waterfall) would rest, because we do, *elsewhere*, in mutually exclusive circumstances, have just such a perception. This is what we see when a dam breaks and water rushes wildly in all directions. Obviously this is *not* a component in what one (on this perceptual model) would conceive of as the "complete" (form-with-content) perception of a waterfall. A dam breaking and a waterfall are simply and obviously different things; they do not share a simple perceptual ingredient.

Perhaps this argument is unfair to Langer, in that it insists on too rigid a distinction between form and content and restricts the perception of form exclusively to this special abstracting mode of perception. Given her general view of perception, however, it is hard to see how this defense could be sustained. Behind her specific theory of aesthetic perception lies the familiar general view that we perceive known objects rather than unrecognizable sense-data in all specific instances of seeing and recognizing because we have, early in our perceptual histories, abstracted the forms of things and retained these as concepts of those things. With this mental catalogue, our new or current perceptions fall into the forms abstracted from our previous experiences. At first we abstract the form unconsciously, she says, and later use it to bring order to otherwise chaotic sensory experiences by assembling those experiences under concepts.[35] It is then far from unfair to search for an understanding of the pre-formal or pre-abstracted experience. It is in fact precisely this, and only this, which would demonstrate the importance of this mode of perception.

A waterfall is not, however, composed of formless rushing water upon which an illusion of form—a virtual image—is built. Nor does a seashell seem to be a mass of variously colored, hard, plasterlike material, whose concave and convex sides we "see" above the mere mass or content. We might, at an imitation-seashell factory, see long flat rolls of this hard, colored, plasterlike substance rolling off a machine, and ask what it is. We might hear the foreman at that moment say happily, "There they are; twenty new shells!" We may then marvel that the flat sheet will soon, inside another machine, be cut up and formed into shells like those we saw in the front display case. But it takes no argument to show that our perception of a seashell on the beach contains nothing of this story. Our seeing of one is not transformed into the seeing of the other through an act of abstraction.

Langer says, however, that the disinterested state is an essential condition for the abstraction, whatever it is, to take place. This disinterested state is achieved by lifting the aesthetic object out of its ordinary practical surroundings and divorcing it from its usual connotations in life. Let us see how this could operate.

---

35. See Langer's *Philosophy in a New Key*, pp. 89–90 and p. 146, for her discussion of this issue.

An object of potential aesthetic interest, say a coffee cup, can be elevated out of its functional role—that is, one may cease to see it as the container of coffee, the object that must be carried back into the kitchen and washed—and see it as pure form. This disinterested view of the cup allows its aesthetically significant features to emerge. Whatever else abstraction may be, it is the mental act that permits the emergence of the aesthetic features. There does seem to be something undeniable here, for if we want to appreciate the cup for its particular shape or form, then we should suspend all purely practical considerations. It has become a common practice at this juncture, however, to exclude as well matters of *content*, where this is opposed to pure form, and this is to conflate the distinction between form and function with that between form and content. When the practical interest of the cup—its function—is ruled out on grounds of aesthetic irrelevance, one feels fairly confident that a reasonable move is being made in the attempt to shed light on the special way we see objects of art. It is, however, a much larger and very different point to declare content irrelevant to the question of meaning. In this way the letter and spirit of the rather simple point regarding the cup is first distorted and then inflated, the former through the conflation of content and function, and the latter by elevating it to the status of a first principle of aesthetic perception. Let me give an example.

In the Tomb of Lorenzo de Medici in Florence, Michelangelo designed with great care the formal organization of elements. Above the sarcophagus on one side of the room we find a statue of a robust, active Medici. On the opposite wall, above the other sarcophagus, is a restful, contemplative Medici. Upon each of the sarcophagi are two reclining statues, representing morning and evening, and day and night. Distinctions and contrasts are balanced within the room, and opposing or contrasting forces are placed so as to counteract each other. Any individual subsection of the overall work (for instance, either wall taken separately), remains unbalanced, but the whole form is perfectly balanced and, once one sees the formal organization, restfully resolved. The perception of this form—the "abstraction" of the formal design of the room—is dependent, however, upon its allegedly irrelevant content or subject matter. We must refer to the content of the design if we are to see its balanced contrasts: active and contemplative, morning and evening, waking and sleeping, and so on. Were we to lift the sculpture in this room above its subject matter, we would at the same time lose access to the form. This, in fact, is perhaps to say too much: it is not that the form depends on the subject matter for its existence; rather, it is not in this case clear how to distinguish one from the other.

The form is the aspect or dimension of the work that we are to abstract; it is this which allegedly carries aesthetic meaning. Langer, on this point, acknowledges a debt to Fry and Bell and thinks it clear why aesthetically relevant form lies beyond description. Indeed, on her view, all matters of content *must* be excluded, because that which is amenable to discursive projection is thereby aesthetically irrelevant, and content is clearly in that category. It appears, however, that in order to *see* what is of central importance to the theory we must rely on the very thing the theory prohibits. To take another case, a disinterested and formally abstracted perception of Picasso's *Guernica* would not yield an uncluttered, undistorted, and immediate recognition of the aesthetic meaning the work possesses. It would yield rather a confusing array of disconnected images and an utter failure to comprehend and to feel the force of the work. There is, however, a clear formal organization in the painting, a three-panel scheme derived from medieval altarpieces. But it is not clear what role this compositional form would play in Langer's account of artistic meaning. With this we arrive at a question parallel to one in the theory of language. Just as that theory inquires into the relation between the proposition and its meaning, we must ask whether the form of the work, e.g., sonata-allegro, rondo, tripartite altarpiece, theme and variations, Sophoclean tragedy, and so forth, is significant in Langer's account. We know that the form holds the key to the unsayable, and yet it appears that one must answer both "absolutely" and "absolutely not" to our question. Why is this?

Taking the latter answer first, it is clear that, given her conception of language acquired from the early Wittgenstein, we should not be able to take discursive account of, or explain, any particular case of artistic meaning. From this Langer concludes that there is nothing we can say in answer to this question. Again, this does not in itself imply that there is also nothing that can be said regarding the *connection* between the particular feeling captured in a work and the form of the work, because the relationship in theory between feeling and form is not itself among those nondiscursive feelings. If, however, we pass over this problem as Langer does, and recall first that the inner life of feeling cannot be fitted properly by language, and second that the significant form of the artwork, like the inner feeling it symbolizes, is nondiscursive (because presentational forms are unsayable), we will arrive at the negative conclusion. The form of the work, to the extent that it is verbally specifiable, cannot itself constitute the "virtual form" of the theory. There is a direct parallel here to the linguistic theory. Wittgenstein had said that the connection between the form of a proposition and the form of the world which it pictures is irrelevant to philosophy— that it is a question for empirical psychology. The relation between feeling and form also remains ultimately unexplained. This is Langer's official position, to which she holds when she has the parallel limitations of the Tractarian account of language clearly in mind, but at other times she seems to suggest otherwise. Perhaps when a work of art rather than a theory of language is foremost in the mind, she seems to rely on the specific formal structure of a work, e.g., sonata-allegro form, as that which gives content to the idea of a symbol of feeling. This clearly leads to our other and far less mystifying answer above—"absolutely."

Langer says that a musical performance will be good "if a virtuoso is free of confusing emotions [and is able to] think in musical forms only and [of] their import."[36] It would appear from this that it is the musical form itself, such as the theme-and-variations structure, that carries the aesthetic significance or meaning. In this connection Langer cites the case of Schubert, who told his students that the meaning of the piece cannot be grasped until the form is seen clearly, but at this point the first in a sequence of similar problems arises.

36. Langer, *Feeling and Form*, p. 146.

It may well be that sound musical performance depends on musical form, but this fact, when integrated into Langer's general account of artistic meaning, does more harm than good. The level of analysis at which "form" is to be understood remains in question, but if the overall structural form is meant, insuperable problems appear. All pieces written in theme-and-variations form would have the same meaning, since they would necessarily, in virtue of that form, symbolize the same feeling. So the *Goldberg Variations* would have the same meaning, or at least the same "vital import," as, say, Fernando Sor's *Variations on a Theme of Mozart.* Any theory that produces this result has failed, as a quick listening to those two works in succession will make obvious. There are, however, worse aspects of the same problem. For example, the form of one part of Shakespeare's *Timon of Athens* is clearly a theme and variations. Timon has fallen into irreparable financial ruin, and his previous courtly acquaintances come to visit him in sequence, having heard that he has yet a little more gold. Now, if a particular feeling is symbolized by the structural form, and if the *Goldberg Variations* were poured into that same form, then that part of *Timon* and the *Goldberg Variations* must have the same meaning because they refer to or symbolize the same feeling. This conclusion can only operate as a reductio; it is prima facie clear that *Timon* has nothing to do with the *Goldberg Variations*.

With the possibility of a role for large-scale form looking increasingly hopeless, perhaps we should turn to a consideration of small-scale formal significance. It may be objected, in Langer's defense, that the large form is not the proper unit of meaning, and that in music it is the phrase, or at least the smaller-scale formal analysis of phrase structure, which will reveal the connection between form and feeling.

As might be predicted, however, the problem of the sameness of meaning still appears, although at a lower level. If the phrase structure of the exposition of one orchestral work in sonata-allegro form turns out to be identical to that of another, then here again there is no way for Langer to claim consistently that the two different works do not symbolize the same feeling and thus carry the same artistic meaning. If we find, say, a first theme in the tonic key, with antecedent-consequent phrase structure, followed by a transition figure to the second theme on the dominant with similar phrase structure in the first work, and find this again and again in other works, then within the confines of this analytical scheme we are committed to much more than we otherwise would be—which is simply that the works have the same form and the same phrase structure. We would be committed to the far stronger claim that they have, as was the case with the larger forms, the same meaning. If this is the proper level of analysis on which to make out the feeling-form connection, then there must be one specific feeling whose felt form corresponds to, or is mirrored by, antecedent-consequent phrase structure. At this point we descend to the next lower level of analysis.

Here it might be claimed that it is the particular intervallic structure and contour of the phrase that is the proper unit of meaning. Thus the symbol would operate, rather than at the level of antecedent-consequent structure, at the level of a descending major third, followed by an ascending second, followed by a descending minor third. Here again, however, this particular intervallic form is not unique to the opening bars of Beethoven's *Fifth Symphony*. This sequence of intervals occurs in many other passages in music, and it frequently occurs in improvised music. We must then ask whether the opening section of the *Fifth Symphony* and the improviser's solo line have the same meaning, and it is abundantly clear that they do not. The same problem pursues us to any level of formal analysis, and thus sends us back empty-handed to the question: What does form, as we know it in works of art, have to do with the feeling-form connection in Langer's theory? We must return to the previous answer, and reply: nothing. This is just to say that within this theory the word "form" is being employed in some unrecognizable or systematically elusive way. We should also recognize that in making all works of art essentially works of form, many aesthetically crucial distinctions that we do in fact make between works are blurred or obliterated. Mendelssohn's *Midsummer Night's Dream*, which follows a perfectly predictable path, and through-composed pieces, which unfold in the absence of any formal design that predates the content of the composition, are all seen as the embodiments of form. Renaissance portraiture and the late-period Turner are similarly run together. A Bach fugue, a bel canto aria, and Gregorian Chant are homogenized into a mixture of works that share "vital form." There are issues of great interest concerning the *differences* of forms in these cases but, first, such differences are lost to the generality of the theory, and second, it is in the end impossible to clarify the significance of the form for the meaning of the work. The doctrine of unsayability, at least when given this theoretical formulation, conceals at its core an element of impenetrable unclarity.

FORM, in its abstraction and in its morphological mirroring of emotion, is central to Langer's explanation of art, yet a clear understanding of the role played by either abstraction or form in the creation or appreciation of art remains a mystery. The paradoxical tension we discovered earlier, that art is the language of the unsayable, cannot be resolved. Langer's explanation of the expressive power of art rests on the assimilation of art to the *Tractatus* theory of language, which has in turn generated the presumption that if art is to have meaning or significance, it must acquire this meaning by mirroring or symbolizing some other thing—a state of affairs that in the case of art would be internal. Thus the work of art itself, on this conception of meaning, is in a sense relegated to a position of secondary importance; the meaning behind the work, or what the work symbolizes, is of central aesthetic interest. The word, taken on the atomistic theory to be a mere dead sign, must get its life by reaching out to another thing, its meaning. And the work of art, it is thought, must operate in the same way in getting its life and expressive power.

Indeed, the last thing I want to deny is that art possesses expressive power and meaning, but it can be denied that this particular attempt to explain that power and meaning is adequate to the task. Wittgenstein came to see his early view of language as deeply misleading, and fundamentally ill-formulated in terms of the sign and its life.[37] The above considerations suggest that such a model

---

37. See, for instance, the early parts of Ludwig Wittgenstein, *The Blue and Brown Books* (Oxford: Basil Blackwell, 1958), pp. 5–11.

applied to art also ultimately obscures more than it can illuminate, and that the conception of artistic meaning housed in this theory must not merely be altered but exchanged for another. That alternative conception could be as radically different as the late Wittgensteinian conception of meaning is from the early one, a conception that escapes the dualistic categories of inner feeling and outer symbol.[38] Another theorist of artistic expression, R. G. Collingwood, built his aesthetic theory on somewhat different linguistic foundations; it is his view to which we turn next.

38. This alternative conception of meaning in art of course calls for its own discussion, which I will take up in following chapters; I have also discussed this at greater length in my *Meaning and Interpretation: Wittgenstein, Henry James, and Literary Knowledge* (Ithaca: Cornell University Press, 1994).

2 Art as Thought

The belief that art is a language, or that it is in a deep sense analogous to language, is among the most pervasive of assumptions in the theory of art. In this chapter I reconsider, both for intrinsic interest and as an exemplary case of a more general theoretical and critical direction, R. G. Collingwood's merger of language and art, specifically the notion that art and language are essentially alike in serving as physical expressions of preexistent mental or imaginary objects.

After a fresh examination of Collingwood's actual reasoning—which will itself shed light on one of the many frequently presumed but rarely clarified analogies between language and art—I will discuss this alleged dualistic correspondence, first in language, in connection with some remarks of Wittgenstein on the link between thinking and saying, and second in art, by considering particular cases that seem to hold promise as illustrations of the analogous correspondence between thoughts and works. My strategy is again based on the conviction that the nature of artistic meaning can be illuminated by reference to linguistic meaning only if we first clarify with considerable precision the particular theory of language employed for the analogy. Care is necessary here because the analogy we choose will shape, perhaps to a greater extent than is often realized, our consequent conceptions of the communicative, expressive, and meaningful dimensions of art.

COLLINGWOOD AND AESTHETIC PERCEPTION

In *The Principles of Art* Collingwood reaches the conclusion that art must be (1) imaginative, and (2) expressive. In those respects, art is not merely analogous but in fact identical to language.[1] "What kind of thing must art be, if it is to have the two characteristics of being expressive and imaginative? The answer is: Art must be language."[2] That Collingwood said this is widely known; precisely why he made this claim, however, is somewhat less generally appreciated. Essential to Collingwood's view of the mind is the distinction between the "psychical" level and the "imaginative" level of experience, a distinction derived from Hume's contrast between impressions and ideas. At the psychical level we are passive receptors of sense impressions, which are as yet unrefined by formulation into an imaginary object. Through an imaginative act, those unsophisticated impressions are then transformed into an "idea." That idea, which exists only at the imaginative level of experience, is, in keeping with the empiricist strain in Collingwood's thought, constructed out of the crude, unprocessed sense impressions, and it is that imaginative construction which may then go on to be externalized or expressed. Thus experience, at the psychical level, consists only of raw material. Here one does not recognize familiar people, things, or places, but only patches of color and light, auditory impressions, olfactory impressions, and so on, all still dissociated. It is the ideas, again in accordance with the traditional empiricist view, that render this chaos coherent. Associations are made between particular impressions, and expectations are established; things, people, and places are created out of the sensory chaos and become familiar and recognizable, through the mentally creative act of synthesis achieved at the imaginative level.

Up to this point this is a very familiar philosophical story, and one might ask what precisely it has to do with the assimilation of art to language. The answer is that the assimilation is effected through the introduction of both a common element and a com-

1. R. G. Collingwood, *The Principles of Art* (Oxford: Oxford University Press, 1938), p. 273.
2. Ibid.

mon process, and it is at that point that Collingwood's theory departs from the familiar.

Each raw sensum, he claims, is infused with an emotional charge. Thus, for Collingwood, if we are perceiving it follows that we are feeling as well: cogito, ergo sentio. At the psychical level of experience, those charges, like the impressions to which they are conjoined, are also crude and as yet unrefined or unspecified. Thus the perceiver, if he were able to speak at this prelinguistic level, would utter, "I feel, I know not what."[3] It is only when the crude emotion is processed by imagination and thus brought to the level of imaginative experience that it is specified. This way of casting the matter is, however, in a way slightly untrue to Collingwood's somewhat elusive, and perhaps theoretically oscillating account. The emotion is not only specified or brought into clearer focus; it is—he insists—in part created by the imagination. Only the emotional charge, a sort of generalized perceptual current, is originally present, and it is this which is sculpted in the imagination into a particular emotion. Thus he says, "At the level of imaginative experience, the crude emotion of the psychical level is translated into idealized emotion, or the so-called aesthetic emotion, which is thus not an emotion preexisting to the expression of it, but the emotional charge on the experience of expressing a given emotion, felt as a new coloring which that emotion receives in being expressed."[4] This process accounts for the transition from "I feel, I know not what" to, for instance, "When I see that old white covered bridge I feel a vague longing for earlier days, when we...." In this case, directing our attention toward the old bridge produces the raw impressions: white patches, dark areas, the sounds made by what we cannot yet describe as the babbling brook underneath, and so on. All of those impressions come with a raw emotional charge, but, as with the bridge and brook, they have not yet achieved the status of specifiable ideas of the imagination. When the experience is elevated to the imaginative level, however, we do recognize all those things, and we also recognize the specific emotional charac-

3. Ibid.
4. Ibid., p. 274.

ter that only the idea possesses.[5] Here it becomes clearer why, for
Collingwood, perceiving is feeling. Every sensation has an emotional coloring in the same way it has, say, a shape; and just as, at
the imaginative level we see the shape as a bridge, we feel the emotional coloring as, for example, longing. It is also becoming clearer
why art and language are for Collingwood not analogous, but rather
two instances of essentially the same phenomenon. The white
patches, dark areas, and so forth, constitute the impressions, with
their crude emotional charge attached; the imagination assembles
the impressions and charge into a coherent idea. That idea, now
assembled, in turn gives rise to a particular emotion, and a result
ensues. This result, whether it be language or art, is the expression
or externalization of the inner object of the imagination. Just after
the passage quoted, Collingwood says, "Similarly, the psycho-phys-
ical activity on which the given emotion was a charge is converted
into a controlled activity of the organism, dominated by the consciousness which controls it, and this activity is language or art."[6]
The active role played by the imagination here cannot be overem-
phasized; the initial cause which leads to the twin effects of language or art is an object *created* in the imagination out of the raw
material of sensory impressions and emotional charges. Thus the
imaginary object occupies the same place in the explanatory
schema for art and for language; this location of the imaginary
object within the explanatory schema is—and here is the conceptual core of Collingwood's connection between art and language—
the element they hold in common:

> It [this activity which is language or art] is an imaginative experi-
> ence as distinct from a merely psycho-physical one, not in the
> sense that it involves nothing psycho-physical, for it always and

5. There is a remote context in which this language has ready application. If we
were taken to the bridge drugged, at first we would see only white patches, dark areas,
and hear noises. Then, as the drug wears off, we begin to make out the bridge and the
babbling water. With this, let us suppose, comes a vague longing. But this linguistic
criticism is perhaps premature; I am interested here in merely showing the progression
from Collingwood's metaphysics of experience to his philosophy of language, and how
it culminates in his aesthetic theory.

6. Collingwood, *Principles of Art*, p. 274.

necessarily does involve such elements, but in the sense that none of these elements survive in their crude state; they are all converted into ideas and incorporated into an experience which as a whole, as generated and presided over by consciousness, is an imaginative experience.[7]

It is through this analysis of perceptual experience that Collingwood's initial conclusion is reached. Art, like language, is in its essence both imaginative and expressive. The element shared by language and art—that which can move outward to one or the other—is the object of imagination. The common process that both undergo is the process of expression: from raw to refined experience, impressions to ideas, from patches and undifferentiated emotional charges to imaginary objects. The result is an external representation in the form of an utterance or a work of art. It is important to bear in mind for the following discussion of the idealist definition of the nature of artworks that expression, for Collingwood, is a two-fold process. First—this is the imaginative act—the imaginary object which is still to be expressed is created in the imagination out of the raw sensory particulars. Second, that imaginary object—and here is the expressive act—finds, contingently, its outward manifestation.

In what follows I want to focus on what we may now identify as the crucial component essential and peculiar to idealist theories of art. Having followed Collingwood's argument we have arrived at the notion of an invariable one-to-one correspondence between an imaginary object or a particular mental state and its outward manifestation in language or art. Collingwood's theory thus implies that for every utterance in language there is a mental experience or event—the imaginary object—of which the utterance is, presuming the work is successful, the perfect outward expression. His theory also implies, of course, that the imaginary object temporally as well as logically *precedes* the expression. Similarly, for every physical object which we designate an artwork there is a determinate state of mind—the imaginary object—for which the physical work

7. Ibid., p. 274.

serves as an outward mirror. In short, just as thinking is believed to stand behind speaking, so thinking is presumed to stand behind a work of art, in a one-to-one relationship with it.

very pointed

"YES, THIS PEN IS BLUNT"

This passage from Wittgenstein provides the materials for an investigation into the dualistic correspondence between thought and word:

> Is thinking a kind of speaking? One would like to say it is what distinguishes speech with thought from talking without thinking.—And so it seems to be an accompaniment of speech. A process, which may accompany something else, or can go on by itself.
>
> Say: "Yes, this pen is blunt. Oh well, it'll do." First, thinking it; then without thought; then just think the thought without the words.—Well, while doing some writing I might test the point of my pen, make a face—and then go on with a gesture of resignation.—I might also act in such a way while taking various measurements that an onlooker would say I had—without words—thought: If two magnitudes are equal to a third, they are equal to one another.—But what constitutes thought here is not some process which has to accompany the words if they are not to be spoken without thought.[8]

Bearing in mind that linguistic correspondence serves as the general conceptual model for aesthetic idealism and that word and work are each believed to bear the same relationship to thought, I will consider some particular cases suggested by this passage in detail and examine its philosophical force.

First, imagine skimming newspaper headlines looking for a specific article. With this kind of haste, fly over the lines, "Yes, this pen is blunt. Oh, well, it'll do." Second, imagine yourself about to

8. Wittgenstein, *Philosophical Investigations*, 3d ed., trans. G.E.M. Anscombe (New York: Macmillan, 1958), sec. 330.

make your stage debut with this one line. You're seated at the desk, on the stage, and the curtains are about to go up. You run over the line slowly and deliberately, "hearing" yourself say it in your mind's ear again and again. Finally, curtain up, you say it, precisely as the director wanted it said. Third, imagine a tyrannical executive addressing a personal secretary who has brought him some documents to sign. "This pen is *blunt*!" the executive roars, and then murmurs, "Oh well, it'll do," and signs the papers. Fourth, imagine just having gone to the department office to get a new pen and finding that the new one is no better than the old. The secretary sees you get the pen, and later comes to your office to get your signature. The pen doesn't work well, and so the secretary says, "I thought you got a new one—why don't you use it instead?" At that moment the secretary sees the old one discarded and says, "Oh, is *that* it?" "Yes," you reply, "*this* pen is blunt. Oh well, it'll do," and you go on with the signatures. Fifth, imagine a much abused office worker replying to what he takes to be a stupid question, "Yes, this pen is blunt," seething all the while. For good measure, the office worker mocks the supervisor's favorite phrase, adding, "Oh well, it'll do," and, grumbling, returns to the task.

Those five cases, if we are to locate all cases within the categories of "thinking it" or "saying it without thought," which are the first two of the three categories Wittgenstein has established, must be identified as "thinking it." This list could be continued indefinitely, but without further comment at this point, let us turn to the second category, that of speaking "without thought." What sort of case might illustrate that category? The following example holds at least preliminary promise.

A spy weapon—a "pen"—has been invented that ejects a poison needle. One spy observes his absent-minded colleague scratching out a memo with this instrument. The first spy asks, "Isn't that pen perhaps a bit blunt?" for the bluntness of the weapon is the only way to distinguish it from its normal standard-issue counterpart. Furiously scribbling, obviously in a great hurry, the second spy replies, without looking up and without stopping writing, "Yes, this pen is blunt. Oh well, it'll do." Suddenly, a moment later, with a start, number two shouts, "Oh! Blunt!" and drops the weapon. This

is decidedly a case of a thoughtlessly spoken line, but whether it is
a case of saying it "without thought" in the requisite sense is less
clear, because it is not obvious that a given mental process that is
normally present has been subtracted. It is rather that the special
significance of "blunt," a significance that arises out of the details of
this assuredly rather curious case, has been not subtracted but simply forgotten. Thus even a rather extreme and obviously tailor-made
case fails to illustrate properly the second category, that of speaking
"without thought." Thought and speech seem not to be detachable
in the way implied by the idealist correspondence theory.

To press the point further, let us suppose that in order to reveal to
the audience that a secret letter is being written feverishly by a the-
atrical character, a stage director has the letter writer on stage say
those lines very blandly and thoughtlessly, with a false sounding
"Oh well," to indicate that the character is entirely preoccupied by
the thought of getting the letter off. Now, the letter writer does say
the line thoughtlessly and does not really listen to the offer of a new
pen. The writer is wholly absorbed in scribbling the letter. This
case, however, would not be accurately described as one mental
entity or state, the "I've-got-to-get-the-letter-off" state, occupying
the space of, and thereby eliminating, the "Yes-this-pen-is-blunt"
state. The explanation of the case is thus not that the conceptual
room for the mental entity—what we are regarding on this view as
the meaning—of "Yes, this pen is blunt" was already taken by the
"letter-off" meaning. Hence, and here is the significance for the idealist conception and its implicit presumption of the separability of
thought from word, it could not be adequately explained as a case in
which the words are present without their normally conjoined
thoughts. Although it initially seems to provide a clear case of "talking without thinking," on closer inspection the case fails to give
content to these categories. Here again thinking and saying do not,
under investigation, conform to the simple laws of addition and subtraction.

Wittgenstein's third category, of particular interest for the art-
language analogy as it applies to artistic conception, is that of just
thinking the thought without the words. This is illustrated by the
writer who makes a face, shrugs his shoulders, and goes on. If he is

asked, "Did you just now think that the pen was blunt, but that it would do?" the answer is probably affirmative. But we must further ask if whatever went through the mind of the writer in this case also accompanied the thought in all cases above in the first section, those placed (with reservations) into the category of speaking "with thought." It is obvious that there was no such common element indisputably present in all these cases, a mental entity which led outward to its physical expression in the form of those words. And this is precisely Wittgenstein's point in the next example, where an onlooker gives an account of what someone wielding a tape measure thought while measuring. If the measurer is asked whether or not he thought of the formula "If two magnitudes are equal to a third, they are equal to one another," he may well answer in the affirmative. This may, however, amount to no more than his *using* the formula, which he has done in building countless times a day for years. The thought he has in measuring is not the complex thought that the young student tries to assemble, piece by piece, upon first hearing this formula having to do with two lengths equalling a third and so on. Thus Wittgenstein concludes, "But what constitutes thought here is not some process which has to accompany the words if they are not to be spoken without thought."

If the two kinds of entities, the mental meaning and its outward expression, are connected by the one-to-one correspondence which we arrived at above, we should be able to proceed unproblematically through the three categories: thinking while saying, then saying without thought, and lastly thinking alone. We discover, however, that this is the very thing we cannot in fact do. The initially promising cases fail in the end, because what goes through or what is in the mind when the various events described occur is not the specific mental phenomenon that is necessarily present in cases in which we speak "with thought." The illusion of sense resident within these clearly cut categories of speaking with thought, talking without thinking, and thinking without words is nourished by the simple intelligibility of the notion of speaking thoughtfully, but that is not equivalent to the present philosophical notion of speaking "with thought." Moreover, the connection between an "imaginary object" and the line spoken is prima facie questionable: images of disliked supervisors, or of a sea of faces in the audience, or of the person who delivers the mail and a clockface, or of the printed newspaper headline sought after, or of the tyrant-executive's favorite restaurant to which he will return after signing the papers, or a hundred other things, may have been in the minds of the speakers. It is even possible that in the case of the person explaining the bad pen to the department secretary, nothing of this imaginary sort was in the mind at all. All of the present section is in a sense preliminary, as it is concerned not with the theory of art itself, but with the conception of language upon which the theory of art is modeled. It is, however, enough to render deeply suspicious the doctrine of the correspondence between an expression in the form of language and the independent object, process, or state in the mind which led to it. The attempt to trace back from the outward expression to its inner source seems to lead not to an isolable imaginary object, but rather to a range of contextual complexities which the idealist theory cannot hope to accommodate. Indeed, such complexities are not dreamed of within the limits imposed by the rigorous categories of thought and word. The attempt does, however, make clearer Wittgenstein's remark in the section just preceding the one we have been considering: "When I think in language, there aren't 'meanings' going through my mind in addition to the verbal expressions: the language is itself the vehicle of thought."[9]

THE INNER CONFLICTS OF
AESTHETIC IDEALISM

The object of the previous section was to make out the correspondence between the utterance and the mental object by isolating the elements and tracing back to the mental from the physical, from the outer effect to the inner cause. The correspondence was not, however, successfully elucidated. The attempt to isolate the

9. Ibid., sec. 329.

distinct components of expression and imaginary object, roughly of words and meanings, proved to be a systematically unclear enterprise. The analogy between language and art, when it is developed along idealist lines, appears thus irreparably unclear, and will prove a misleading analogy to the extent that the correspondence between mental meaning and verbal expression is unquestioningly presumed.

In this section I bypass the problematic correspondence of imaginary object and language, with its disquieting implications for the analogy between language and art, and I focus instead on the link between the imaginary object and the artwork. Perhaps this second of Collingwood's twin effects will yield a better result.

One place in which it is quite natural to speak within the categories of the conception—whether equivalent to the imaginary object or not—and the finished work is not where one is the perfect expression of the other, but where they *differ*. In the lower chapel in Assisi, behind one of the Simone Martini frescoes, there was found a cartoon, a working sketch, that had the architectural background on the opposite side from the actual painting. It did not balance with the adjacent painting, and so Martini had exchanged sides freehand—without another cartoon from which to work. Here there is room to speak of the original idea and the final work. First, however, the idea is itself a drawing—a cartoon—and not a mental image; second, the change was made after the actual physical process of execution had begun; and, third, there is no evidence that Martini was working from a first image—a mental one—which served as the model prior to the execution of the cartoon. Thus the issue of idea and execution goes back only to the cartoon; it does not lead off into the realm of the immaterial.

There is a set of Holbein drawings that for the artist were merely sketches in which to work out plans, problems, and details for the later oils that, at least in some cases, followed. Some questions arise here. First, it was here—at the sketching stage—that Holbein worked out the problems and details that he knew would arise in the painting. Like many artists, however, he used this method precisely because he did not know exactly what he would do in oil, or exactly what problems he would face in execution. It would be ludicrous to suggest on these grounds that Holbein suffered from a mental weakness that was, given his occupation, particularly unfortunate; the existence of these sketches cannot in any case be attributed to a weak imagination. Second, we must ask why, if the idealist view is correct, these works, the sketches, although greatly treasured, are accorded a second-class position in relation to the oil portraits that followed. These works are, after all, in a sort of artistic halfway house between mind and matter, and are thus that much closer to the imaginary object, which on the idealist view is the object of real aesthetic interest. The idealist might now insist that his theory has been done an injustice because the sketch is, and was for Holbein, just that and nothing more: it is the finished oil that matches, at least to a much greater extent, the original object in the mind of Holbein. That last claim, however, begs the question. By what criteria are we to determine that the final oil bears a greater resemblance to the imaginary object? Perhaps the full articulations of the oil—the detail, the care, the color, the slight alterations in placement, and so forth—are all nothing more than distortions of the original, added *after* the fact, after the more true-to-mind sketch.

At this point one might raise a more philosophically sobering objection: It is not merely that the idealist theory fails to tell us which work to treasure, but that it asks us to determine the relative values of two artworks by assessing their proximity to the mind of Holbein—a procedure that is patently absurd.

The precise nature of this embedded absurdity should be more delicately unearthed. Let us suppose there is a scholarly debate regarding the performance of a piece of early music. *Musica ficta* is, roughly, the practice of adding accidentals that allow a departure by a scale step from the six-note mode or scale in which a given piece is otherwise contained. Some performers and scholars question whether this is, in a number of particular cases, authentic practice—that is, whether the original music was actually performed with those added accidentals, or whether they are a later editorial fiction. The issue is usually an unproblematic one, but seen through the eyes of the idealist, it generates some curious difficulties. First, why are the musicologists looking for shreds of evidence concerning performance *practice*? The idealist would say it is at least a place to start: the music as it was performed was the external expression of the imaginary object, and that object is our ultimate aesthetic concern. The musicologists, however, regard conclusive evidence of performance as the place to *end*, whereas the idealist does not, or if he is to follow consistently the dictates of his own theory, *should* not.

Assume that a confusion regarding *musica ficta* occurred at the earliest possible point, between the composition of the first motet and the first performance of that motet. The composer is looking over her just finished manuscript, which is to be performed that evening. Regrettably, she is struck down at that moment, quill in hand, and happens to make a mark just above the highest of the six tones of the mode as she falls to the ground. In the confusion of the sad event her new manuscript is shelved. Later, the new choirmaster and resident composer come in, get out the manuscript, and "discover" the "new device," which allows an escape from the six tones. Seeing it as a daring and ingenious step forward, they immediately put it into practice, and the new composer henceforth utilizes the device to its fullest. The course of music history is, in this imaginary case, altered by an accidental mark. The piece is performed, from its first performance, with the accidental, and becomes well-known and much-performed throughout the centuries. For the musicologist, these facts, although they expose a scandalous, or at least curious, origin of the new compositional device, are easily accommodated as an unusual story behind a particular seminal piece. The idealist, however, is committed to a number of rather more shocking conclusions. The actual piece has in fact never been performed, and it cannot be the case that *another* piece was performed, since that piece originated in the mind of no one. Whatever it is that people have been singing for hundreds of years, it cannot attain the status of a piece of music, because it is not the expression of a mental object. The idealist must, then, embrace the claim that the "piece" performed was not a piece at all, but rather a purely physical tonal accident. Indeed, on idealist grounds this "piece," as it stalks through the art world without a prior mental counterpart, must accept the status of an aesthetic zombie. This consequence is both inevitable and absurd; the motet was quite evidently a piece of music, albeit with a curious provenance, and it was performed. The idealist must also claim that, as the piece has never been performed, a fortiori none of the particular performances were especially beautiful, and in fact all critical comments made about the "piece" must evaporate into a cloud of nonsense; they must wander as adjectives in search of a subject. Yet, let us further suppose, we do in fact know of a choir which performs the work to perfection. If practices have grown up around the piece—monastic, musical, historical, and so forth—that entire world should, on strict idealist grounds, collapse into the empty space erroneously thought to be occupied by the piece.[10] Yet the special kinds of repercussions that the idealist must predict are never felt; the work of art at the core of these practices is not vaporized merely because it fails to correspond to a composer's imagination. We may indeed see the work differently, but it is certainly not true that we cease seeing it at all.

A number of conceptual conflicts arise once the position of the idealist is taken up. First, there is the problem concerning the specificity of imaginary objects.[11] In accompanying a vocalist, the experienced performer will watch and listen for the breath intake and movements of the head of the vocalist in order to synchronize the entrances perfectly. Singers, however, most assuredly vary in their entrances from one performance to the next. If pianist Gerald Moore could have heard recordings of Schubert songs performed by Schubert himself, would it have been a better thing for Moore to place the piece exactly, to the millisecond, as Schubert played it,

---

10. There is another ultimately less plausible position the idealist can take here. The idealist can—and sometimes will—say that if there is anything we take as a work, then there will exist, de facto, a mental creator of that work, however closely the physical embodiment follows the mental envisagement. For example, the new choirmaster was the creator of the work; in jazz improvisation or in free cadenzas, the performer is the creator, creating immediately prior to the performance. This aesthetic manifestation of linguistic mentalism I will take up explicitly in Chapters 4, 5, and 6 below; for the present I will note that the only real ground for postulating such ideal entities in cases like these is that the idealist's theory requires them.

11. This question is raised by Richard Wollheim in *Art and Its Objects*, 2d ed. (Cambridge: Cambridge University Press, 1980), sec. 22.

regardless of Fischer-Dieskau's entrance? The criterion of excellence is correspondence between physical realization and mental ideal, so it should be simply an unfortunate aspect of the physical world if the singer is left stranded on a note: the actual work allegedly proves itself impervious to the abuses of performance. This certainly is nonsense. Moore and Fischer-Dieskau could not have made the music they did if they had proceeded in any such fashion. Could it be suggested that they are not really artists and that they do not in truth know the real work?[12] Again, of course, this serves as a reductio. If those two musicians are not artists and do not know Schubert, no one does—a fact that the idealist would surely admit. This admission, however, strikes a damaging blow to the theory of the imaginary work of art. If there are various and equally good, but different, interpretations of the imaginary object, then the idealist must also (1) admit that the work—the real one in the mind—is a hazy, variable, unclear work, or (2) take back the criterion of excellence, that of the correspondence between the outward expression and its imaginary predecessor. Neither admission is possible. If the idealist opts for the first choice, the physical object is given priority over the imaginary object, which amounts to nothing short of a total capitulation. With the second choice, the idealist sacrifices the significance of the imaginary object, leaving it as a lever attached to nothing.

The theoretical urgency of this problem concerning imaginative specificity can be more clearly revealed through detailed particular cases. Suppose that two musicians are performing a jazz composition that includes improvisational sections. In rehearsal Smith had discovered that over a particular dominant chord an ascending line works out nicely in her improvisation. Now, in performance, as she embarks on this passage, she hears that Jones has spontaneously altered his dominant chord by adding a raised ninth. Smith recognizes upon hearing it that the alteration has implications for her ascending melody. Rather than the major third she will have to play a minor third, the pitch one half step lower than the note she

12. Collingwood is in fact driven at one point to just such extremes, when he suggests that musicians are mere artisans who make "noise." See his discussion of the nature of the musical work, *Principles of Art*, pp. 139–41.

planned. The raised ninth of Jones equals the minor third of Smith, and if Smith does not make the change she will cause a severe dissonance—a clash of a half step between the competing major and minor thirds—which she most certainly does not want. The line she intended has a sweet melodic character, and she wants to preserve that. She thus makes the adjustment in mid-performance, plays the altered ascending line, achieves her purpose, and in a flash is on to the next phrase. Now what will, and must, the idealist say? Does Smith's performance possess the virtue of fidelity to the imaginary object? There are two answers to this question, depending on our conception of the mental work.

If we regard the particular notes of the piece as part of the imaginary object, then Smith has damaged the music by blurring the correspondence. If, on the other hand, we decide that she has in fact saved the performance, then other more serious problems arise. For, from this case, it must follow that the particular notes do not matter, and the question of correspondence is thus diffused and banished to the rather nebulous realm of aesthetic descriptions like "sweet melodic character." Here the idealist faces a dilemma. It is an obvious truth that Smith has given a better performance by adjusting the note to suit the chord; not doing so would have resulted in a clearly audible mistake, marring the performance. For the idealist, however, this implies that the given notes of a composition are strangely irrelevant to the authentic work; the genius of Bach's counterpoint, for instance, would be relegated to a position of secondary importance, being replaced by "the sense of necessary forward motion" or some similar description.[13] Idealism, at this juncture, compels us to carry out the aesthetic equivalent of trying to retain the shadow while disposing of the object that casts it.

This position, however, marks the point of entry into a deeper problem, an inherent tension in the idea of the work of art as imag-

13. Many further cases could bring out similar confusions concerning the identification of a necessarily nonspecific object with the work of art. For instance, in what way does the cadenza in a piano concerto fit into the work? In the raga, are the *scales* which serve as the basis of the improvisation the real imaginary object? It is, after all, only these scales which are rigidly determined in advance; countless similar questions arise in recent visual art.

inary object. If we construe the imaginary object as a mental entity essentially like the physical work, then we picture the object as being conceived by the artist *in* the materials or medium in which it is to be realized. Here we view the mental construction of the imaginary object as analogous to our conception of the birch in the back yard, or the aroma of freshly ground coffee, or the bark of a dog. Clearly, in these cases, the tree, the coffee, and the dog come first. It is not only false, but indeed senseless, to suppose that the thought of them comes before the experience: it is senseless to suppose that the imagination creates a space for them, which is later filled by the actual sensory experiences. With such cases of imagination in mind, one naturally tries to understand the imaginative act central to aesthetic idealism in the same terms. It would appear, then, that the artist knows his materials and is a master of his medium before he begins the mental creation of the art object; it is thus a particular assemblage of those materials which he envisions as the work. To take one example, Collingwood says, "If a man has made up a tune but has not written it down or sung it or played it or done anything which could make it public property, we say that the tune exists only in his mind, or only in his head, or is an imaginary tune."[14] Knowledge of the materials of music clearly precedes the imaginary work.

A more strict adherence to the letter of the theory, however, will show that the materials cannot in fact enjoy that psychological priority. If the object is imagined in terms of its medium or realization, then, to put it simply, we know too much too soon. We saw that the imaginary object is a result of the refinement of a raw emotional charge that comes in conjunction with its raw sensory data. Such data and that charge are preimaginative and are preexpressive: they have not yet taken one of the twin channels of expression, language or art. The process of refinement, common to both language and art, gives to the emotion a specificity it otherwise lacks; it is this that constitutes the imaginary object, and only so constituted can the object be expressed. Indeed, this is Collingwood's meaning in the statement, "Expressing an emotion

14. Collingwood, *Principles of Art*, pp. 131–32.

is the same thing as becoming conscious of it."[15] The incompatibility is evident. If Collingwood assimilates art to his model of language, then the imaginary object could not be a thing envisioned in terms of its expressive medium, because the expression allegedly proceeds from the inside outward. So there may be imagined works of art for which the materials of the genre provide both mental and physical components, but they could not be the imaginary objects which constitute the real works of art and which are identical to utterances in language. If this is the case, then we ultimately have no idea how to understand such an object. Any description of it in terms of material, e.g., ascending passages, blue or rose colors, marble or granite, oils or watercolors, violin or oboe, and so forth, must be ruled out. How, without such distinctions and qualities, can a work of art be described? Collingwood does oscillate between a view of the imaginary object as conceived in terms of ideas, and one in which their emotional charges are the essential element, but neither option does the job. We may here state the simple truism—which in this context assumes considerable argumentative power—that without the specific notes of a Bach fugue we simply are not thinking of *that* fugue. The imaginary object, as the real work of art, can only be conceived in the wrong terms.

What moral can be extracted from the previous considerations? We saw initially how Collingwood reached his conclusion that art is both imaginative and expressive and that, through common ingredients and a similar process or genesis, art is not merely like language, it *is* a language. These conclusions depended, however, on the existence of one-to-one relationships both between speaking and thinking and between art and thought. Art and language, Collingwood claimed, are alike by virtue of those relationships. Every word or sentence traces back to the thought it serves to express, and every artwork traces back to a specific state of mind— an imaginary object—which it expresses. By following out the implications of a passage of Wittgenstein on meaning in language, and by tracing the artwork back to its imaginative predecessor, we

15. Ibid., pp. 182–83.

found the theoretically crucial relationships between thought and expression to be conspicuously absent.

THERE are many helpful and illuminating ways in which to draw analogies between art and language. When an analogy is spelled out, however, in dualistic terms and a correspondence between the inner work and the outer physical realization is thought to stand parallel to the meaning in the mind behind the acoustical utterance, this analogy is ultimately more misleading than illuminating.[16] It only generates an untenable model of art out of an untenable and conceptually mischievous model of language. Initially idealism promises much in the explanation of art, but it is a promise made under the illusion that there exist simple and direct correspondences, in language, between thinking and saying, and in art, between thinking and creating. We saw above why Wittgenstein said that "the language is itself the vehicle of thought." To employ the analogy between art and language in another way, we might say, against the central tenet of aesthetic idealism, that the materials are themselves the vehicles of art.

Art has also frequently been construed as a vehicle for feeling, or as a system of external signs that carry emotional significance from an artist to a perceiver. C. J. Ducasse was one of those who both built his theory, although not always explicitly, on a philosophy of language and who gave clear expression to this way of construing artistic meaning. It is to his view that we turn in the next chapter.

16. The analogy is misleading because it encourages an ascent to theoretical generalities rather than a descent to critical particularities. For example, the distinctions we make in actual contexts of musical composition between fortuitous compositional developments arrived at by chance or sudden insight and genuine compositional ideation or pre-sonic reflection are lost to the larger claims of idealism, yet it is precisely these situated and particular distinctions that ensure the intelligibility of concepts like "compositional ideation."

3   The Language of Feeling

Art, to the minds of many, is the language of the emotions. Like many prevalent views in aesthetic theory, this one initially appears to be both obviously true and conceptually harmless, but like most sweeping claims, it simultaneously houses truth and falsehood. Beneath the apparently unobjectionable claim lies a powerfully influential analogy between art and language, or, more specifically, between art and a certain conception of language. In this chapter I first identify the most common conception of language employed in this particular variant of the analogy and make explicit its implications for the understanding of art. I then turn to a consideration of some cases of aesthetic experience which provide a testing ground for that theory, and finally I come back around to examine the very idea of the experience of meaning in language upon which the art-language analogy, in this formulation, ultimately depends.

The particular conception of language I investigate is perhaps best expressed by Locke; its implications are most directly and unhesitatingly explored by Ducasse in his still-influential *Philosophy of Art*; the experiential subtleties that surround linguistic comprehension and understanding were examined with the greatest precision by Wittgenstein. The first question, then, is how "language," when it appears in the assertion "Art is the language of the emotions," is meant.

DUCASSE AND THE LOCKEIAN CONCEPTION OF
ARTISTIC MEANING

Locke's description of the nature and function of language best articulates the conception of linguistic meaning that is here fundamental; for this reason it is worth quoting at length:

> Man, though he have great variety of thoughts, and such from which others as well as himself might receive profit and delight; yet they are all within his own breast, invisible and hidden from others, nor can of themselves be made to appear. The comfort and advantage of society not being to be had without communication of thoughts, it was necessary that man should find out some external sensible signs, whereof those invisible ideas, which his thoughts are made up of, might be made known to others. For this purpose nothing was so fit, either for plenty or quickness, as those articulate sounds, with which so much ease and variety he found himself able to make. Thus we may conceive how *words*, which were by nature so well adapted to that purpose, came to be made use of by men as the signs of their ideas; for then there would be but one language amongst all men, but by a voluntary imposition, whereby such a word is made arbitrarily the mark of such an idea. The use, then, of words, is to be sensible marks of ideas; and the ideas they stand for are their proper and immediate signification.
>
> The use men have of these marks being either to record their own thoughts, for the assistance of their own memory; or, as it were, to bring out their ideas, and lay them before the view of others; words, in their primary or immediate signification, stand for nothing but *the ideas in the mind of him that uses them . . .* and let me add, that unless a man's words excite the same ideas in the hearer which he makes them stand for in speaking, he does not speak intelligibly.[1]

What are the components of this view? Among the conclusions we might extract from the foregoing passage are: (1) thoughts are, at

1. John Locke, *An Essay Concerning Human Understanding* (1690; reprint, New York: Dover, 1959), bk. 3, chap. 2, sec. 8, pp. 8–9, 13.

least in the first instance, "hidden from others" in that they are private mental occurrences ("within his own breast") that as yet have no linguistic form ("cannot of themselves by made to appear"); (2) "sensible signs" were invented to stand for those thoughts (the "invisible ideas") in the physical world; (3) articulate sounds—words—are those signs, which the speaker utters; and (4) the connection between the two entities, one mental (the idea) and one physical (the sign), is arbitrary, made by "voluntary imposition." These four components put us in a position to understand Locke's general conclusion that the significance of a word is the idea that it stands for in the mind of the speaker, and that successful communication is the result of exciting the same ideas in the hearer through the employment of the materials of words.

Our first task is to see how the claim that art is the language of the emotions relates to Locke's conception of language. The relation consists in their shared model of idea-excitation which is thought to operate, in both language and art, as a type of meaning-mechanism. Although the aesthetic variant of the theory is directly expressed by Ducasse, the well-known remarks of William James regarding the emotionally evocative characteristic of words provide an illuminating intermediate point between Locke's theory of language and the corresponding theory of art.

James tells us that "we feel [a word's] meaning as it passes," and that "there is not a conjunction or preposition, and hardly an adverbial phrase, syntactic form, or inflection of voice, in human speech, that does not express some shading or other of relation which we at some moment actually feel to exist between the larger objects of our thought. . . . We ought to say a feeling of *and*, and feeling of *if*, a feeling of *but* and a feeling of *by*, quite as readily as we say a feeling of *blue* or a feeling of *cold*."[2]

---

2. William James, *Principles of Psychology*, vol. 1 (London, 1890), p. 281 and pp. 245–46, quoted in P. B. Lewis, "Wittgenstein on Words and Music," *British Journal of Aesthetics* 17 (1977): 111–121. I am indebted to Lewis's work here both as a valuable source of references on topics treated in this chapter and for suggesting further directions to take in investigating the parallels between artistic and linguistic meaning. James's point is discussed by Wittgenstein in *The Blue and Brown Books* (Oxford: Basil Blackwell, 1958), p. 78.

The thesis is abundantly clear: a specific idea or feeling is excited in the mind of the hearer by the otherwise lifeless sign[3] that serves as its signifier. This is strikingly reminiscent of a well-known passage of Ducasse: "Art is the critically controlled purposive activity which aims to create an object having the capacity to reflect to its creator, when he contemplates it with interest in its emotional import, the feeling-images that had dictated the specific form and content he gave the object."[4]

This particular analogy between language and art is thus gaining in specificity: the work of art stands parallel to the word within the shared idea-excitation model of meaning.[5] The "feeling-image" of the artist occupies precisely the same place in the explanatory schema as Locke's "idea" in the mind of the speaker. On this view, when a speaker communicates to us, he excites ideas in our minds which, if communication succeeds, are the same as those behind his words. Similarly, when an artist successfully communicates to his audience, it is also through the excitation of ideas or "feeling-images" just as James described this function in language. The deepest and most fundamental similarity between Locke and Ducasse can best be brought into focus through an examination of what Ducasse states directly about language. It is no coincidence that, in the course of expounding his theory of art, he turns almost immediately to the question "What essentially is language?" He answers that it is the "intentional *expression* of an inner state" and in further explaining that remark makes reference to "the antecedent presence of an inner state," and the "antecedent inner state which eventuates its overt utterance." He claims that "the antecedent inner state meant is a psychical one. And the evidence for asserting its existence is that of introspection."[6] Here, like Locke before him,

3. This way of putting the matter, i.e., as a question of linguistic sign and its life, derives from Wittgenstein, *The Blue and Brown Books*, pp. 5–7.

4. Curt Ducasse, "Art and the Language of the Emotions," *Journal of Aesthetics and Art Criticism* 23 (1964): 109–12, reprinted in *Aesthetics and the Arts*, ed. Lee A. Jacobus (New York: McGraw-Hill, 1968), pp. 47–52; quotation from p. 52.

5. This reliance on language as a model for aesthetic theory is common among expression theorists and, as we shall see in following chapters, is by no means restricted to pre-Wittgensteinian theorists.

6. Ducasse, *Philosophy of Art* (1929; reprint, New York: Dover, 1966), p. 32.

Ducasse is persuaded that linguistic meaning is of an essentially inner and purely mental nature, and thus that the meaning of a word is prior to and separable from its expression. On this view, the outward expression is not a *necessary* part of language; one way to express this would be to say that a wholly unexternalized language, comprehensible only to the speaker, should be readily intelligible.[7] Of the examination he is conducting into the nature of language, Ducasse states:

> What it reveals is that (developed) language is an (intuitional) *external expression of an inner psychical state.* Expression of one's meaning in words may be undertaken with the further intention of conveying that meaning to someone else, and possibly of affecting his behavior through this. But it may fail to effect this conveyance of meaning, and yet it remains speech. Moreover, expression of one's meaning in words may be undertaken without any intention of conveying the meaning, then or eventually, to another, even supposing that other to be one's own future self (as when one writes not a letter, but a memorandum or record for one's own use).[8]

Indeed, Locke claimed in the passage quoted earlier that the use people "have of these marks [is] either to record their own thoughts, for the assistance of their own meaning, or, as it were, to bring out their ideas, and lay them before the view of others." For both authors the external sign, or the expression, is conceived in the same way, i.e., as an outward object which can be contingently attached to its inner significance and which may be an isolated object itself subject to comparison. Having written a sentence, or having assembled a group of signs, Ducasse asks himself, "Is this the meaning that I *was* trying to express? And, inasmuch as, upon comparison, I judge that it is, I let the sentence stand as written."[9]

7. For a helpful discussion of this issue, specifically within the philosophy of language, see B. Armstrong, "Wittgenstein on Private Language: It Takes Two to Talk," *Philosophical Investigations* 7 (1984): 46–62.

8. Ducasse, *Philosophy of Art*, pp. 34–35.

9. Ibid., p. 33. Just before this quotation, he writes that "there was antecedently present in my consciousness a thought, which it was my problem to express in words."

It is clear that, as a conceptual necessity, for a comparison to take place there must be at least two objects present which are mutually distinguishable.[10] It is also clear why the feeling-images occupy the central position in Ducasse's theory of art, as analogues to the ideas in the minds of the speakers in the corresponding theory of language. Thus his view of art is in this fundamental way identical to his view of language: the external manifestation of the speaker and of the artist, which in the former case are words and in the latter case works, are products of a prior inner mental origin. They are the physical effects of mental causes. The artistic feeling-image, like the linguistic idea, need not force its way outward into the tangible form of an artwork—it may, like the speaker's idea, conceivably remain forever unexpressed, because it is fundamentally prior to (and thus separable from) its expression, and unlike it in kind.[11]

One implication of this view is that, if the perceiver of the artwork can be said to understand the work in the way we allegedly understand words, then the feeling-images of the artist and of the

10. Ducasse also says that "words were [found to be] extraordinarily useful as signals, that is to say as means of communication of certain inner states, viz., meanings" (ibid.). The topic of mental-physical comparisons and their connection with aesthetic perception and aesthetic creativity will be more fully discussed in Chapter 4. On the philosophical motivation to adopt this misleading linguistic dualism, see Ludwig Wittgenstein, *Philosophical Investigations*, 3d ed., trans. G. E. M. Anscombe (New York: Macmillan, 1958), sec. 334: " 'So you really wanted to say. . . .'—We use this phrase in order to lead someone from one form of expression to another. One is tempted to use the following picture: what he really 'wanted to say,' what he 'meant' was already *present somewhere* in his mind before we gave it expression."

11. There is, however, at the same time a difference between Ducasse's views of language and of art, or, more accurately, a partial difference. The difference concerns the arbitrariness of the sign. In the case of language it is clear that Ducasse, like Locke, takes the signs—the words—of the language to be connected in an utterly arbitrary way with the ideas they serve to express in the mind. Locke speaks of the "voluntary imposition" that accounted for the connection between idea and sign, and Ducasse speaks of the "invented" signs. In the case of art, however, Ducasse does refer to "the feeling-images that had dictated the specific form and content he [the artist] gave the object." Here it sounds as if there is an artistic parallel to the "natural connection" Locke said there could not be in language because we do not speak one universal language. For the present, however, we may proceed, having established that Ducasse's theory of art is constructed around the central idea of an external artwork firing in the mind of the beholder an inner feeling-image, and that in this it is perfectly analogous to Locke's theory of language where outward signs form in the minds of the hearers inward ideas.

perceiver must match, just as, for Locke, "unless a man's words excite the same ideas in the hearer which he makes them stand for in speaking, he does not speak intelligibly." Indeed, cementing the analogy, Ducasse asserts that "the conclusions reached above concerning the language of meaning, and the considerations upon which they were based, apply equally to the language of feeling, that is to say, art."[12]

This theory of language has, of course, been subjected to a great deal of investigation, particularly by Wittgenstein.[13] We will return to his work on this view of linguistic meaning in Chapter 6; it is sufficient for present purposes to show what the theory of language is to which art is being held up for comparison and to show how that implicitly held theory of language itself determines the subsequent conception of artistic meaning. It is, however, worth noting in passing that the theory is by no means obviously true in the way it may initially seem. It is true, indeed, that words may fire ideas in the hearer's mind, but those fired ideas are rarely associated with the meaning of the word. For example, upon hearing the word "indubitably" one may be reminded of, not the image of certainty, but the image of an acquaintance who often used the word, an image of the well-known portrait of Descartes, a hand of G. E. Moore, or countless other things. Similarly, a feeling may be fired in us upon the hearing of a word, but that feeling, as in the case of hearing the name of an object distinctly related in our experience to someone lost to us, is by no means equivalent to the meaning of the word. Directly stated, the claim, "Every time I hear X I feel Y" is perfectly intelligible and defensible; the claim, "The meaning of X is my feeling of Y" is far less so. To take one illustration, a prison warden may ask an inmate, "What do the words 'operation tunnel' mean to you?" What the words do in fact mean to the hearer depend on the contextual circumstances, which in this case include the fact that this individual and his fellow inmates have been working for months at digging their way out. What the inmate is caused to *feel* by this question, i.e., simultaneous alarm, fear, and

12. Ducasse, *Philosophy of Art*, p. 36.
13. See, for example, Wittgenstein, *The Blue and Brown Books*.

disappointment, have nothing to do with the meanings of the *words* "operation" and "tunnel," just as the warden's thoughts of his certainty of the inmate's guilt, or his doubt about the inmate's guilt, or his feeling of uncertainty due to his decision to proceed on the basis of an anonymous and unreliable tip, or his reflections on his success in this case, or any other similar thoughts or sentiments are not constituents of the strict definitions of these words.

In a second example, a thought highly specific to a person's legal troubles may be fired by the legal phrase "party of the first part"; here the specific thought is in one sense part of the meaning of the phrase, and in another sense—since it is a thought specific to that person—*not* part of the meaning. And in this case a feeling of gloom and a feeling of vulnerability to financial catastrophe may overcome the hearer of the phrase, along with the specific thought attached to the phrase, so both thought and feelings are fired here, in ways making it unclear whether to count these as parts of the meaning of the phrase or not. But in any event, the specific thought and the feelings of gloom and vulnerability are not in any standard sense constituents of the meaning of the phrase "party of the first part." As a third example, a person may be too quick to judge, and learn that first impressions of people can be inaccurate; here the name of a person, say "John," initially misjudged, can serve later not merely as the name of that person but as a reminder, in rather specific circumstances, of the danger of rendering judgments too quickly. In this case, a friend may utter the name "John," first, in reference to John, second, as a reminder of the initial misleading impression, third, as a warning not to judge too quickly another person now present, and so forth. For the hearer, the utterance "John" may fire these three thoughts as well as memories of the setting of their first meeting, other persons present at that meeting, and any of countless other thoughts or feelings associated with that initial encounter. If we ask the speaker of the name "John" if she *meant* any or all of these things, we will of course get unpredictably mixed answers. And of particular interest to the linguistic theory presently under consideration, we may well get the answer "Well, yes, I suppose I did mean that, although I had not exactly thought of the matter in those terms," which makes clear that the psychological constitution of the speaker does not—contrary to the dictates of this theory—circumscribe the possible meanings of the utterance.

Moreover, as a more general point against the theory, in these cases communication *should*, if the theory of language is accurate, break down, as the idea fired in the perceiver is different from that originating in the mind of the speaker. It most definitely does not; linguistic comprehension is not precluded by mismatched cognitive or emotional responses.

Although these few examples and critical remarks are intended to suggest that the internal coherence of the conception of language to which art is being conjoined cannot itself be relied upon to provide a stable conceptual foundation, the primary exploration here must concern itself with art. Indeed, a staunch defender of this formulation of the art-language analogy might claim that the model of artistic communication it engenders is enlightening quite apart from its accuracy or applicability as a theory of language. To pursue this point we must turn to some sample locutions in the language of art.

ART AND IDEA-EXCITATION

As examples of emotional states given rise by works of art, consider the following cases:

1. Paintings of the French Baroque Court may leave more than a shade of anger in a political activist wandering through a gallery. She may admire the paintings, and let us further suppose that she has invested considerable labor in familiarizing herself with the criticism surrounding these works. She finds, however, that she cannot help but be reminded of the dismal lives of the masses upon which this delicate courtly existence rested. This unexpected feeling has struck her for the first time in the presence of the paintings, and she tries to drive the feeling from her mind and concentrate on the paintings, but as soon as she turns to another painting glorifying the Sun King, the same feeling overcomes her. She proceeds to the paintings of the residences but, unhappily, finds herself pos-

sessed by the feeling again. She finally accepts that she simply cannot see the paintings through the feeling, and so goes to a room in
which she is at home, the room containing *The Raft of the Medusa*,
in which the poor souls clinging to the raft in the turbulent sea are
passed by a large, secure, undamaged ship.

2. At a concert two students of musical analysis are seated
together. One has finished his work in counterpoint for early the following morning, the other has not. Midway through the Bach piece,
the second whispers to the first that he has to leave the concert; he
cannot enjoy the music. The music only serves as a reminder of his
unfinished work, and even the soothing effect of music proves
unequal to his nerves. Leaving the concert hall, he goes to a practice
studio, taking his music notebook, and his worry, with him. He had
honestly tried to listen, but every time he heard two independent
melodic lines moving contrapuntally his anxiety only worsened.

3. A student of architectural history travels to Rome for a few
days and is devoting one day to each style period, i.e., Monday she
sees the ancient buildings, Tuesday the Romanesque, Thursday the
Renaissance, and so forth. When she finally gets to the modern
period, her chosen field of specialization, she finds that she now
feels vaguely saddened in the presence of those works; she cannot
overcome a feeling, arising out of the works, of loss. She tries to
force herself free of the feeling and spends a few days attempting to
recapture her initial enthusiasm for the modern style, but having
seen all that came before, she finds she cannot. Unable to see any
recent building without this unexpected and irrepressible sense of
aesthetic absence, she travels north and becomes instead a scholar
of Florentine Renaissance architecture.

4. A traveler goes into a gallery exhibiting Dutch still lifes and
town scenes and is overcome by a feeling that he missed his era,
that he was born much too late. He is especially taken by one particular work and stands before it, utterly absorbed, for some time.
He finally leaves it, but with an odd feeling of longing for the past.
He is gripped by an emotion resembling nostalgia, a paradoxical
feeling of desire to return to a time he was never in.

5. A violinist attends a reigning maestro's recital and notices on
the program a little étude that she studied very briefly years earlier.

She had always thought it to be a purely technical exercise con-
trived for the development of a certain technique, and she is more
than surprised to see it on the program, but when the piece is performed, the violinist is stunned. The master performer has revealed
the inner coherence and beauty of the miniature étude and elevated
it to a position of musical authority she presumed it could never, in
the hands of anyone, achieve. As each successive phrase flows out
of the instrument, the listener's desire once again to play this
piece—or, rather, to perform it for the first time—strengthens. She
tries to listen attentively to the rest of the program with the same
degree of interest and care, but the feeling that she must return to
the étude again and the mental activity stimulated by the feeling,
i.e., the repeated "hearing" of it in her mind's ear, substantially blur
her perception of the rest of the recital.

6. On a solitary stroll through Venice, a man is jolted out of his
reflections upon turning a corner and suddenly overhearing a piece
of music which is, in his mind, distinctly associated with a person
he once knew. His mind is instantly flooded with powerful images.

Now, what can be said of these six examples as illustrations of
the theory that art is the language of emotion? Although feelings
are fired by the works of art, one might be inclined initially to
claim that the examples are quite clearly not illustrations. Most
involve feelings that are irrelevant to the work or works of art being
seen or heard; we certainly would not argue that a perceiver understood a particular work if he came away from it uttering the sorts
of things we might imagine the characters in these cases to say.
The matter is not, however, and as we shall see could not be, so easily dismissed.

We know that the analogy with language implies that the works
serve as vehicles for the communication of feelings whose origins
are in the inner life of the artist. We also know that the analogy carries with it a corresponding conception of artistic understanding.
The artwork has been understood—i.e., the content, or, if we are to
preserve the integrity of the analogy with language, what must be
called the meaning of the work, has been derived from it—when
the feeling is excited in the mind of the beholder. What then is to
be said of the prerevolutionary French paintings? The viewer was

undoubtedly left with a certain feeling from viewing them, a feeling so strong that she lost the ability to do the very thing she came to do—to see, and to derive enjoyment from, the paintings. The theory here legislates as follows: This viewer does not understand the paintings, because she has been struck by a feeling other than that which originated in the mind of the artist; the communication process in art has here resulted in the variety of unintelligibility of which Locke wrote. Simply put, the wires are crossed. But are we entitled to reach this conclusion so quickly? Let us suppose, *ex hypothesi*, that this viewer has studied the paintings in depth. There is not a question about them to which she does not know the answer, nor is a question asked that does not itself provoke a discussion of many related concerns about the paintings and their provenance. Thus there may well be a number of things to say about this viewer, but the claim that she does not understand the works is not among them. She understands them well; her problem lies in being unable to see them through the filter of her feeling. What must in this case be identified as her understanding of the work is, against the prediction of the theory, unrelated to the feeling fired by the work.

There are, at this juncture, more difficult questions to face. What is to be said, if this way of construing the analogy is maintained, of a history teacher who takes students to see the paintings in order to show the students what life in the French court was like? A theorist speaking in defense of the analogy might here object on the grounds that the paintings are expressive works of art; they were not painted in the lowly interest of mere historical documentation. That objection, however, invites more trouble. Do we now uncover another unargued assumption that follows from the analogy? The theory seems also to bring in its wake a reductive and unitary account of *why* works of art are created: as a corollary of the theory we are driven to the conclusion that works of art are created to store and transmit feelings. In this way we are also led to a fundamental concern with the contents of the mind of the artist: but for what purpose, we must then ask, was a portrait of Louis XIV commissioned? If our critical interests gravitate toward the minds of the painters, a good deal of caution is needed in any wholesale

exclusion of apparently nonaesthetic considerations such as historical documentation, because it is very likely that this in fact was
precisely what Louis had in mind when he commissioned the portrait. Once the artist accepted the commission under those conditions, how would he then describe his task? If art is defined on the
model of linguistic expression, then the mere recording of historical appearance ought obviously to be irrelevant; a speaker in the act
of speaking is not equivalent to a historian in the act of documentation. In this case, however, we see that deliberate historical documentation does in fact have to be considered after all, as a
consequence of the theory which would initially prohibit an inclusion of such nonaesthetic motives on grounds of irrelevance.

The second case, in which the counterpoint assignment has
remained undone, presents a problem of a different variety. The student is at the concert, listening to the distinct melodic lines of the
music. According to the theory, he is hearing the signs the composer
has used to communicate feeling. He listens to the top voice against
the lower voice, and hears that upper voice starting on a high pitch,
descending toward a meeting with the lower voice which is moving
upward toward it in contrary motion. The high voice turns upward,
and now moves away from the lower voice, but the student's mood
does not lift with the melodic line.[14] His feeling is now moving in
contrary motion to the top voice; the sinking feeling of unfinished
work overwhelms him. What does the analogy theorist say now of
this case? He will want to say, keeping a safe distance, that the student cannot listen, because he is, quite unproblematically, too ner-
vous. But that answer cannot suffice. The student hears the music,
and is in fact attending to it very closely. It thus cannot be claimed
that he is not hearing the music. He does hear it, and with painstak-
ing, and in this case pain-evoking, attention to melodic detail. So
the first, and somewhat dismissive, explanation fails. The listener's
problem is not that he cannot listen, if "listen" here means to hear

14. I have invented this connection between rising and falling lines and rising and
falling feelings for the purpose of this example, but even this simple and direct correspondence between sign and feeling goes beyond the theory itself, which never makes
clear precisely what the connection is between feeling-images and the materials of art
in question.

and comprehend compositional structure. The theorist might next say that the student is hearing, or perhaps more accurately, over-hearing the signs—the materials the composer used to communicate the feeling—but that here, too, the mechanism has misfired. This answer may seem an attractive way to salvage the hypothesis, but it cannot withstand the slightest scrutiny. The insurmountable problem is that the student *does* hear what we, again through the analogy, are encouraged to refer to as the meaning of the work. This becomes clear if we trace the problem back to its parentage in the linguistic case. To accomplish this we must take this student out of the concert hall and place him in a restaurant, where he overhears a conversation in Japanese, not one word of which he understands. According to the theory, he hears the signs but cannot simultaneously decode the meanings arbitrarily attached to them. If we now ask whether the cases in the concert hall and the restaurant are exactly parallel, as they should be according to the foregoing explanation, the answer is clearly that they are not. The student at the concert hears musical lines moving ahead, each one with a strong melodic identity and standing in various relations to the others; he does *not* hear a meaningless or incoherent succession of pitches that are devoid of direction, propulsion, and cadence, or without a teleological aspect. He hears all those musical qualities, and what he hears makes perfect sense to him. Whatever his problem is, it is not a problem parallel to that which he faced in overhearing the conversation in Japanese. In the restaurant his aural experience is linguistically unintelligible, whereas his experience at the concert is musically coherent. Thus, as the cases in art and language are not parallel, their explanations, which according to this particular construal of language proceed in terms of signs detached from meanings, will not be identical.

In the third example we might say of the architectural historian, in explaining her change of field, that she has arrived against her will at a new way of seeing works in the modern style. She has also come to see in a new way the Renaissance works that had in photographs failed to grip her. There is nothing conceptually troublesome in the latter point for the Lockeian analogy theorist, but what can be said of the former? The problem is this: the student now sees something about the modern buildings strong enough to motivate her to change her field, and what she now sees is undeniably one component of her aesthetic experience. Yet on the model supplied by a Lockeian variant of the language analogy, we cannot acknowledge the student's new perception as one part of the experience, because what she now sees is something that the buildings, in contrast with their Renaissance forerunners, *lack*.[15] The distinctive feeling given rise by these works is not occasioned by an utterance in the language of art. It is occasioned, against the theory, by no artistic utterance at all. The feeling of disillusionment with modernism could not in fact arise within the strict confines of the analogy theory; rather than signs without meanings we would here have the impossible architectural equivalent of meanings without signs. What all of this brings to the surface is that we are given, along with the language analogy, a unitary definition of the aesthetic experience as a process of decoding the signs of which the work consists and the experience of the feeling resulting from that decoding or reading. The present case presents to the theory an indisputable part of the aesthetic experience for which theory simply has no place and no explanation.

The foregoing point is amplified in the fourth example, in which the traveler finds himself vaguely longing for a bygone period of Holland which he never in fact witnessed. Here what the viewer derives from the paintings is indeed a feeling or an image of what life in Amsterdam was like at that time. The conditions of the theory, then, seem to be fulfilled. The artist, let us suppose, was trying to capture on canvas the spirit of the age. Judged by Locke's conditions for successful communication, the artist has succeeded: the viewer is possessed by that feeling. The viewer's feelings, however, cannot be described without mentioning his longing for the past; indeed, it is the paradoxical longing along with his newly acquired sense of the spirit of the age which so affects him. So how can we, again within the boundaries of the analogy theory, explain this case? To say that the feeling of nostalgic longing must have been part of the painter's initial feeling is patently absurd: he was not

15. The objection cannot be made that this depends purely on an (alleged) error of criticism, that of criticizing something for what it is not, because this is in any case a part of the student's experience of these buildings which must be given a full account.

longing for those times, he was in them. Yet that feeling, inspired in the viewer but not originating in the artist, is again the dimension of this viewer's aesthetic experience which must be acknowledged by any successful theory of artistic communication and which could not be acknowledged by this one.

The fifth example brings another kind of difficulty to light. At first glance, we might well want to say, along with the analogy theorist, that the desire of the violinist to reconsider and perform anew the unappreciated étude cannot be included as part of the musical communication taking place; on the contrary, the desire is in fact getting in the way of and thus preventing the communication which would otherwise occur. But can the accusation of aesthetic irrelevance be made with any conviction from the vantage point of the analogy theory? We here arrive at a familiar skeptical problem of intention: How can we ascertain whether or not the composer intended to write precisely such an étude, one that develops certain techniques and yet also inspires through its charm an overwhelming desire to be played? The urgent problem is that the theory provides no criteria with which to determine the inclusion or exclusion of possible intentions. How are boundaries to be drawn between what is to be included as part of the artist's feeling-image, and hence an essential part of the experience of the meaning of the work, and what is not? It is true that this case does fill the general requirements of the theory, insofar as the listener hears the work and is taken over by a certain feeling. At first glance, the feeling generated in the hearer appears plainly irrelevant to aesthetic experience, while on second thought it appears to be perhaps the best illustration of the analogy theory yet considered. But the theory cannot tell us which, because it does not demarcate the boundaries of aesthetically significant intentions. Within this conception of the language of art we are unable to distinguish meaningful assertions from irrelevant interruptions.

In the last example, in which images are brought to the mind of the stroller in Venice by the music, the emphasis shifts from feelings to images as the ends of artistic communication. Here, one finds an indisputable case of image evocation resulting from the hearing of music, while at the same time the critical irrelevance of such intensely personal images to a true appreciation of the work is obvious. The images are caused by the work, so the meaning-mechanism seems to be in operation, but the images are not in fact the *result* of communication. They are, contrary to the Lockeian requirements of intelligible communication, private to the mind of the hearer, attached by personal association or projection.

A Wagnerian leitmotif, for example, may call to mind specific images through extramusical association and, as the association was intended by Wagner and is shared by the listener, the analogy theory can happily accommodate the case. In our last example, however, the musical phrases seem to have acquired meaning—the emotionally significant remembrance—in the absence of what Locke called a "voluntary imposition" on the part of the composer. It is true that the personal meaning which the music has acquired may be of biographical interest, but it has no critical relevance to the work. The fact remains, however, that it is one way in which music can assume significance, a kind of significance which is perhaps more common than theorists and critics want to acknowledge. Although the analogy theorist, due to the surprising combination of signs and meaning without intentions, must proclaim this variety of artistic meaning impossible, it most assuredly is not.

Someone might interject at this point that the particular analogy between art and language presently under consideration is being asked to bear too much weight. In spite of the foregoing detailed objections, such a defender might claim that the analogy, quite generally, still holds. All that is necessary is to think of people talking to each other. Simply think what happens when people understand a *word*: the same thing happens when they understand a *work*. It is with this rather puzzling objection in mind that we must now turn to some comments Wittgenstein makes about experiencing the meaning of a word.

EXPERIENCING MEANING IN WORDS AND WORKS

It is undeniable that the analogy between language and art enforces the belief that we experience the meaning of a work of art just as we experience the meaning of a word. It is true that the phrase "experiencing the meaning of a word" does not have applications that spring readily to mind, but it is clear, given the Lockeian presumptions in the philosophy of language upon which this type of analogy theorist relies, that any answer to a question concerning meaning in language will necessarily involve references to mental experiences. On that view, after all, a meaning *is* a mental experience, so if art is to possess meaning then it, too, must induce mental experiences.

The analogy theorist, who objected to the more detailed puzzling over the art-language analogy above, wants to explain art in precisely this way. It is perfectly obvious: we look at or listen to the work of art and derive from it what it means, just as we hear the word spoken and experience its meaning. Nothing could be more simple. But is it or could it be so simple? Here the salient feature of the theory is that our experience of the word or of the artwork occurs above and beyond the acoustical word or the material work. We know that, for the analogy theorist, understanding a word is an inner process or event that accompanies the hearing of it, just as the aesthetic experience is a parallel inner process that accompanies seeing, hearing, or reading of any work. Thus the question now facing the analogy theorist is: How are we to characterize that experience and how might it be isolated and identified in order to render it fully comprehensible.

Let us look at a few cases in which our notions of a word and its meaning seem to have some application to this difficult question. First, there is a sense in which a word can be felt to "fit" its meaning. Wittgenstein, in discussing the experience of understanding in language, gives the example of someone saying, "I feel as if the name 'Schubert' fitted Schubert's works and Schubert's face."[16] Can one progress from this point, at which there is a glimmer of sense to the notion of experiencing the meaning of the word "Schubert," to the full understanding we are in search of? Given only the one cryptic line concerning the sense of fittingness of a name to a face and a body of musical works, the analogy theorist might seize

16. Ludwig Wittgenstein, *Philosophical Investigations*, 3d ed., trans. G. E. M. Anscombe (New York: Macmillan, 1958), p. 215. Here I follow the direction suggested in Lewis's paper "Wittgenstein on Words and Music."

the example and employ it in support of the Locke-Ducasse view. Indeed, such a theorist may claim that it demonstrates exactly what is wanted, i.e., that the experience of the word—the meaning—has been associated in many past instances with its sign, "Schubert," and that now we are, as intelligible speakers and comprehending hearers, in a position to experience that fit. If, however, Wittgenstein's remark is more fully investigated and considered in the light of some other related passages, deeper confusions implicit in this conception of meaning can be unearthed. In what context, we must ask, would the name "Schubert" possess such a sense of fittingness?

Suppose that at a musicological conference we attend a paper entitled "Beethoven and Schubert." When we get to the lecture room, there is a delay. Finally someone comes rushing into the room carrying a paper, and we settle back to hear it. It turns out, however, that the author could not come, and that the paper is going to be read by the author's research assistant who, though a good speaker, knows nothing about Beethoven and Schubert. He apologizes, saying that he just finished typing the paper that instant, having had a handwritten copy of the manuscript passed on to him from a colleague of the author only that morning. Unknown to him, the colleague, infamous for practical jokes, reversed the composers' names throughout the paper, leaving them correct only in the closing line. The assistant begins: "The young Beethoven greatly admired the grand master of music in Vienna, and was in fact very intimidated by him. When Beethoven wrote, for instance, 'The Trout,' he . . ." Everyone in the room suffers a jarring sensation and, recovering from the shock, realizes what has happened. The listeners politely resolve, with no little amount of rustling, shuffling, and whispering, simply to hear "Schubert" as "Beethoven," and vice versa. Excerpts known and loved as the essential Schubert are played on cue by an assistant and discussed with critical and analytical acuity but under the name of Beethoven. Finally, at the conclusion of the paper, the names are finally heard in the right places. As the research assistant reads, "And, in conclusion, it may be said that Schubert's 'Trout' has . . . ," he vaguely wonders why there issues forth from the entire audience a sudden sigh of relief.

Now, is this a case of experiencing the meaning of a word in which sign and meaning "fit"? The analogy theorist will answer in the affirmative, having heard the collective sigh of relief as the outward evidence of the inner experience. Can the sound from the audience support such an interpretation? First among the many problems with the example is that it is surely an extremely unusual, if not wildly implausible, case. It is seen and understood only in marked contrast to the normal case in which "Schubert" means Schubert, and the analogy is supposed to rest upon the normal case. Do we, then, experience in the same way the meanings of all the other words in the papers at the musicological conference where the names are in order? No corresponding experiences occur there; it is simply phenomenologically obvious that there is not a continuous sense or experience of linguistic fittingness. A second and more important objection is that, in the interest of giving content to the analogy, the case ought to be identifiable as one of experiencing the *meaning* of a word. It is not, for the reason that the explanation which in fact arises out of this case, i.e., "Somehow the names got mixed up," is not by any means prima facie equivalent to "He exchanged the meanings of the words." It would thus take a separate and further argument to show that we are here talking about *meanings*, where meaning is understood as a mental entity. This leads into the third problem, which concerns the very distinction between a word and its meaning. Is it clear that we have separable entities of different ontological natures? Is it clear that we can add and subtract, or arbitrarily mix and match, using words and meanings as isolated particulars? If the fundamental issue is not clear, then the power of this particular analogy between language and art is considerably weakened.

Wittgenstein writes:

> "The word falls," one is tempted to explain, "into a mould of my mind *long* prepared for it." But as I don't perceive both the word and the mould, the metaphor of the word's fitting a mould can't allude to an experience of comparing the hollow and the solid shape before they are fitted together, but rather to an experience

of seeing the solid shape accentuated by a particular background.[17]

What is the significance of this cryptic remark for our problem of the experience of meaning? First, the "mould" must correspond to the multitude of thoughts concerning Schubert, but independently of the name "Schubert." That is, not only a face, but an entire constellation of thoughts, without a name: all we know, think, and feel about Schubert. Second, the "solid" corresponds to the name or the mere sign "Schubert," or, more accurately, "S-c-h-u-b-e-r-t," considered in isolation from any and all of those thoughts of Schubert. Wittgenstein's conclusion is that the separation cannot in fact be intelligibly drawn; the temptation we feel is towards incoherence, it being impossible to "perceive both the word and the mould" in isolation from each other. How could the analogy theorist get us to call Schubert to mind without ever saying "Schubert"? It might be done in a musicological version of a charade game, but of course here the theorist is still operating with signs. To make the distinction good, the theorist has to be able to think of Schubert (the mould) without thinking "Schubert" (the solid). This conceptual subtraction cannot be effected. When we think of the man and his name, "the solid shape is accentuated by a particular background"—words that initially suggest the possibility of a separation which further investigation reveals to be impossible. Thus the present direction in our pursuit of the experience of a word's meaning has not helped us understand the meaning of a work of art, but has rather exposed a further confusion in the view of language upon which such a version of the art-language analogy rests. We, quite simply, do not yet have an experience in language to which the experience of meaning in art can be compared.

If conceptual subtraction is impossible, perhaps addition, where sign and mental experience are both present, will fare better. It is clear that necessary conditions for "signhood" have been established by the theory of language under consideration. Signs must be

---

17. Wittgenstein, *The Blue and Brown Books*, p. 170.

arbitrary, possessing in and of themselves no intrinsic meaning. Alone, they are merely senseless blasts of sound[18] and it is only through the addition of or connection to the mental component that they acquire meaning. The analogy theorist might insist that at least these minimal conditions for signhood have been met and

18. See, for example, Searle's development of this theory in *Speech Acts* (Cambridge: Cambridge University Press, 1969); see especially pp. 16–21, where "a noise or mark on a piece of paper" that is an instance of linguistic communication is distinguished from non-linguistic phenomena by its having been "produced with certain kinds of intentions" (p. 16). On the matter of the alleged arbitrariness of the sign, consider Wittgenstein's case of repeating a word over and over so that one feels that the "word lost its meaning and became a mere sound" (*Philosophical Investigations*, p. 214). Upon twenty or thirty fast repetitions of "beagle," for example, the word comes to sound like a pair of nonsense syllables; it, indeed, becomes mere sound. In response to the question "What is your favorite dog?," however, it seems to dart back into place, its nonsensical air vanishing; on the second hearing of the word in context we can no longer hear its nonsensical sound. Does this example reveal the essential arbitrariness of the sign? Any proponent of the theory under review here will (prematurely) answer yes. Through repetition, it will be claimed, a wedge was driven between the sign and its meaning, paring the meaning off the back of the sign, and the recontextualization of the word brought the two elements back together. And of course works of art and their meanings will correspondingly be construed as detachable. In fact, it is only seemingly obvious that the two components, arbitrary sign and meaning, have been rejoined at the moment of usage. If the sign is defined as lifeless and intrinsically meaningless, and if the life is given by the associated meaning, then precisely such a lifeless acoustical blast must be present as half of the whole when the whole—the combination of sign and meaning—reappears in context. But it is precisely the nonsensical air of "beagle" that has vanished, and along with it the identifying mark of the arbitrary sign's presence. As long as the word is defined as a composite including the arbitrary sign as the physical bearer of the mental meaning, and as long as the *arbitrary* air is conspicuously absent in the actual employment of the word, then the conception of language here serving as an analogical base for artistic meaning eludes comprehension. To put it briefly, if we have the word that we understand in context, we do not have the sign (the noise or acoustical blast), and vice versa. If we are unable to articulate what was subtracted by repetition, or what was added by recontextualization, then we have ultimately very little in the way of an analogical foundation for an understanding of artistic meaning.

Although this is not the place to pursue the matter at length, I note in passing that these matters in particular (as well as Wittgenstein's later work on the misformulation of the problem of linguistic meaning in terms of the sign and its life) significantly reduce the explanatory value of semiotic aesthetics. For the linguistic foundation of this direction, see *Semiotics: An Introductory Anthology*, ed. Robert E. Innis (Bloomington: Indiana University Press, 1985), especially pp. 24–27, where Ferdinand de Saussure's claim that the word, the "linguistic sign," unites "not a thing and a name, but a concept and a sound-image" is discussed, along with his belief in the "indissoluble union of the two components."

thus that this theory of communication does at least in this sense have application.

A banker named A. E. Kellog meets with a familiar loan applicant and agrees to lend some money. The grateful borrower says, "Well, A. E., I owe you." Later that day in a singing lesson, the teacher asks which vowel sounds the borrower will practice, and our friend replies, "Well, A.E.I.O.U." The case is of interest to the theorist because it does indeed seem to show that the signs are arbitrarily associated with meanings. This man, he will claim, said the same thing in both cases but meant different things, i.e., he employed the same intrinsically meaningless signs but, as an intentional contingency, attached them to different ideas. This claim, however, is in fact indefensible if not hostile to the point the analogy theorist wants to make. In order to give content to the additive model of signs and meanings, we would need to preserve the sense of arbitrariness as a component added to the possessor of significance, the attached mental meaning. There is, of course, no sense in which what the borrower said in either case is *arbitrary* or fundamentally meaningless. It appears that when we have people speaking in contexts we have a rather conspicuous absence of linguistic signs; the necessary condition of arbitrariness of signhood has thus by no means been met.

Nevertheless, the theorist might argue that, regardless of the state of arbitrariness of the signs, we are in fact in search of the *experience* of meaning, and that this is shown by the fact that we can take a word one way or another: this, finally, is enough to place the art-language analogy on a firm foundation. The theorist might remind us of a remark of Wittgenstein's: "You can say the word 'March' to yourself and mean it at one time as an imperative at another as the name of a month."[19]

Just after this passage, however, Wittgenstein adds, "And now say 'March!'—and then 'March *no further!*'—Does the *same* experience accompany the word both times—are you sure?"[20] Here we arrive at the final problem with the idea of the experience of mean-

19. Wittgenstein, *Philosophical Investigations*, p. 215.
20. Ibid.

ing which lies at the heart of this analogy. It is clear that "March" *means* the same in both cases; there is no confusion here between a military command and the name of a month. Yet the experiences which accompany the hearing of these different cases are obviously correspondingly different. Here what must on the theory be identified as the same sign, with the same meaning, gives rise to different experiences. This of course implies that the experience of the word, however that is to be described, and the word's meaning, are *not* identical. Yet it is, after all, the very meanings which are allegedly experienced. Thus even if we do locate an experience attached to words, we still have not necessarily located the experience of meaning.

Elsewhere Wittgenstein writes, "Ask yourself: 'When I said "Give me an apple *and* a pear, *and* leave the room," had I the same feeling when I pronounced the two words 'and'?' "[21] As intelligible speakers on the Lockeian model we ought, of course, to have had the same feeling associated in each case to the sign "and," which would be followed by a decoding of the feeling by the hearer. If, however, we again consult experience, it is clear that this theoretical prediction is not fulfilled in linguistic practice.

To make the point clearer, suppose we are charged with caring for a group of children who have made their craving for ice cream very clear. With their special interest in mind they inquire into the schedule for the afternoon. They are answered, "We'll go to town, . . . and stop by the playground, . . . and go to the park, . . . *and* then get some ice cream." "And get ice cream!" they all excitedly repeat to each other. Each of these "and's" obviously differs. There is something very much like a crescendo, or a building of tension, through the progression of them. Moreover, the "and's" the children repeat are all unlike those forming the crescendo. This would be simply impossible within the strict confines of the theory under consideration. The theorist here cannot accommodate these kinds of cases without saying that since the experience of each "and" is different, each of these is in fact, against the appearances, a different word with a different meaning. This conclusion is clearly

21. Wittgenstein, *The Blue and Brown Books*, p. 79.

absurd; for all their differences, they are not different words. As for their meanings, one does not know quite what to say, because to this point nothing that could definitely answer to the name "the meaning" has been located; it most assuredly is not tied to the only variety of experience we have been able to specify.

WE are finally in a position to reach a conclusion concerning this particular variant of the art-language analogy. On this construal of language, nothing is itself clearly specifiable as the object, allegedly transported in linguistic communication via the meaning-mechanism we have discussed: we have not been able to find a linguistic meaning to which the meaning of a work of art is believed to exist as an analogue. The elusive target of much aesthetic theory and criticism is, when construed on Lockeian grounds, a mythical entity born of a misleading analogy. The question what is the meaning of a work of art, where "meaning" carries an implicit analogy with language and where in turn language implies a fundamental separability of meaning from materials, is a question that ought to be treated with extreme caution. If an entity of a suspiciously ill-defined metaphysical nature is presumed to exist as the meaning of a work, aesthetic discussion will not proceed along fundamental lines: instead of asking what we mean by artistic "meaning," we merely ask what critical approach best captures that meaning. It is, and ought to be, an undeniable truth that art possesses meaning, and it is similarly undeniable that art exhibits an expressive aspect, but the assertion that art is the *language* of the emotions, where language is elucidated in the terms considered here, conceals delicate falsehoods within unassailable truths. In the most general sense, however, language is certainly an intentional activity, and in this respect it resembles art. Thus we turn to intentional considerations in the next three chapters.

4 Artistic Intention and Mental Image

At one point in the *Philosophical Investigations*, Wittgenstein remarks that "it is clear that one can want to speak without speaking. Just as one can want to dance without dancing. And when we think about this, we grasp at the *image* of dancing, speaking, etc."[1] If we continue Wittgenstein's quotation by adding "painting, composing, sculpting, writing, designing," and so on, we place ourselves at still another problematical, but potentially illuminating, point of intersection between the philosophy of language and aesthetic theory.

point of this / study work.

THE ALLEGED INTENTIONAL OBJECT

When we think about artistic intention and creation it seems almost inevitable—as in the parallel linguistic case—to invoke at some point images of already existent works. Why should this be the case? We begin, perhaps, by thinking of a particular work of art, such as Picasso's *Les Demoiselles d'Avignon*. Next we reflect that, in order for the work to exist, the artist must have *wanted* to paint that particular work. We are then in a position to duplicate mentally the physical world of artworks by attributing to the minds of their creators mental works which existed prior to, and which in a sense caused, their physical realization. What assumptions under-

---

1. *Philosophical Investigations*, 3d ed., trans. G. E. M. Anscombe (New York: Macmillan, 1958), sec. 338.

lie this progression of thought and make it seem, from this particular perspective, inevitable?

This question can be answered, I think, by elucidating what is
involved in the very idea of wanting, for example, to paint a picture.
Wanting, in connection with the creation of artworks, does seem to
entail some reference to a prior image, because this image serves as
the object of the want: it is the image that renders the want intelligible. We cannot comprehend "I want, and yet there is nothing I
want," or "I want, but what I want is nothing." These are specimens
of nonsense precisely because the want reaches out, not to something as yet unknown, which would be understandable, but rather
to nothing at all. Stated directly, wanting has a necessary conceptual
connection with its object. Why, however, should the object of the
want be conceived, perhaps unwittingly, in the simplest possible
way, which is as a mental representation or image of the completed
painting itself? One explanation for this is that the concept of wanting is taken to be unitary, so that all cases, even the exceedingly
complex ones such as wanting or intending in art, are modeled on
the very simple cases, such as, for instance, wanting a peach. If the
idea of wanting is reduced and unified in this way, the view that art
images precede art objects becomes more plausible the more one
reflects upon it. When we see peaches at the market and find ourselves wanting one, the want is clearly directed toward an already
existent object. The artist's case, however, is in a striking way
unlike this; the artist is the creator of the object. The work of art
does not exist before the want as the peach exists before we see it.
Yet both are undeniably cases of wanting and if, again, the possibility of an object is necessary to the intelligibility of the want, then
the work must, in some sense, exist. If the work does not exist physically, as it most assuredly does not in cases of wanting or intending
to create, then, this line of reasoning concludes, the work must exist
in the only way it can, which is, of course, mentally.[2]

2. There is a potentially instructive ambiguity here concerning the example of
wanting a peach. We might indeed want the particular peach before us in the market
now, and thus want a preexisting particular, or we might, away from any peaches,
want a ripe and sweet peach. In this latter case, of course, it does not follow that there
exists a peach fitting this description from the mere psychological truth that we want

This view has not had to struggle along in relative obscurity without distinguished exponents. In the development of his famous argument Anselm says, "When a painter considers beforehand what he is going to paint, he has it in his understanding."[3] Alberti refers to "the painter . . . [who] can represent with his hand what he has conceived with his mind."[4] An early instance of the intention-as-image view in both art and language can be found in the Pythagorean philosopher Archytas, who thought, as A. C. Crombie reports, "that man had first to conceive in his mind both what he wanted to explain, and what he wanted to make or do."[5] In Vitruvius's *De architectura* we read of artists who want to "put into practice through a burning desire to produce in sensible works with their own hands that which they have thought out with the mind."[6] Dürer claimed that "a good painter is inwardly full of figures,"[7] and we also know of Leonardo's repeated assertions that "art must begin in the mind before it can issue through the

---

one; nor does it follow that there exists a fully articulated and detailed imaginary peach. All that follows is what the want already implies—that we want a peach of that description. Now suppose that an artist wants to paint a portrait of Jones in oils. This description "a portrait of Jones in oils" does imply a good deal, i.e., it invokes a representational genre of portraiture, a specific medium for that representation, and so forth. So the artist can want to paint a portrait of Jones in a way directly analogous to that of wanting a peach satisfying the description "ripe and sweet;" i.e., the artist may assemble paint, brushes, canvas, sitter, arrange lighting, and so on, but without the psychological truth of the presence of this "artistic want" implying the existence of an imaginary counterpart of the completed portrait in the mind of the artist. Simply stated, the psychological fact of wanting does not *itself* argue in favor of aesthetic idealism. Moreover, even a cursory investigation into the concept of wanting shows that it is not a unitary phenomenon, and so non-artistic wanting itself is not a single, identifiable experience that could serve as a clear and stable model for artistic wanting. To put the matter linguistically, "wanting" is not a word that gets its meaning through reference to a single mental phenomenon.

3. Anselm, *Proslogion*, chap. 2, reprinted in *The Existence of God*, ed. John Hick (New York: Macmillan, 1964), p. 26.

4. Leon Battista Alberti, *On Painting and Sculpture*, ed. and trans. Cecil Grayson (London: Phaidon Press, 1972), p. 58, quoted in A. C. Crombie, "Science and the Arts in the Renaissance: The Search for Truth and Certainty, Old and New," *History of Science* 18 (1980): 233–46, this quotation p. 233.

5. See Crombie, "Science and the Arts," p. 237.

6. Ibid.

7. Erwin Panofsky, *The Life and Art of Albrecht Dürer* (Princeton: Princeton University Press, 1955), pp. 252–53.

hands."[8] Nor should one think this idea died young. André Breton claimed that "the plastic work of art . . . will either refer to a *purely interior model* or cease to exist."[9] The belief that visual artworks are the outward manifestations of mental images can as well be found quite readily in art criticism; indeed, one can see it plainly enough behind the critical cliché "brilliantly conceived and executed," where these two terms are thought to be not merely temporally but also ontologically distinct phenomena, the one involving mental envisagement and the other physical embodiment.

The image view in language is characterized succinctly by Wittgenstein's interlocutor in the section just preceding the one quoted above: "But didn't I already intend the whole construction of the sentence (for example) at its beginning? So surely it already existed in my mind before I said it out loud!"[10] It is, then, precisely this view of intention, in its aesthetic form, and the accompanying sense that matters could not be otherwise, which should be examined now.

Let us consider a case in which the question of the relation between intention and the completed work seems to be naturally invited. The architect of the Tower of Pisa possesses an unusual sort of fame. His work is admired; yet we would not know of him or of his work were it not for an aspect of the tower that is wholly unintentional. As things stand, his fame rests on his mistake; he is the recipient of a sort of aesthetic luck. We may suppose that the tower

8. Leonardo da Vinci, *Treatise on Painting, Codex Urbinas Latinus 1270*, trans. A. P. McMahon (Princeton: Princeton University Press, 1956), p. 35, quoted in Crombie, "Science and the Arts," p. 238.

9. André Breton, *What Is Surrealism?*, trans. David Gascoyne (London: Faber and Faber, 1936), reprinted in *Theories of Modern Art*, ed. Herschel B. Chipp (Berkeley: University of California Press, 1968), p. 406. I have here only very briefly cited a few notable instances of this general view; one source of many fuller cases is Erwin Panofsky, *Idea: A Concept in Art Theory* (1924), trans. Joseph J. S. Peake (New York: Harper and Row, 1968). To take one example, Cicero, under the influence of the Platonic Doctrine of Forms, claims that Phidias, "when he produced his Zeus or his Athena, did not look at a human being whom he could imitate, but in his own mind there lived a sublime notion of beauty; this he beheld, on this he fixed his attention, and according to its likeness he directed his art and hand." Encapsulating Cicero's conception of artistic creativity, Panofsky states that in the artist's "own mind there dwells a glorious prototype of beauty upon which he, as a creator, may cast his inner eye" (pp. 12–13).

10. Wittgenstein, *Philosophical Investigations*, sec. 337; see also sec. 334.

fulfills his intentions with regard to the particular variety and placement of the columns and capitals, the number of stories, and so on,
but it is of course the way in which the tower stands that is of interest, and this was clearly not part of his intentional scheme or design.

This work of architecture appears to provide a case in which we
can coherently discuss the artist's creation within the rather clear-
cut categories of mind and matter, specifically (1) his intentions, of
which he is ultimately the sole possessor, and (2) the publicly
observable work, which may or may not fulfill or embody the
intentions. We could determine in this case, if we were to assemble
an exhaustive list of the features of the work, e.g., the choice of
stone, its particular appearance, and so forth, in which category
each of these particular features belongs. It is the leaning, of course,
the most salient aspect of the work, which is not intentional.

This dualistic intention-into-work conception of artistic creation
projects itself, however, all too easily over numerous further examples. We may, for instance, go to hear an improvising pianist and
come away amazed at his ability, as one would say under the influence of the intentionalist conceptual template, to play anything he
thinks, spontaneously and flawlessly, without mediation. Here we
see the player and his instrument as the vehicle for the externalization of the musical ideas that the player-as-intender has quite
literally preconceived. Similarly, in watching a composer engaged
in the skills of his craft, we may find ourselves amazed at what we
see as his masterful ability to commit immediately to manuscript
paper anything at all that comes to mind; he can instantly notate
anything he thinks, instantly rendering the mental in material
form. We may encounter an allusion to an artist's intentions in a
critical passage that states that the Sistine Chapel ceiling is a profound visual realization of an intricate theological program. In all of
these cases it is natural enough to posit an image of the work, or, as
in the Sistine ceiling case, a complex set of images, when we think
about the creation of the work. It is, however, as will become clear
below, one thing to say that the Sistine Chapel ceiling was painted
according to a theological program, and quite another to suggest
that a fully articulated conception in the mind of Michelangelo was
the mental predecessor of the work.

There is still another, and perhaps more simple, motivation for using the intentionalist template: a work does indeed come out in one way rather than another, although the other way is perfectly conceivable and within the capabilities of the artist. With this observation in mind, it is very easy to think that from all the possible works the artist has conceived, he has chosen to externalize the one standing before us. In Wittgenstein's characterization of the position, the sentence must have existed complete in the mind prior to its utterance because the speaker must, after all, have intended the whole construction. In a similar fashion we can easily assume that prior to its fabrication the artist must have had the intention that corresponds to the work. If we accept this notion of intention-as-image, it is then a short step to the uncritically held belief that a question of intention is invariably appropriate in connection with any existing work of art. This entire direction of thought brings us, willingly or otherwise, face to face with the general question entirely familiar to aesthetic theory, "What is the relevance of the artist's intention to the understanding or appreciation of a work of art?"[11]

DUALISTIC CRITICISM

Among the most widely known answers to this question was that of Beardsley and Wimsatt[12] and the New Critics, who assumed the ready intelligibility of the notions of "the artist's

11. See, for example, Henry David Aiken, "The Aesthetic Relevance of Artists' Intentions," *Journal of Philosophy* 52 (1955): 742–53, reprinted in *Art and Philosophy*, ed. W. E. Kennick (New York: St. Martin's, 1974), pp. 403–412; Theodore Redpath, "The Meaning of a Poem," in *Problems in Aesthetics*, ed. Morris Weitz (New York: Macmillan, 1970), pp. 360–72; Frank Cioffi, "Intention and Interpretation in Criticism," *Proceedings of the Aristotelian Society* 64 (1963–64): 85–106; Anthony Savile, "The Place of Intention in the Concept of Art," in Harold Osborne, *Aesthetics* (Oxford: Oxford University Press, 1972), pp. 158–76; Stanley Cavell, "A Matter of Meaning It," in his *Must We Mean What We Say?* (Cambridge: Cambridge University Press, 1976), pp. 213–37; Berel Lang, "The Intentional Fallacy Revisited," *British Journal of Aesthetics* 14 (1974): 306–314; and Mark Roskill, "On the 'Intention' and 'Meaning' of Works of Art," *British Journal of Aesthetics* 17 (1977): 99–110.

12. W. K. Wimsatt and Monroe C. Beardsley, "The Intentional Fallacy" in *The Verbal Icon: Studies in the Meaning of Poetry* (Lexington: University of Kentucky Press, 1954), pp. 3–18.

intention" and, in opposition to this, the "work of art," and confidently asserted that information regarding the artist's intentions is aesthetically irrelevant and indeed pernicious. We should not look to features external to the work for help in coming to an understanding of the work. It is, however, precisely this drastically simplified and misleading dualistic conceptual scheme, resting beneath the question to which New Criticism was one answer, that leads us to feel that the general question of the relevance of intention is both critically crucial and theoretically inevitable; in this sense too this dualistic conceptual scheme perfectly parallels the position of Wittgenstein's interlocutor, who employs the dualistic scheme in thinking about language. If, however, there is no uniform and exhaustive collection of descriptions of a mental image which could be regarded as an artistic intention, and no work itself which is the direct result of the artist's intention and which answers to those descriptions, then there would be simply no point in trying to answer the general question concerning the critical relevance of intention. Lacking such descriptions we, quite literally, would not know what we were talking about in asking the question.

It in fact takes surprisingly little attention to detail to disturb the equilibrium of the two-entity scheme. The jazz pianist Bill Evans states:

> There is a Japanese visual art in which the artist is forced to be spontaneous. He must paint on a thin stretched parchment with a special brush and black water paint in such a way that an unnatural or interrupted stroke will destroy the line or break through the parchment. Erasures or changes are impossible. These artists must practice a particular discipline, that of allowing the idea to express itself in communication with their hands in such a direct way that deliberation cannot interfere. . . . This conviction that direct deed is the most meaningful reflection, I believe, has prompted the evolution of the extremely severe and unique disciplines of the jazz or improvising musician.[13]

13. Bill Evans, "Improvisation in Jazz," liner notes for Miles Davis, *Kind of Blue* (Columbia LP PC 8163, 1959).

"Forced to be spontaneous," "interrupted strokes will destroy the line," "erasures are impossible," "in such a way that deliberation cannot interfere"—all of these phrases can rather forcibly alter our initial conception of what the musician (as well as the Japanese painter) is doing. They describe a medium which *itself* precludes even the possibility of working within the two-entity scheme. Put simply, the rigors of spontaneity prohibit it.

It is true, however, that one could here argue that these phrases are forceful, but in the opposite direction, reinforcing rather than refuting the initial independence and eventual correspondence between image and work. If the artist has thought very carefully about the specific image he wants to create, and if he has that image very clearly in mind before he picks up the brush, then he can proceed to paint without erasure or change precisely *because* these deliberations were made, with specific alterations being adopted or discarded, prior to the act of painting. The work thus embodies the artist's intention without need for erasure, deliberation in execution, interrupted strokes, or change. In response to this it must be pointed out that it is an improvising musician here drawing the parallel with a form of visual art, and that, even if the visual analogue of improvisation can be redescribed in dualistic terms, the improvisation itself never could be. Indeed, part of the challenge to the improviser is to invent musically coherent melodic lines over changing harmonic structures which, in their specific realization, often cannot be anticipated; the similarly unpredictable rhythmic dimension also enforces spontaneity. In the musical case, then, erasures are impossible and an interrupted stroke will destroy the (melodic) line, in a setting where the line is itself, very often, shaped *as it proceeds*. What Evans says of his own work does differ considerably from the speech we would have been inclined to attribute to him under the influence of the two-entity scheme which is the aesthetic form of the intentionalist template in the philosophy of language.

The musician's response to our astonishment that he can play exactly what he thinks might resemble the puzzlement of an orator if someone were to exclaim after her speech, "It was unbelievable! You were able to follow perfectly the rules of grammar, word order, sentence construction, and so on while going along at a phenomenal rate—your mastery of the art is so complete that we were altogether unaware of your effort!" The orator might well honestly and correctly respond, with no small degree of puzzlement, that the rules of grammar were the farthest thing from her mind as she spoke and that her effort most certainly should remain undetected, because it was not there. Yet, on the disputed view of intention, we would surely have included the following of rules as one of the descriptions which gives content to the image of the work in the mind of the creator, and necessarily so. After all, the work does in fact exhibit the particular characteristic of following grammatical rules, and the work is only the physical counterpart of the artist's intention, so, inferring mental facts from physical evidence, the intention must have had the following of the rules of grammar among its constituents. To say that this was not part of the inner, intentional work would be to say, on the image model, that the physical work was unsuccessful to the extent that characteristics were present and observable which were not part of the intention, just as unintended features are prominent in the Tower of Pisa case. Instead of constituting one admirable aspect of the speech, conformity to a rule would then have to be counted as an accidental or inadvertent result of some distortion, some mismatch, between intention and work. The improvising musician and the composer, who follow the rules of harmony, provide parallel cases.[14]

Evans's testimony is often echoed in the notes and biographies of conductors, composers, painters, poets, and sculptors. The conductor Herbert von Karajan tells of his surprise at discovering, against his initial plans, that the tempos had to be changed in one of his recordings of Beethoven's symphonies, and Stravinsky refers to himself as the "vessel" through which the *Rite of Spring* passed, which, in conjunction with the image model, seems a curiously pas-

14. See Robert E. Barela, "A Paradigm of Art," *Journal of the Theory and Criticism of the Visual Arts* 1 (1982): 7–19, and especially pp. 10–17, for a discussion of the ways in which artists of a given style or school stand parallel, as followers of internalized rules, to native speakers of a language.

sive way to put the matter.[15] Sculpture is perhaps the art in which the intentionalist view has the greatest intuitive plausibility, because here we are quite sure that the artist doesn't merely chisel away and see what happens, but rather that, before hammering the chisel (or igniting the torch), the artist must know exactly what he wants. Indeed, under the influence of Plotinus, Michelangelo spoke of "releasing" the sculpture from the block of stone. Consider, however, the statement of David Smith: "I cannot conceive a work and buy material for it. . . . Rarely the Grand Conception, but a preoccupation with parts. I start with one part, then a unit of parts, until a whole appears . . . The order of the whole can be perceived but not planned."[16] From this glance at a few cases it begins to appear that the artist need not have any intentional work, understood in terms of an image which can be completely captured by a collection of descriptions, in mind at all. Indeed, when artists do have ideas of the way the work will be carried out in mind, the very character of these ideas often fails to conform to the intentionalist template. In painting *Les Demoiselles d'Avignon* Picasso may well have had a strong visual image in mind, but it might have been a primitive face mask, rather than an image of the completed work.[17] Picasso also describes

15. The countless references to artistic or creative discoveries in the writings, statements, and journals of artists, where the discovery in question reverses or revises an initial plan of artistic execution, collectively constitute a massive empirical refutation of the intentional theory under consideration here; if this template-theory were true, no such discovery would ever be made because the given materials of the art in question would never "resist" the initial intention. For the Stravinsky example, see Robert Craft and Igor Stravinsky, *Expositions and Developments* (London: Faber and Faber, 1962), pp. 147–48. For the von Karajan example, see "Karajan Talks about Music with Irving Kolodkin," published with von Karajan's recording of Beethoven's Nine Symphonies with the Berlin Philharmonic (Polydor International, GmbH: nos. 2563 795-802, 1977); see particularly his remark, "To speak, if I may, of the metronomic indication. We have tried to follow it very closely. Sometimes it just doesn't go. I think many will be shocked by the first movement of the 'Eroica'—it is really fast."

16. David Smith, "Notes on My Work," *Arts* 34 (1960): 44, reprinted in *Theories of Modern Art*, ed. Chipp, pp. 576–77.

17. For a detailed discussion of a case in which the inspiration for a work takes the form of images from previous work of other artists, specifically, the combined influence of de'Barbari's *Apollo and Diana* and the *Apollo Belvedere* on Dürer's *Adam and Eve*, see Robert E. Barela and Joseph E. Young, "Deep and Surface Structures in Albrecht Dürer's *Adam and Eve* Engraving and Lorser Feitelson's 1968 *Untitled* Acrylic Painting," *Journal of the Theory and Criticism of the Visual Arts* 1 (1982): 21–38, especially 24–27.

his painting *Friendship* as involving a long and agonizing working out of technical problems bequeathed to him by Cézanne and Braque. He gave the work its title long after its completion, and it would surely be wrong to suppose that his intention in this work could be adequately represented by reference to a mental image. His intention was to conquer the problems passed on to him and to assimilate their solutions into his style, which quite evidently has nothing to do with an articulated imaginary object; indeed, the very idea of working things out *in art* is incompatible with the intentionalist picture.[18] In the same way, the fact that artists often learn things about their own works after completing them deepens the suspiciousness of the view that artistic creation should be viewed as a process of making choices on every matter that could serve as the subject of deliberation. This is strikingly illustrated by the case of T. S. Eliot, who readily admitted that he could be taught many things about the content of his own work.[19]

It would be wrong to take these remarks and quotations as definitely proving one thesis against another, for artists may be confused or deluded about their beliefs and practices, and quotations and anecdotes could no doubt be brought forward to support the intentionalist model as well. They are assembled here for the particular purpose of showing that the two-entity view of intentions and works is in fact far from inevitable; one can easily characterize

18. There are, of course, models of intention other than the one under review here which are not incompatible with a process of working things out in execution; see, for example, Barela, "A Paradigm of Art," pp. 13–14, and "The Visual Arts as Language," *Journal of the Theory and Criticism of the Visual Arts* 1 (1982): 149–67, especially 160–64, in which artistic performatives, most of which do not involve mental images, determine the artist's intention. For example, Warhol's intention to criticize an implicit aesthetic elitism is not *itself* an image of a soup-can, and the intention to define a style in contrast to abstract expressionism is not *itself* a multiple image of Marilyn Monroe.

19. In addition to the example of the well-known work on the drafts of the *Waste Land* with Ezra Pound, see Eliot's remarks on his own interpretation of Tennyson: "It happens now and then that a poet by some strange accident expresses the mood of his generation, at the same time that he is expressing a mood of his own which is quite remote from that of his generation . . . I get a very different impression from *In Memoriam* from that which Tennyson's contemporaries seem to have got." In *Selected Prose of T. S. Eliot*, ed. Frank Kermode (New York: Harcourt Brace Jovanovich, 1975), pp. 243–44. See also Kermode's remark: "Usually he disavowed the author's intentional control" (p. 6, n. 15).

numerous aspects of the process of artistic creation without relying on it and, moreover, when it is brought into play, other crucial details concerning intentions are obscured.

A few sections after the one with which we began, Wittgenstein remarks: "One cannot guess how a word functions. One has to *look at* its use and learn from that."[20] What, then, are some of the ways in which we can ask questions concerning an artist's intentions in particular cases and receive satisfactory answers? This is, of course, by no means intended to be an exhaustive catalogue, but rather merely a few cases in which specific problems of intention can arise.

First of all, we are sometimes interested in assessing the success of the artist in working toward technical goals or overcoming technical difficulties. In asking, "Did you intend to play that B-flat in the Bach piece, or did you mean to play a B-natural?" it is clear what answer is being sought. The same is true of the question "Did you intend to pause after that phrase?" Here the answer may be "No, I ran out of breath," or "Yes, I felt the phrase called for a division at that point." In neither case is there any temptation to push matters further than this to discover something about the relation between the piece, or the interpretation of it, and the intention or mental image thought to stand behind it, and if such a question were asked it would not be at all clear how to proceed in answering it.

Second, a question about the intention of an artist may arise on account of the strangeness or unusual character of the piece. A person might ask for an opinion on what John Cage intends by his *4:33* (the length of time for which the performer sits, silently, at the piano). Again, as curious audience members we know exactly what kind of answer to expect, such as, "Cage means to challenge traditional performer-audience relationships," or "Cage is determined to awaken us to the music of the natural sonic environment"; debilitating stage fright, or rather severe technical incompetence, are plainly ruled out, as are any other answers that proceed in terms of an image of the actual performance.

Third, a question of intention may arise where a work of art is assumed to be conveying a political, moral, or religious message.

20. Wittgenstein, *Philosophical Investigations*, sec. 340.

Milton in *Paradise Lost* is said by some to have meant that Man was appreciably better off after the Fall than before. In *The Raft of the Medusa* Géricault may have intended to capture in a single canvas the abuse of the lower classes by the self-interested upper classes. Here the issue is whether the artist was concerned with a specific doctrine or idea and put it into the work. Again, it is clear what is to be taken as an answer to this kind of question about intention. Once again, however, the answers do not rely on comparisons involving Milton's or Géricault's preexistent mental images.

Finally, there are cases such as the Masonic symbolism in Mozart's music and the allusions to Freudian theory in Nabokov. Although these particular cases are perhaps rather clear, one can easily imagine a question arising whether the author was explicitly portraying in a specific passage an instance of libidinal sublimation or not. In such cases images may play central roles. Again, this question is hardly sufficient to prompt any question concerning the relationship between an image and a physical object, or of the connection between two entities that occupy distinct ontological categories.

At this point we should ask whether there is anything conceptually significant which all of these cases of intention (the intention to play a B-flat, the intention to alter performer-audience relationships, the intention to register a protest against political oppression, and the intentional reference to Freudian or Masonic doctrines) have in common. If not—and it is not in any way clear they do—it is difficult to see how the general question of the relevance of intention at which we arrived at the end of the preceding section could be made authentically comprehensible. Moreover, we are now in a position to see that even if there were such a common element it would surely not take form as an articulated mental image, which in each case is indispensable to the forming of an intention.[21]

---

21. This is not, however, intended to effect a sweeping behavioristic exclusion of all mental aspects of artistic creativity; there are ways of preserving the mental without simultaneously relying on the mental image. The artist's intention, for example, might well include complex sets of unexamined presumptions about the art world along with sets of specific communicative artistic gestures, none of which requires any reference to an image for a full elucidation of them.

Someone sympathetic in perhaps a more refined way with the central tenet of New Criticism (a tenet by no means isolated to that phase of critical history) might reply that we need not suppose the existence of this rather suspicious metaphysical entity "The Artist's Intention" which is conceived of as an image of the completed work. The point to be taken to heart, this critic might insist, is that *none* of the specific artist's intentions, whether they are images of the work or intentions of some other kind, should be taken into account in an attempt to understand the work or to assign it a value. The missed note, Cage's silence, *The Raft of the Medusa*, and *Despair* must stand on their own; the New Critic will say that these works are not to be accorded greater value in virtue of details we may know about what the artist explicitly intended or meant in the work. The piece was not better performed because B-natural was intended. Cage's piece is not rendered a greater work by our adopting the view that musical relationships need changing, and to appreciate Géricault's painting we need know nothing of French political history; such knowledge, the critic might claim, may actually inhibit a genuinely aesthetic response to the work.[22] Similarly, reading Nabokov's *Despair* in Freudian terms may distract our attention from the real work thought to constitute the core of hard literary fact around which layers of subjective interpretation revolve.

The difficulty with this line of argument is that it rests on the doubtful and equally problematic assumption that we can distinguish between external evidence (that which concerns the artist's intentions or alleged intentions) and internal evidence (that which concerns the work itself) in any clear and consistent fashion. Here, in addition to the problems encountered with the mental half of this distinction, we are presented as well with the problem of understanding what is meant by the other of the two aesthetic entities—the work itself. Here we must ask what would be required for

22. This claim is in fact often made in connection with the theory of the aesthetic attitude and noncognitive or disinterested aesthetic perception; see, for example, Jerome Stolnitz, *Aesthetics and the Philosophy of Art* (New York: Houghton Mifflin, 1960), pp. 32–42, reprinted in *Introductory Readings in Aesthetics*, ed. John Hospers (New York: Free Press, 1969), pp. 17–27.

us to be able to see a work in strictly formal terms, or as standing independently of all extratextual considerations. An appreciator able to perform this perceptual feat would, for example, have to read a text without experiencing any association between, among other things, words or phrases and past experiences. No sentiments, feelings, thoughts, places, events, relationships, satisfactions, or disappointments could be allowed to enter into the appreciation of the work. The reader would have to have a vocabulary that contained no favored words or particularly meaningful phrases and could possess no predisposition to put things in certain ways. Otherwise, the reader's affinity for a particular writer might depend on the merely coincidental fact that the writer shared these particular linguistic or expressive idiosyncrasies. Of course, it was recognized by New Critics that we cannot prevent ourselves from experiencing these kinds of associations. My claim, closer to the philosophy of language than to literary criticism, is simply that the notion of a neutral *description* of the work which would be read by a reader who had also managed to discount external evidence is an unattainable ideal. Moreover, if any such description were attainable it would prove ultimately undesirable anyway. I. A. Richards described ways in which the values and idiosyncrasies of his students got in the way of their understanding poetry,[23] but he did not attempt to give a description of an isolated aesthetic object, the work itself. Similarly, he did not attempt to describe the reader who perceived exclusively that which is internal to a work. One might ask what a description of the work itself, for example, of Bernini's *Ecstasy of St. Teresa*, would include. The moral to be drawn from a case such as this is that it is not clear where the boundary is to be drawn between internal evidence and external evidence, and it is not clear by what criteria we should make these decisions. One can see how difficult this problem becomes when we ask what parts of the religious, cultural, social, and art-historical backgrounds of Bernini's work must be present to the mind of the perceiver who can truly be said to understand the expressions on the faces of the two figures portrayed in this work. For instance,

23. I. A. Richards, *Practical Criticism* (London: Kegan Paul, 1929).

it is fairly clear that we need considerably more than that contained by the description "a little fellow with wings stabbing an
ecstatic woman in the heart with an arrow." When we now go on
to ask what more, precisely, is needed, we begin to suspect rather
strongly that the answer is not in any case going to involve critically relevant facts that are clearly internal, just as descriptions of
an elaborated intentional object of Bernini's are not relevant either.
Whatever background is necessary for the critical illumination of
this work, it is not going to be entirely captured or explained in
these terms.

Perhaps one reason that it has often been tacitly assumed that
art can be exhaustively described in some altogether neutral set
of terms is that any other view is felt to threaten the possibility
of objective critical judgment. The extreme claim in this direction would hold that if objective description is possible, then a
picture can in fact and in itself be no more than a collection of
patches of color on canvas and a musical composition nothing
more than a combination of sounds of various timbres and
pitches, both of which are the external counterparts of the prior
intentional creation. This fear is, once brought into the light of
day, obviously irrational and the view obviously absurd. The
kinds of corrections of another person's reading of a work of art
with which we are familiar do not presuppose the existence of
any such neutral and abstract entity. The musicologist may reply
to the student who is puzzled by a reference to death in an otherwise jolly Elizabethan lute song, "In that lusty age, this reference is anything but what it might seem; in this context 'death'
has a sexual meaning." Someone who read George Eliot as rec-
ommending a passive resignation to Fate would require correction, as would someone who found Stravinsky's *Rite of Spring*
rather dated, considering it was composed last year. It does not
follow, however, from the mere possibility of correction that the
work of art is exhaustively captured by some finite set of true
factual statements about it which in turn describe an intentional
object.

Few will dispute that a poem, a novel, a painting, or a composition may mean a good deal more to a person of forty than to that

same person at twenty, but how can such a fact be explained on the supposition that the work itself lies under the critical and interpretive accretions and distortions superimposed on it? We may indeed come to understand the language of a poet, but this need not mean that we comprehend an overall intention, particularly where intention is given the definition we have discussed above—a definition that unfolds according to what Wittgenstein calls a "misleading picture." In spite of one's desires for theoretical concision, the question whether documentary evidence of the artist's intentions or the kind of evidence provided by the art historian can contribute to an understanding of the work will have different answers in different cases.

Yet *music* still seems different, in that it appears to require an elaborated intentional object in order to provide the identity of the musical work and to illuminate the nature of the compositional process itself. Whether or not it is different is the topic of the next section.

MUSIC AND IMAGINATION

When we inquired into the nature of works of art in Chapter 2 we saw that there is a good deal of evidence against aesthetic idealism, the view that artworks are, in the final analysis, imaginary objects in the minds of their creators. To reset the stage, we know that the National Gallery not only contingently but in some sense necessarily weighs more than merely the sum of the empty building, the people in it, and the assorted fixtures. This sum must also include the weight of canvases, the oils on them, carved stone and marble, and so on, all of which add up to substantially more than nothing, which is at least the approximate weight of imaginary things. We know that it takes considerably more than a verbal utterance or acoustical blast to transport an artwork, and we also know that a visit to the gallery is not going to amount to an afternoon spent with wax figures of unicorns, flying horses, present and bald kings of France or, for that matter, talking teapots. Against the idealist theory intuition strongly protests that if works of art are imaginary objects, they cannot be the things we go to see in the gallery; and if they are imaginary objects then, like a waxen Peter Pan, they are surely not art. Mellon and Meinong simply have different kinds of collections.

When we inquire specifically into the nature of musical works, however, aesthetic idealism seems to possess a much greater intuitive plausibility. Bach's meticulous contrapuntal calculation, Bartok's problem-solving quartets, Schönberg's twelve-tone designs, and Wagner's carefully premeditated placement of leitmotifs all seem to emphasize the mental over the material; calculating, problem solving, designing, and premeditating simply do not fall into a natural category along with things that take place in the physical world such as earthquakes and eclipses. In fact, a melody can be transported via the acoustical blast. Reflections such as these propel one quite rapidly towards the view that, behind the perhaps misleading and certainly multifarious world of musical performance there lies a more pure world of musical thought, populated with the imaginary objects of an ideal reality to which all the aural flux impossibly, and in many performances recklessly, aspires. Indeed, does not the very possibility of poor performances or misinterpretations imply the existence of these immaterial standards of excellence, ultimately private to the mind of the composer? What we have arrived at here is an aesthetic correspondence theory, or the idea, examined above with arts other than music, that there exist one-to-one dualistic relationships between that which is heard and that which is thought. Let me follow Wittgenstein's recommendation to "look and see," and investigate this musical theory by considering some examples in which thought and imagination do in fact operate.[24]

1. Someone is trying to recall the opening theme of Beethoven's *Fifth Symphony*; it seems to be on the tip of her tongue, but she cannot quite remember it. She knows it begins with a note repeated

24. See in this connection Wittgenstein's admonition to "*look and see* whether there is anything common to all" of the multifarious "proceedings that we call 'games'" in *Philosophical Investigations*, sec. 66, and the subsequent discussion of "family resemblances" in sec. 67.

three times and decides to work through the intervals systematically in her mind's ear until she hits on it. Her first effort—three
notes followed by an ascent of a half step—immediately strikes her
not only as wrong, but as moving in the wrong direction. She tries
again, this time with a descent of a half step, which is still wrong,
but closer, she feels. At last she tries with a descent of a third. It
clicks into place and the rest of the theme returns to her; she
knows how to go on.

Now, in this case, the woman searching for the passage uses her
imagination; she thinks in pitches to find the passage. She is shuffling pitches around, like a person with a forgotten name on the
tip of the tongue running through the alphabet in search of the
first letter, but she is thinking in pitches only so long as she is trying to find something she has not yet gotten. Does she, in the
same way, think in pitches when the rest of the passage instanta-
neously comes to her? One may feel some diffidence at saying
anything here, but it is at least clear that she does not think or
imagine the pitch configuration in the same way as she does with
her search method. Indeed, one may say, in a manner reminiscent
of Gilbert Ryle, that with regard to the latter notes in the phrase
that come back suddenly she did not have to think in pitches,
because she did not have to think at all.[25] In any case, the notion
that there is one kind of thinking or imagining of, or in, music
that is suitable for the correspondence theory is already cast into
doubt.

2. A group of music students are thinking of their upcoming
examination in Baroque music, and one asks another if he knows
the melody to Bach's *Cantata 147*. The answer is yes—the other
sings it straight off. We may be inclined to suppose that he also
thought of the melody in pitches. But in this case, unlike the previous one, he did not imagine the melody at all; he simply sang it
without imagining or thinking it; our understanding of his singing
it does not necessarily depend for its cogency on our conceiving of
him as thinking or imagining.

25. See Gilbert Ryle, *The Concept of Mind* (New York: Barnes and Noble, 1949),
especially pp. 32–60.

To be sure, there are cases in which we hear singing without imagination, or at least unimaginative singing, and there are cases in which we have performances without thought, or thoughtless performances, but this student's singing of the cantata melody is not such a case.

3. Here is a case in which thought undeniably plays a part: on two successive evenings we hear recitals in which the same piece, a theme and variations, is performed. On the first evening the performer simply runs through the notes. The piece amounts to an unimpressive homogeneous string of undifferentiated, undistinguished pitches. Our only clue that the piece is a theme and variations is the title on the program. The following evening, another performer transforms the piece for us. Dynamic shadings, variations in tempo, clear phrasing, and many other subtleties of interpretation give the theme and each of its variations a unique and recognizable character.

The first performance was a mere demonstration of technique, if that. The first performer revealed what he saw in the work—a succession of notes; his playing was, for this reason, thoughtless and unimaginative. The second performer, by contrast, gave a thoughtful and imaginative performance, revealing the structural coherence that she perceived in the piece. Now, in these cases, thought does not enter into consideration as the idealist would predict it. Even though as a critical remark we may say that the piece was not really performed on the first night, the simple indisputable fact remains that the piece is present on both nights. Directly stated, thought and the work are not inseparable.

4. In this case, imagination plays another kind of part: a piece is being composed collectively by a group of composers. The form in which the composers are writing requires a modulation to a new key for the middle section, and it is suggested that they quickly and efficiently accomplish this by simply stating the dominant chord of the new key just at the end of the first section, thus setting up the resolution to the new tonic at the prescribed place. All except one agree. She, after a moment's reflection, suggests a much smoother modulation employing a pivot chord—a chord common to both the old and new keys—prior to the new dominant. All immediately

agree, congratulate her on her good idea, and the unimaginative modulation is replaced by the new one.

In this case it is clear that the piece could have been written in the unimaginative way, without the pivot chord, yet it would still have been in a definitional sense the same composition, just as an arrangement of a piece, although it may incorporate alterations, is still an arrangement of *that* piece. In the present example, with the addition of the pivot chord, the piece has an imaginative passage it otherwise would not have had. When asked about the difference—a question specifically concerning the imagination—the composers in the workshop will point not to the entire piece, which is hardly an answer at all, but to that particular passage.

5. A critic may object to an orchestral piece on the ground that it is "mere texture." It may be entirely composed of varying orchestral colors but devoid of any strictly musical development or musical logic. The piece may indeed have simply no thought at all in it, but again, the piece enjoys a certain sovereignty with regard to thought, and it is this sovereignty that is incompatible with the idealist view. Conversely, a critic may criticize the piece for having, like a canvas with only a bright yellow square, too much thought behind it, i.e., she may object to its being born purely of art theory. Here also, of course, the connection between art and thought is not at all what the idealist view would imply. Sound and thought here have a far more complicated relationship than a simple mutual reliance between conception and execution.

6. A composer in the group mentioned above may be vaguely dissatisfied with a certain cadence. He objects to it, saying that the individual voices do not lead from one to the next smoothly enough. He says, "I think, although I don't know what it is yet, that there is another way to do it." Now, already he is beyond a doubt giving thought to the work, and yet there is not yet a work, in terms of the idealist's view of that entity, to which he is giving thought. He thinks there is another way, but he does not yet see what this could be. In the previous cases we have seen both works without thought or imagination and works with a kind of thought

or imagination not accounted for by the theory. Here, however, thought is undeniably present, and it is thought about the work or any part of the work, as it is thought about doing the cadence some other way, a way not yet identified. The correspondence breaks down in both directions, i.e., both from sound inward to thought and from thought outward to sound.

7. Now the composer suddenly sees what he has been looking for: rather than the dominant chord in the cadence he was going to use unsatisfactorily, he can substitute a dominant chord one half step above the tonic to which the dominant resolves. He sees that both dominant chords contain the same internal interval of a tri-tone, and it is this that generates the dominant function of the chords. He makes the substitution, the cadence is much smoother, and the work is completed. Now, however, this thought—everything about the tri-tone and the dominant function—has been necessary to the completion of this particular work. The thought, we may say, has "gone into" the work. On the idealist view, is this—the thought involving the principle of the chord substitution—to be a permanent part of the work? Apparently the idealist is committed to saying that it is, and yet when performers perform the piece, and when audiences hear it, in order to understand that final cadence, i.e., hear it as a cadence, do they need to hear it also as a substitute chord, holding in mind the original dominant chord just "behind" it, so that the two internal notes common to both chords overlap? This was the thought, or at least one way to represent the musical thought, that was essential to the composing of the work, but no such imaginary overlapping of chords, or thinking of one chord as a substitution of its predecessor, is essential to hearing that this is a final cadence. Thus, hearing and understanding the work is not, contrary to the conception of criticism as the recreation of the artist's intention, identical with a reconstruction of the thought that went into it.

What conclusions can be drawn from the foregoing detailed cases with regard to our general problem of intention and the musical variant of aesthetic intentionalism suggesting that musical works are intentional or imaginative entities? We have seen cases in which thought and imagination do enter into creating, performing, hearing, and understanding pieces of music. None of these cases, however, served to illustrate the theory of the correspondence between mental envisagement and tonal embodiment. Thought and imagination do enter into the creation and criticism of music in a multitude of ways but, as it now appears, in ways either incompatible with the correspondence theory or at least not explained by that theory. In many cases the strict application of the theory to the case could only result in obliterating the distinctions we actually do make regarding thought and imagination, and these distinctions, as seen in the examples, are themselves essential to our understanding of those cases as involving imagination and thought in the first place. Not all musical works or their performances are thoughtful and imaginative, and although many are, those are not thoughtful and imaginative in a uniform way that appears in every case.

Ryle has discussed the compulsion to make the case of thinking analogous to that of fence-mending, singing, and testimonial writing: no fence-mending without hammering; no singing without sound-making; no testimonial writing without marks on paper; no thinking without _____.[26] The craving to fill this blank goes, of course, by the name of essentialism. As a result of the same kind of craving the aesthetic intentionalist of the particular variety under consideration here feels that, if we mean anything at all by "music," there must be something to fill the space in "No music without _____." His next response is to fill in this blank with "imagination." As our glance at a few cases has suggested, however, this concept is far too ill-behaved to sit peaceably in such a position.

THE crucial point in the preceding discussion is the one that stands parallel to Wittgenstein's remark about intention in language: "But here we are constructing a misleading picture of 'intending', that is, of the use of this word. An intention is embedded in its situation,

---

26. Ryle, "A Puzzling Element in the Notion of Thinking," in *Studies in the Philosophy of Thought and Action*, ed. P. F. Strawson (Oxford: Oxford University Press, 1968), pp. 7–23.

in human customs and institutions."[27] Specifically, intelligible discussions of the artist's intentions will not concern the relations between an image of the work itself in the mind of the artist and a physical object purported to be the material embodiment of that image. For it is not clear that such an image need play any role in the creation of art; nor is it clear what this image would be or how to describe it if it did play such a role; lastly it is not clear that the accompanying philosophical notion of "the work" is any less of a mythical product of conceptual vertigo produced by an indifference to actual cases of artistic creation and criticism. In the same discussion Wittgenstein also remarks that "an unsuitable type of expression is a sure means of remaining in a state of confusion. It as it were bars the way out."[28] I am suggesting that the phrase "the artist's intention," when viewed as an embodied image rather than an embedded custom, can very easily become such an expression. The next question, however, is what significance Wittgenstein's philosophy of language holds, not for the understanding or critical analysis of a work of art, but for the process of artistic creativity itself.

27. Wittgenstein, *Philosophical Investigations*, sec. 337. The culturally embedded nature of artistic intention is naturally best shown through a detailed consideration of the ways intention functions rather than through an attempt to describe this embeddedness generally. To take a few brief examples: Dali's deliberate intention to obfuscate meaning can, once grasped as artistic intention, clarify meaning. Miro's intention to get the viewer to see the work as a freely associated collection of images can reveal the distinctive coherence of the work. Beckman's stated specific intentions can prove thoroughly helpful in a context where the larger intention is to allow pure form to communicate emotion without the mediation of the artist's thought, consistent with an expressionist program. Propositionally encapsulated intentions can transform the unintelligible into the comprehensible in contexts of conceptual art, insofar as these asserted intentions render the aim or the point of the object visible. Mondrian's artistic platonism, as an intentional program, serves as a contrast to, and thus makes salient distinctive features of, Morandi's very different variety of intentional platonism, both of which provide a critically significant background for the comprehension of Zuccari's extreme mannerism, itself the result of still another variety of platonism.
28. Ibid., sec. 339.

5　Against Creation as Translation

A good deal of discussion of the problem of creativity in aesthetics has presupposed the familiar philosophical distinction between the phenomenologically private and the physically public; in this respect it of course mirrors a good deal of work in the philosophy of language. The creative process in art has often been viewed as a sequence of events through which an inner entity, a particular feeling or emotion, is given external realization. This way of construing artistic creation also nourishes a familiar, and from this theoretical vantage point, seemingly intractable problem—how can a private feeling be instilled into an inanimate physical object?

The acceptability and, indeed, the intelligibility of the dualistic categories resting beneath this conception of artistic creation have been, of course, called into question by Wittgenstein within the domains of the philosophy of language and the philosophy of mind. The precise consequences of his remarks for aesthetic theory, however, and particularly for our understanding of the creative process, are often left unspecified. In this chapter, then, I consider some passages from Wittgenstein concerning expression and intention in language and clarify their significance for philosophical discussions of creativity. I will show that it is misguided,[1] although misguided in instructive ways, to see creativity as a matter of the artist's

---

1. This conclusion in aesthetics stands parallel to the conclusion in the philosophy of language that the "sign" does not get its "life" from some prior private mental content. See Wittgenstein's discussion in *The Blue and Brown Books* (Oxford: Basil Blackwell, 1958), pp. 4–11.

clothing a preexisting feeling in a material shell or of reproducing an inner object of any ontological variety in outer form. A careful dismantling of the elements that make this approach seem plausible will itself point to a better way of understanding creativity. Wittgenstein's remarks provide as well the grounds for a reappraisal of the role of the medium in artistic creation.

THE TRANSLATION MODEL

Although the view of the creative process I want to discuss, which I shall call "the translation model," can be found, explicitly or implicitly, in the utterances of many theorists, critics, and artists,[2] I will use one of the most concise formulations of this model, the famous passage of T. S. Eliot, as a point of departure: "The only way of expressing an emotion in the form of art is by finding an 'objective correlative'; in other words, a set of objects, a

2. This dualistic pattern of thought was perhaps most clearly articulated by the theorists of the Symbolist movement. During this period this model of creativity became for these theorists not merely one aspect of artistic activity, but the very essence of art itself, and since that time the model has retained its power as a central influence on thought about art. For example, the painter and theorist Maurice Denis wrote: "We have substituted for the idea of 'nature seen through a temperament,' the theory of equivalence or of the symbol; we asserted that the emotions or spiritual states caused by any spectacle bring to the imagination of the artist symbols or plastic equivalents. These are capable of reproducing emotions or states of the spirit without it being necessary to provide the *copy* of the initial spectacle; thus for each state of our sensibility there must be a corresponding objective harmony capable of expressing it." "De Gauguin et de Van Gogh au Classicisme," *L'Occident* (Paris, May 1909), reprinted as "Subjective and Objective Deformation" in *Theories of Modern Art*, ed. and trans. Herschel B. Chipp (Berkeley: University of California Press, 1968), pp. 105–6. The translation model also appears implicitly in the critic G.-Albert Aurier's manifesto "Symbolism in Painting: Paul Gauguin." In this essay a number of characteristics of the new art are listed; among other things works of art must be *"Ideist*, for its unique ideal will be the expression of the Idea, . . . *Symbolist*, for it will express this Idea by means of forms," and *"Subjective*, for the object will never be considered as an object but as the sign of an idea perceived by the subject." "Le Symbolisme en peinture; Paul Gauguin," *Mercure de France* 2 (Paris, 1891), trans. H. R. Rookmaaker and Herschel B. Chipp, and reprinted in *Theories of Modern Art*, ed. Chipp, p. 92. To understand fully what Aurier means by "idea" one would have to review the Neoplatonic strain in his thought; nevertheless it is apparent that the translation model is at work—the material object is subservient to and follows the prior subjective content. Earlier, Gauguin

situation, a chain of events which shall be the formula of that *particular* emotion."[3]

On this view the artist, perhaps a sculptor, faces the task of shaping his stone after the model—say Balzac—presently sitting in his studio. But he also has to pay heed to another model, the inner one that allegedly serves as the model for the emotional content or impact of the work. He has a particular outer subject, Balzac, and he has as well an inner subject, a *"particular* emotion," which is recollected in tranquility or held before his inner gaze in some similar fashion and which is to become the expressive content of the work, the feeling captured by the physical object. Thus, on the translation model of artistic creation, the given artistic medium in which an artist is working is assigned a subordinate role; indeed, the materials now play a supporting role to the particular emotion. We are thus directed by this model to look, not at what is on the painter's canvas, or the sculptor's pedestal, or composer's score, but rather in a sense through or behind these things, to the emotive significance of which the materials are the supporting outward correlate. As a way of encapsulating the implications of the translation model we might say that the physical materials are now merely *evidence* for the inner aesthetic meaning or emotional content which lies behind, and that our interpretive task is to read between the physical lines or behind the physical materials in search of the particular emotive content. As we shall see, this inferential conception of criticism is the result of a prior conception of private meaning, and as such is yet another meeting point within aesthetics of the philosophy of mind and the philosophy of language. We will return to these matters explicitly in Chapter 6; for the present we should ask the following question. Do artistic materials, and

---

himself revealed in a letter the extent to which his thought conformed to this theoretical template: "Above all don't sweat over a canvas; a great emotion can be translated instantly, dream about it and seek for it the simplest form." Letter to Emile Schuffenecker, Copenhagen, 14 January 1885, in *Lettres de Gauguin à sa femme et à ses amis*, ed. Maurice Malingue (Paris, Grasset, 1949), pp. 44–47, reprinted as "Feeling and Thought" in *Theories of Modern Art*, ed. Chipp, p. 59.

3. *Selected Prose of T. S. Eliot*, ed. Frank Kermode (New York: Harcourt Brace Jovanovich, 1975), p. 48.

does the art medium, deserve to be made subservient in the way this translation model requires? Are the materials—the painter's colors, the composer's pitches, and the poet's words—nothing more than elements so arranged as to constitute the formula of a given emotion? Are they within this context only the bearers of, and in no part the makers of, artistic meaning in their own right?

One can, of course, easily be led to believe that the translation model for the creation of works of art must be the only one able to do justice to the facts. Indeed, the very facts called to mind when considering the process of artistic creation seem naturally to invite, and in fact almost to demand, an explanation which proceeds along the lines of this model. Imagine a defender of the translation model inviting us to consider in turn three well-known works of art, a Dürer engraving, a Beethoven symphony, and a Michelangelo sculpture. Dürer's *Melancholia*, we are told, is uncontroversially expressive of a particular deep melancholy, a kind of entrapment in an unpleasant present and an utter inability to take action now with a view to a future greater good. Had Dürer not known in advance what it was he wanted to express, the defender might argue, he could not have executed the work in the way he in fact did. Dürer did not, after all, just execute the work, and then ask himself or his colleagues what it looked like, finally settling on the title it now bears. Any such story as this would obviously fail to do justice to both the skills and the intentions of artists. Beethoven's *Ninth Symphony*, in turn, contains an unmistakable sense at its conclusion of final triumph—surely Beethoven must have intended to capture precisely this feeling of exaltation in the work. Again, it is ludicrous to say, in direct opposition to the translation model, that Beethoven simply worked out the pitches and found the quality of the work there after the fact. Finally, the translation theorist may point to Michelangelo's *David* and insist that the gesture indicates not merely a piece of carved stone, but the physical counterpart of the emotional intent behind the work. The particular nobility of spirit conjoined to a sense of autonomous power, he will say, was precisely what Michelangelo intended to capture and put on display and which served, during the process of creation, as his inner model.

These cases apparently provide a set of facts which call for the translation model; in each of them it appears that a specific inner feeling is translated into material form. Indeed, it appears that a dualistic explanation of creation is incontrovertible, precisely because each work is materially embodied and carries an emotional impact. As we shall see, however, these facts do indeed induce translation-model theorizing, but they are far from establishing its truth. This can be seen through an exploration of a significant confusion first identified in Wittgenstein's *The Blue and Brown Books*.[4] In the following I would like to show the remarkable power this confusion has in connection with the problem of creation and then apply the distinction Wittgenstein enunciated in diffusing its power to mislead.[5]

THE TRANSITIVE-INTRANSITIVE CONFLATION

Wittgenstein distinguishes between what he calls the "transitive" and "intransitive" uses of the words "peculiar" and "particular." He says: "Now the use of the word 'particular' is apt to produce a kind of delusion and roughly speaking this delusion is produced by the double usage of this word. On the one hand, we may say, it is used preliminary to a specification, description, comparison; on the other hand, as what one might describe as an emphasis. The first usage I shall call the transitive one, the second the intransitive one."[6] Wittgenstein illustrates this difference by asking us to contrast two sorts of remarks. In the first case one might say, "I have noticed the way in which A enters the room." The important thing here is that upon request the speaker can go on to provide a description of A to which he is calling attention. There is room for this further description—"He always sticks his head into the room before coming in"—implicit in the original

4. Wittgenstein, *The Blue and Brown Books*, pp. 158–65.

5. I am here much indebted to Richard Wollheim's brief but illuminating discussion of this distinction of Wittgenstein's and its relation to art in *Art and Its Objects*, 2d ed. (Cambridge University Press, 1980), pp. 93–96, and 110–12.

6. Wittgenstein, *The Blue and Brown Books*, p. 158.

remark. By contrast, consider the remark: "I've now been observing the way A sits and smokes." Here, Wittgenstein tells us, the speaker need not be prepared to provide a further description of A's particular way of sitting and smoking *independently* of A. One way of explaining the remark is simply to say that it means nothing more than "I've been observing A as he sat and smoked," which, by contrast with the first case, is to provide no further description. The point is that although we do in fact speak of the particular way in which A does X, " 'the way' can't in this case be separated from him [the person who sat and smoked]."[7]

To return to the analogous artistic case, suppose then that a critic says, "This Dürer expresses so perfectly and forcefully that particular feeling of deep melancholy." If the question is now asked *"What* feeling?" one might quite naturally reply, pointing again to the engraving with a shrug of the shoulders, "Well . . . , *that* feeling." This is a way of replying which is in fact intransitive, and indeed this intransitivity accounts for the naturalness of the response, i.e. its lack of art-theoretical significance. The translation theorist, if present, might artificially, or through a distinctively theoretical motivation, insist that the question "What feeling?" in fact deploys a transitive use (where the question is taken to mean "What *particular* feeling?") and through this insistence on the transitive use of "particular," the theorist forces philosophical significance into the otherwise innocent, or theoretically noncommittal, lines. Having thus forced the issue through insisting on transitivity, the translation theorist can then return to those initial intuitions regarding the necessity of the translation model in the Dürer, Beethoven, and Michelangelo cases with renewed confidence. Although I have made this process sound deliberate, these conceptual sleights of hand might well be carried out unwittingly; indeed, this process constitutes an exemplary instance of being misled by grammatical appearance or, as Wittgenstein refers to it, by the surface grammar of our expressions. Operating a philosophical apparatus while under the influence of a misleading form of words, the theorist believed that two entities were being pointed out: the per-

---

7. All the brief quotations in this paragraph are from ibid., p. 160.

fectly tangible carved stone and the less tangible but equally present nobility of spirit with autonomous power. Let us further investigate the source of this grammatical-optical illusion. In reference to the smoker and his particular way of smoking, Wittgenstein says:

> We are inclined to answer the question "What way do you mean?" by "*This* way", instead of answering: "I didn't refer to any particular feature; I was just contemplating his position". My expression made it appear as though I was pointing out something *about* his way of sitting, . . . whereas what makes me use the word "particular" here is that by my attitude towards the phenomenon I am laying an emphasis on it: I am concentrating on it, or retracing it in my mind, or drawing it, etc.[8]

The crux of the distinction, then, lies in our ability in the transitive case to provide further explanations and descriptions of the "particular feature"; in the intransitive case there exist no such further identifying descriptions. There is, in the intransitive case, nothing *apart* from the phenomenon under consideration to be captured by a further description. In order to clarify this distinction Wittgenstein invites us to consider the sentence, "By 'kilogram' I mean the weight of one litre of water." This kind of explanation is of the general type: "By 'A' I mean 'B', where B is an explanation of A." The contrasting remark, similar in form or grammatical surface structure but different in content, is, "I said that I was sick of it and meant it." Now, we may well be inclined to go on and ask, following this remark, "*What* did you mean?" The answer Wittgenstein suggests one might give to this question again reveals the curious power of the confusion between the transitive and intransitive cases. He observes that the answer "by what I said I meant what I said" is a way of answering within the general form, "By saying 'A' I mean 'B'." We are reminded, however, that in fact we use expressions such as "I mean what I mean" to tell someone that there *is* no further explanation, that there remains no further

8. Ibid.

explanatory room in which to move. The point is that as a result of this confusion we are trying in the artistic case to ask a question strikingly similar to that notable—and senseless—linguistic curiosity, "What sentence is formed by this sequence of words?" It is indeed precisely a question of this type we would be asking if, after hearing the Beethoven symphony, we asked: *What* feeling of triumph? Yet if the translation model were correct, this would surely be *the* essential question in the criticism and understanding of a work of art, one we should be able to ask intelligibly and answer coherently.[9]

We can now see that it was at least in part this confusion between transitive and intransitive uses that generated the apparent need for the translation model in the above initial reflections of the translation theorist. Again, the theorist points to the three works and claims, quite rightly, that the works capture *these particular* feelings. There remains, however, one further specific belief of the translation theorist that must be directly addressed, namely that the particular feeling or emotive content of a work must be identifiable independently of the work itself. To pursue this side of the matter, Wittgenstein draws a slyly smiling face and observes that we may "feel inclined to say: 'Surely I don't see mere dashes. I see a face with a *particular* expression.'" Again, this is in fact *not* said as a prelude to further descriptions or details; it rather draws attention within this conversational context to the face. To construe this case, however, as a transitive use makes one think that there remains a latent further description, and that this further description would in fact be a description of a separate entity independent from the face itself. We are led to think, Wittgenstein argues, that, in trying to explain what we *mean* by "This face has a particular expression," we could point to something *other* than the face. "But," he adds, "if I had to point to anything in this place it would have to be the drawing I am looking at." This illicit act of aesthetic reification is encouraged by the fact that we speak of the face as *having* an expression, suggesting that there is an entity separable from the face to which we could point in giving the meaning of the

9. All the direct quotations in this paragraph are from ibid., pp. 160–61.

words "a particular expression." Comparing the phrase "This face *has* a particular expression" with the phrase "This *is* a peculiar face" helps to disentangle this element of confusion; there is not the urge to posit an independent expressive entity in the latter case, because "is" denotes identity or one thing, whereas "has" suggests one thing possessing something else, which in the present case would amount to a physical artifact possessing a separately identifiable emotional expression. Thus Wittgenstein says, reminding us of the larger philosophical power of a smaller exchange of words, "What a thing *is*, we mean, is bound up with it; what it *has* can be separated from it."[10]

The translation theorist, then, points to the Dürer engraving, the Beethoven symphony, and the Michelangelo sculpture and thinks that the gesture indicates two ontologically distinct entities in each case—the materials of the given medium *and* the particular feeling of melancholy, triumph, and nobility of spirit. Moreover, the theorist believes that these indisputable facts of the case, which can only be adequately accounted for on the translation model, naturally give rise to the theory. Indeed, the theorist may think these conclusions so obvious that the use of the word "theory" seems unnecessary. Nevertheless, the facts the theorist assembles and relies upon, i.e., these three works of art which indisputably capture particular feelings, do not themselves demand a dualistic explanation, because it is far from an indisputable fact at this point that two separable and distinct entities are being pointed out in each case. Two entities of contrasting ontological natures are not mentally compared or held together in the perception of the Dürer, the Michelangelo, or the Beethoven works, any more than they are in the perception of Wittgenstein's cartoon face. We do not identify the particular feelings of melancholy, triumph, and nobility by comparing what we see physically of the artwork with what we "see" emotionally in the mind's eye—although we can be led to believe that we do this through an implicit insistence on the transitive meaning of "particular feeling" and the resultant conception of correlated inward feelings and outward objects. As we have seen,

10. All quotations in this paragraph are from ibid., p. 162.

this perhaps unwitting insistence, itself motivated by grammatical confusion, underwrites the entire conception of artistic creation as translation. Wittgenstein observes in this connection: "And in letting the face impress itself on me and contemplating its 'particular impression', no two things of the multiplicity of a face are compared with each other; there is only *one* which is laden with emphasis. Absorbing its expression, I don't find a prototype of this expression in my mind; rather, I, as it were, cut a seal from the impression."[11]

To summarize this section, the transitive-intransitive conflation results in a picture of (a) an original entity, the mind's emotive prototype, and (b) a second entity, the physical artwork, which serves as the former entity's outward correlate. Both of these categorically distinct entities initially appear necessary but in fact do not play the part envisioned for them in our perception of works of art. Although this picture of artistic creation implies that we should be able to ask the crucial question *"What* feeling?" in response to a phrase such as "Look how Dürer has captured that particular feeling of melancholy," we have seen that this question demands logico-linguistic room for its asking that the circumstances do not allow, i.e., it is a question that asks about the precise nature and function of a nonexistent entity. The translation theorist will here say, "But surely the Beethoven *says* something—and simply listening to the piece proves that." This is, of course, correct; it does. Extreme caution is needed, however, to avoid going beyond what the intransitive use itself dictates; part of the difficulty, indeed, is— as Wittgenstein characterized problems in philosophy generally— saying what we know and no more. Wittgenstein marks this boundary by saying that "that same illusion possesses us even more strongly if repeating a tune to ourselves and letting it make its full impression on us, we say 'This tune says *something*', and it is as though I had to find *what* it says."[12] The illusion is not that the tune says something, but that what it says is independent of the specific materials in which it is said and thus that the specific tune

11. Ibid., p. 165.
12. Ibid., p. 166.

before us is itself only one instantiation, or indeed translation, of that prior emotive content.

ON FINDING THE RIGHT EXPRESSION

I now turn to some questions Wittgenstein asks in the *Philosophical Investigations* and discuss the relevance of those questions for the validity of the translation model in artistic creativity. Wittgenstein asks, "What happens when we make an effort—say in writing a letter—to find the right expression for our thoughts?" This search for the right expression is a familiar experience and as such is another kind of case which lends intuitive plausibility to the translation model. Wittgenstein remarks that "this phrase compares the process to one of translating or describing: the thoughts are already there (perhaps were there in advance) and we merely look for their expression." This stands as the perfect linguistic analogue to the artistic model because it is implied, in the formulation of the question itself, that the letter writer possesses the inner content, which is only awaiting the creation of its external counterpart for its expression. "This picture," Wittgenstein continues, "is more or less appropriate in different cases."[13] This, as far as it goes, seems undeniable; in cases in which actual translation or something very much like translation is in fact being carried out, the characterization of the process in terms of "finding the right expression for the thought" is philosophically harmless. As one example, one might discover, upon having written an invitation and having read it over, that the tone is not quite right, or one might find that a particular turn of phrase used in a letter does not quite capture the intended sentiment; such cases are philosophically harmless because they do not themselves require the positing of the independent prior feeling as distinct from the actual written language. In these cases, in order to recognize that one has got the phrase wrong one does not *compare* feeling with writing; rather

---

13. Quotations from Ludwig Wittgenstein, *Philosophical Investigations*, 3d ed., trans. G. E. M. Anscombe (New York: Macmillan, 1958), sec. 335.

one sees that the particular emotional tone of the writing *itself* is not what one wanted. Not all cases of writing or of artistic creation are fundamentally like translation, however, and to characterize artistic work in terms of the initial thought and the finding of its external correlate is surely not philosophically inert. To cast the very question concerning such cases of "finding the right expression" within the categories of the thought or the feeling and its external expression in the subordinated medium is already to prejudice the case strongly in favor of the translation model. Thus to ask the question in art parallel to Wittgenstein's question, namely, "What happens when we make an effort—say in composing—to find the right expression for our thoughts?" is to beg the question, in that the formulation of the question itself presumes the existence of two entities. The conceptual prejudice imposed by the formulation of the question is exposed when Wittgenstein next asks, "But can't all sorts of things happen here?"[14] With various answers to this question come the details that disturb this general picture of creativity.

Considering one of the things that can happen, Wittgenstein says, "I surrender to a mood and the expression *comes.*"[15] This phenomenon is common enough, both in letter writing and in artistic creation, yet it clearly does not fit the translation model. For instance, a composer can struggle for some time with a harmonic problem of modulation. Suddenly, "for no reason," as it may be described, she may see that the way from one harmonic area to another to which she wants to progress is through a diminished chord. A poet may have the same experience with a problematic passage involving a complex rhyme scheme. A novelist may "surrender to the mood" and let a character "say what he wants," permitting himself to write with a free rein. In all of these cases, the work comes to the artist in a way neither predicted by nor allowed for on the translation model, because it is the unleashed materials *themselves* which lead the artist to the desired content, which on the translation model must of conceptual necessity come first.

14. Ibid.
15. Ibid.

Indeed, on the model itself these cases can make no more sense than the idea of producing an English translation of a poem which does not yet exist in Italian.

There remains, however, another common critical practice that lends further intuitive support to the translation model, and this is our tendency to accord the artist a special position in the critical examination of his own work. In a restricted sense this is perfectly justifiable; the artist is, after all, the person who created the work in question. This special position is, however, often given to the artist for more metaphysical reasons, i.e., because of the supposed privileged access that an artist uniquely enjoys in relation to the emotive meaning of the work. The artist is believed to be in a unique position to speak for the meaning of the work because of some special access to the inner, nonpublic model. This stands as the perfect aesthetic parallel to the metaphysical problem of other minds; here the artist is the only one who *knows* what the content is behind the appearances, and for all others it is a matter of educated guesswork. Thus the critic's task is thought to be in all essentials like that of the "other": as the other is thought by some theorists to infer the presence of mental states on the basis of observable physical movements, the critic makes inferences concerning the emotional content of the work on the basis of the physical evidence, e.g., brush strokes, colors, pitches, and so forth. But as Wittgenstein asks, can't all sorts of things happen here?

There are many varieties of cases in which the artist is in the worst possible position to speak for his own work. For example, she may have a hugely inflated view of the significance of her work; she may be blind to its defects; she may not have the perspective to see that it is not strikingly original; and so on. Or she may be excessively modest, believing her work to be insignificant, flawed, and derivative when in fact it is not. An artist can come to change her mind about what a given work means. Or the artist can come to see the work in a new light, e.g., as influenced by others in ways not previously realized. She may become disillusioned with a work and claim that it is worthless and means nothing. (She may be right or wrong about this; it doesn't matter which, as the important fact is that her view *can* change.) Critics may expand her appreciation of her own work, or her psychoanalyst (again rightly or wrongly) may bring her to believe that her work actually concerns past struggles in her life in ways she had not previously considered. The artist may come, with the years, to lose this alleged privileged status; she may view her early work as that of another person, and be unable to remember how she carried out the work in question. Simply put, it is remarkably easy to assemble numerous reminders of actual cases discordant with the privileged critical status the artist is granted under the translation model. More strongly, these cases would in fact be impossible if the translation model were accurate, and they thus operate collectively as a reductio.

Still another aspect of artistic creativity for which the translation model would hold direct implications is the relationship between the artist and his materials. Here too, however, disruptive cases incompatible with the model are readily available, and it is thus not difficult to identify and isolate the discordance between theory and fact within this region of artistic practice.

On the translation model the medium must be regarded as a lifeless collection of materials that are almost magically imbued with life by the artist. Now, there is certainly some truth here, just as there is some truth to the theory of privileged status.[16] Any competent artist does in some sense "breathe life" into his materials, but this truth can be captured and given an explanation without recourse to the translation model, and there exists a ready cluster of examples here as well. A minimalist painter may paint a yellow square on the canvas and "let the materials speak for themselves." Here the artist might describe his activity as presenting the life of the materials themselves rather than communicating through them. A composer can "discover" where a harmonic progression "wants to go" and find how the piece wants to be assembled; he can find something very much like the trajectory of a melody and follow it; he may see how a phrase or theme calls for extension; and so on. He may be able to look at a theme and see the variations in it that the theme itself affords. A sculptor or painter may discover

16. See Mark Roskill, "On the Artist's Privileged Status," *Philosophy* 54 (1979): 187–98.

in the course of the work, and not before it, how a particular feature can be modeled.[17] In music, the cases of experimentation with unresolved dominant seventh chords, dangling leading tones, parallel fifths in the harmonization of a chorale melody, the mistreatment of augmented sixth chords, poor voice-leading away from diminished seventh chords, phrasing imbalances, and the letting of one voice "die" in four-part counterpoint will all serve to illustrate the life possessed by the materials themselves. The last case is especially instructive. A suddenly dropped voice in counterpoint will be recognized as a line that died, regardless of the amount of melodic life in the other lines. The life of the line, if it has to be located somewhere, exists *in* the materials rather than in a less tangible realm. Here one wants to say, substituting one picture of creativity for another, that the composer *discovers* rather than *creates* the life of the melodic lines; this exchange, however, can be of philosophically therapeutic value in showing that the translation model is far from inevitable. Indeed, a discovery of the expressive power and character of an artistic gesture or specific set of materials implies that we do not inject these gestures or materials with expressive life.

We left the discussion of how we find the right expression for our thoughts with Wittgenstein's question, "But can't all sorts of things happen here?" It appears certain that they can, and none of the elements in our two catalogues either supports or requires the translation model. First, those who have what could only be called underprivileged access are often in fact in the best position to judge the significance of a work, or they are at least in a far better position than one would expect from the theory. Secondly, the relations between the artist and his medium do not at all conform to the dic-

17. Actual cases of unanticipated discoveries are common, and in such cases it is abundantly clear that the materials possess a life, but very much a life of their own and not one endowed by the artist; any case of an artist realizing that an alteration *has* to be made illustrates the point. It is of interest to note here that we naturally expect these kinds of midstream discoveries in the work of the novelist, yet philosophers and critics who offer explanations in accordance with the translation model often exclude novelists from consideration, focusing instead on painters, sculptors, and composers— perhaps because writing is a far more familiar activity and is hence less plausibly explained on the translation model.

tates of the theory. But let us return to the next step of Wittgenstein's discussion.

"Now if it were asked: 'Do you have the thought before finding the expression?' what would one have to reply?"[18] What kinds of answers could this question be given? The minimalist may answer that he wanted to discover the effect of the yellow square on the white canvas. The composer may answer that he knew the progression did seem to want to go somewhere harmonically, and that it ended up in the subdominant. Or he may say that he could indeed see the variations promised by the theme, but that he had to work them out one by one. He may answer that he did not have "the thought" at all before "finding the expression," and that he had to pull each reluctant variation out of the theme, note by note. Or he may say that he finally, after many sketches, worked out the melody. He may add that he had the general idea of the melodic contour desired, but that numerous specific problems concerning the melody's relation to the harmony had to be solved one note at a time. The novelist may say that she finally discovered in the final chapter why a detail was set down in the first chapter. The painter may answer that while in progress her canvas gave her the vague impression that something was missing, but that it took another artist to show her precisely what it was that she needed. Another composer may say that she was painfully aware that it was a four-part fugue she was writing, and that she wanted to resolve in the key of E-minor, but that she had not even a hint of the exact resolution until each individual voice resolved itself.

All of these detailed answers, however, do not provide an answer to the general question Wittgenstein is considering: "Do you have the thought before finding the expression?" As answers they are in fact far too specific; they answer specific questions within specific contexts. This in turn reveals how mystifying the general question really is. One does know what form specific answers to specific questions take, but not what form an answer to the general question would take. That question—and this is Wittgenstein's point—which is phrased in terms of "the thought" and "the [corresponding]

18. Wittgenstein, *Philosophical Investigations*, sec. 335.

expression," is constructed out of nothing more than artificial linguistic categories derived from metaphysical dualism. That this is precisely Wittgenstein's point is clear from the next line: "And what [would one have to reply], to the question: 'What did the thought consist in, as it existed before its expression?' " There is, of course, no answer to this question, other than to point to the expression itself—the exact linguistic analogue of pointing to the Dürer, Michelangelo, or Beethoven in answer to the question "What particular feeling?" Thus it appears that in language the thought and the expression are no more separable than the feeling and its expression in art.

I suggested above that the translation model is, if not born of confusion, at least supported by it. It now appears that both the translation model and, more fundamentally, the very question that the model tries to answer stand in the way of conceptual clarity. This is one of many negative conclusions in Wittgensteinian philosophy that is at the same time—but of course in a different sense—a positive conclusion; it removes an obstacle that would otherwise prevent us from achieving a clear view of the richly diverse aesthetic practices that lie before us.

In this chapter we have seen the consequences of failing to distinguish between the transitive and intransitive uses of "particular." This confusion allows us to believe that our aesthetic experience is a translation between two entities: the physical work on the one hand, and on the other a particular, determinate feeling with an identity independent from the work itself. We have also seen the way in which the translation picture is itself misleading by virtue of its dual categories of "expression" and "thought"; by looking at individual cases, I have endeavored to show the distance that separates these categories from actual aesthetic practice and the impossibility of applying one to the other.

There remains, however, one final question. Why should we, apart from the need to remove theoretical obstructions to clear vision, take such great care over such specific points as the transitive-intransitive confusion and the translation model in our thinking about artistic creativity? The answer is, I think, simple enough: many excesses of criticism spring directly from confusions such as these.

The language used by some critics in certain sectors of the arts is in serious disrepair.[19] Countless artists speak about their own works in ways that are anything but illuminating, and often in ways that would, if taken at face value, actually demean their work. Often the words of artists and critics possess merely a contingent connection to the art they describe: the work and the words do not organically connect, and one is left wondering if the words might not have been attached with equal plausibility to any of a hundred other works. Perhaps by subscribing, explicitly or otherwise, to an outmoded if not incoherent view of the creative process, artists and critics are compelled to speak the language prescribed by the translation model, and try to say "what the thought consisted in before its expression," or to say "what the tune says." Moreover, that the dual-model conception is outmoded seems beyond any doubt, quite apart from the question of its internal coherence. There is much experimentation, innovation, and improvisation in recent art, and these new practices simply will not settle comfortably into old theories.

The longing for this kind of organizing explanation in art is of course understandable, and one cannot help but feel sympathetic with any attempt to see behind or into an enigmatic work of art. If, however, the criticism resulting from this attempt itself fails the test—if it lacks the power to transform aesthetic experience by altering what it is we see, hear, or comprehend—we should ask whether or not that criticism is a product whose sole function is to occupy a place reserved for it by a misleading and ultimately inapplicable conceptual model.

In summary, the particular feeling that a given work captures should not, first of all, be understood as a separate preexistent entity which is later embodied in the physical work. Second, the translation model of creativity in art is inadequate; to the extent that contemporary discussions unwittingly presuppose the cate-

19. See, for example, Roger Scruton's revealing discussion of a number of architectural theorists and critics in his *The Aesthetics of Architecture* (Princeton: Princeton University Press, 1979), pp. 37–70.

gories brought along by this model, these discussions cannot further our understanding of art and its creation. Third, intentional criticism about a work which seems to lack the virtue of being necessarily connected to the particular work in question should be held in suspicion, for it may in fact amount to nothing more than an attempt to describe a phantom preexistent entity; it may constitute an ill-fated attempt to translate back into an original that never existed. There may well be an experience, or more likely a complex pattern of experiences, referred to by the phrase "the creative process." As I have tried to show in this chapter, however, to attempt to characterize this experience within the terms and categories of the translation model can only further mystify what is already something of a wonder. Before progressing to the final chapters of this study, where we turn to a discussion of recent aesthetic theory, there remains the issue of linguistic privacy and the correlated conception of artistic meaning; it is thus to this issue that we turn in Chapter 6.

6 The Silence of Aesthetic Solipsism

In the criticism of art and its attendant search for meaning, many are inclined to attribute a distinctively metaphysical priority to the artist, a priority that quickly engages us with implicit theories of the ontological nature of artworks, the nature of artistic meaning itself, and the proper function of criticism. The progression of thought is as follows. Beginning with a critically problematic or conceptually troublesome artwork, we look for the meaning *behind* the work and ask, "What did Kandinsky, Pollock, Joyce, Cage, or Stockhausen, *mean* by that?" The metaphysical assumptions implied by this question are, of course, that (1) the artwork is one thing—a physical artifact—and (2) its meaning—a mental object or conceptual entity—is another, and that (3) because of our aesthetic puzzlement we need criticism that will lead us from the enigmatic outward object back to the clarifying—but hidden—significance. This metaphysical priority granted the artist is a natural analogue to the priority we grant within language, the primary residence of meaning. If someone utters a phrase we do not initially understand or which in various ways puzzles us, for example, "What we cannot speak about we must pass over in silence,"[1] we often ask, in the linguistic case, for an explication of verbal meaning that stands exactly parallel to the criticism we invite in the above artistic case. Thus we stand here at yet another point of intersection between the

---

1. Ludwig Wittgenstein, *Tractatus Logico-Philosophicus* (1922), trans. D. F. Pears and B. F. McGuinness (Humanities Press, 1974), p. 7.

philosophies of art and of language, where a conception of meaning in art is given shape by a prior, if implicitly held, conception of linguistic meaning. To summarize the themes intersecting here: the word stands parallel to the work; the linguistic meaning in the mind of the speaker stands parallel to the artistic meaning in the mind of the artist; and the critic in art stands parallel to the translator or expositor in language.[2]

It is true, of course, that this entire metaphysical construction in the art world, built on the now shaky conceptual foundations of a Cartesian dualism separating mind and matter, is shrouded in suspicion, and it is widely understood that the pall was cast over this construction of art and its criticism in some indirect way by Wittgenstein. It is not clear, however, that his *argument*, carried out not in aesthetics but in the philosophy of language, has been assimilated by the wider art-theoretical community. Indeed, one often encounters the conviction that Wittgenstein certainly did something of the first importance for our conception of meaning in the arts, and that in the postmodern critical and theoretical atmosphere, with its emphasis on artistic languages, a grasp of this contribution is essential to theoretical progress, but along with this conviction comes an uncomfortable feeling of uncertainty—of knowing that the old conceptions of meaning are unacceptable but still not quite knowing why. To clarify Wittgenstein's contribution we must briefly return to the fundamental problem of twentieth-century aesthetic theory already familiar from the first three chapters above, the problem of expression.

THE PARADOX OF EXPRESSION

The problem of expression in art can be succinctly described as something of a paradox; the shroud of mystery covering the word "expression" in the philosophy of art comes from the following conceptual collision:

2. Within the larger geographical metaphor for philosophical investigation we could say that this is the intersection between art and language discussed in Chapter 5, but that it is here approached from another direction.

1. Emotions are private, phenomenologically internal objects that are logically beyond the reach of others; they are not a part of the public, observable physical world to which others have access. They are, in a sense, secrets inviolably kept by ontology.
2. Artworks are physical objects (albeit of a curious sort), objects located in the public, observable, external world. Their existence, we might say, is physical rather than phenomenological, and their existence does not depend—unlike emotions—on the mind that perceives them.
3. Artistic expression is nothing short of the apparently impossible process of merging (1) and (2). Expressive artworks cannot, as ontological impossibilities, exist—and yet they most assuredly, as the empirical fact of the case, do exist.

The problem is a function, of course, of the obvious metaphysical incompatibility of inward emotions and outward objects. We believe on the one hand that there must be an insurmountable ontological barrier separating the two, and yet we know on the evidence of actual expressive works of art that such a barrier, if it exists, has in fact been crossed. Every philosopher (including those we discussed above) who has espoused a version of the expression theory, i.e., that the essential unity of the arts comes from the fact that they serve as outward expressive vehicles for inner emotional states, has puzzled over this paradoxical situation of thinking that it must be one way and seeing that it is in fact the other. This incompatibility, this sense of theoretical impossibility in the face of museums and concert halls full of evidence to the contrary, has provided the universal point of departure for the "classical" expression theorists of philosophical aesthetics. Bernard Bosanquet writes, "How can the feeling be got into the object?"[3] Similarly, Louis Arnaud Reid asks, "How does a body, a nonmental object, come to 'embody' or 'express,' for our aesthetic imagination, values which it does not literally contain? Why should colors and shapes and patterns, sounds and harmonies and rhythms, come to *mean* so

---

3. Bernard Bosanquet, *Three Lectures on Aesthetics* (London: Macmillan, 1915), pp. 8–10.

very much more than they are?"[4] This mysterious move from the private to the public is also what Eugene Veron has in mind when he says that "art is the manifestation of emotion, obtaining external interpretation."[5] Santayana, propelled by the same conceptual tension, refers to the "two terms," of "private and public." He writes, "In all expression we may thus distinguish two terms: the first is the object actually presented, the word, the image, the expressive thing; the second is the object suggested, the further thought, emotion, or image evoked, the thing expressed."[6]

Tolstoy states that in the aesthetic experience people "experience . . . a mental condition," which is produced "by means of certain external signs."[7] Beardsley, in reference to the statement, "This Moorish interior by Matisse is cheerful," writes that what the speaker must mean is, "It makes me cheerful" because "only *people* can be cheerful, strictly speaking."[8] Beardsley is here being strict about the *kinds* of things that can, and the kinds of things that cannot, experience emotions.

Thus the ontological problem itself, as the paradoxical source of philosophical mystery surrounding artistic expression and as the governing question beneath expression theories of art, is clear, as is an underlying dependence upon the metaphysical dualism dividing mind and matter. To begin to assess the damage[9] to this way of

4. Louis Arnauld Reid, *A Study in Aesthetics*, (New York: Macmillan, 1954), pp. 62–3.

5. Eugene Veron, *Aesthetics*, trans. W. H. Armstrong (London: Chapman and Hall, 1878), quoted in H. Gene Blocker, *Philosophy of Art* (New York: Charles Scribner's Sons, 1979), p. 98, in the context of a helpful discussion of artistic expression that incorporates more fully a number of the theorists I am citing here. (See pp. 95–142.)

6. George Santayana, *The Sense of Beauty* (Cambridge: MIT Press, 1988), p. 123.

7. Leo Tolstoy, *What Is Art?* trans. Aylmer Maude (Oxford: Oxford University Press, 1930), p. 123.

8. Monroe Beardsley, *Aesthetics* (New York: Harcourt Brace Jovanovich, 1958), p. 36.

9. See the critical discussion of progress and its culturewide definition as the construction of theoretical edifices in the foreword to Ludwig Wittgenstein, *Philosophical Remarks*, ed. Rush Rhees, trans. Raymond Hargreaves and Roger White (Oxford: Basil Blackwell, 1975), and its draft in Ludwig Wittgenstein, *Culture and Value*, ed. G. H. von Wright and Heikki Nyman, trans. Peter Winch (Oxford: Basil Blackwell, 1980), pp. 6–7. Also see the closing paragraph of Fania Pascal's "A Personal Memoir" in *Recollections of Wittgenstein*, ed. Rush Rhees (Oxford: Oxford University Press, 1984), in which Wittgenstein's antipathy toward the construction of theories on an architectural model is reflected, perhaps unwittingly: "As for me, looking back, I see him bulldozing, year in year out, clearing away the rubble that could only continue to accumulate."

thinking carried out by Wittgenstein in his work on privacy or "private language," we must turn to his diary-keeping genius who invents (or, rather, does *not* invent) a private language. First, however, we must move one step closer to clarity about the connection between that work in the philosophy of mind and language and our initial intuitions concerning the artist's priority and its art-theoretical corollaries.[10]

Picasso's *Guernica* provides a classic case that directly contradicts our theoretical prohibition: it indisputably expresses Picasso's rage at, and the horror of, Franco's inhuman experiment in saturation bombing. The form of explanation, despite its apparently paradoxical content, is quite simply "A expresses X," where A is a public physical object—the painting—and X is a private emotion—rage. Thus the more general puzzlement of the expression theorist is here refined into a particular problem concerning the creative process: How did Picasso put the emotion into the object? A crude explanation, surely ranking among the most theory-driven conclusions imaginable in aesthetics, states that Picasso *felt* rage at the moment of execution, and that it was through the presence of this powerful emotion that he was enabled, in some way still unspecified, to paint *Guernica*.[11] This view, of course, stands as the aesthetic analogue to the conception of natural linguistic expressivity, wherein cries, shrieks, and howls are naturally occurring outward expressions of inner states and other slightly more refined linguistic performances are parasitic on these.[12]

But can this suggestion, in aesthetic form, be taken seriously? Can we imagine that Picasso remained full of rage through all the preliminary sketches, all the intermediate designing, and the final

10. Much of the remainder of this section relies on Ludwig Wittgenstein, *Philosophical Investigations*, 3d ed., trans. G. E. M. Anscombe (New York: Macmillan, 1958), sec. 256–83.

11. For the musical parallel to this picture of artistic expression see J. W. N. Sullivan, *Beethoven: His Spiritual Development* (New York: Knopf, 1927); see especially pp. 38–58 and 116–28.

12. See Wittgenstein, *Philosophical Investigations*, sec. 244, especially the remark: "Here is one possibility: words are connected with the primitive, the natural, expressions of the sensation and used in their place."

detailing? Did he not feel a momentary delight at a certain stroke, or frustration at a technical limitation, or elation at the progress of the work—or anguish in the course of producing it? Any and all of these are possible. The problem may be brought into clearer focus by returning to the linguistic analogue: if the troglodyte is howling at the moon with the wolves but inwardly is optimistically contemplating evolutionary theory, then the outward expression—the howling—is not natural and immediate, but rather mediate and deliberate. Thus this emotion-to-utterance causal chain is broken, and the frustration that an art theorist feels upon realizing that any realistic scenario disturbs the rage-into-paint picture quickly generates a partial refinement of the theory; Picasso was able to recall to mind, or recollect in tranquillity, the rage he initially felt at the bombing. This is the dual-model theory of artistic expression in another form. Here the artist has both an outward and inward model, i.e., Picasso works from both the scene depicted and the feeling generated by that scene.

We know that this view of the inner model has taken a number of forms in aesthetic theory—the "feeling-image" of Ducasse, the "given emotion" of Collingwood, Langer's "envisagement of feeling" yielding the "vital import" of the work, and so on. The crucial point, however, is to see that these various formulations of inner models stand as the artistic analogues to the "private objects," or inner private emotions which, through acts of introspection and related acts of naming, constitute the alleged private meaning of emotion terms. Thus the metaphysical variety of introspection required by the expression theory of the artist in the creation of the work looks very much indeed like that required by Wittgenstein's famous introspective virtuoso, the diary keeper. Before approaching Wittgenstein's argument directly, however, there remains still one more lead to follow in clarifying the parallel between the linguistic privacy theorist and the artistic expression theorist.

Our fundamental concern here is with the view that the artist is in all essentials like a speaker of a language and that the meaning of an artwork is thus like the meaning of a word. The ways in which this analogy can be given detail, however, differ consider-

ably. In Collingwood's theory the work of art was defined in terms
of an inner mental entity private to the artist. It was only in virtue
of this inner mental work that the artist was called an artist at all,
and on that view it is possible that the artist, although perfectly
capable and perhaps even accomplished, never produced an external public instantiation of this inner content.[13] We must here ask,
in spelling out the precise details of the analogy, whether the artist
is to be seen as the analogue to the speaker who is only speaking to
herself inwardly, or rather as the analogue to a speaker who has
thoughts but no language, no vocabulary in which to express them?
On the weaker analogy,[14] the logic of the expression theorist is *not*
parallel to that of the privacy theorist, because the artist, like the
speaker, has already acquired a "language"—she already thinks in
terms of, or elaborates her inner images in terms of, the given
materials of her art, and in this case the entire issue of linguistic
privacy would be irrelevant because disanalogous. The expression
theory in aesthetics does in fact itself dictate that the analogy be
spelled out in the stronger case, where the artist stands parallel to
the "speaker" with thoughts but no language. The two-term
explanatory schema, where work A expresses feeling X, requires
that the inner object expressed be separable from the outer thing
that expresses it. The object must be separable in the same way
that a cause, in order to be understood as a cause, must be isolable
from and prior to its effect. This essentially dualistic schema
demands the separability of the "cause" of the work of art, the
inner object, from the physical work itself. Most important, it
requires that the "cause" of the outward expressive object *precede*
that outward work, be it object of art or verbal utterance. Thus
these two essential conditions—separability and priority—dictate
that the art-language analogy be spelled out, at least within the
domain of expression theory, in the stronger terms. The artist here

13. This implication, of course, approximates a reductio ad absurdum.
14. Here I follow the distinction for the art-language analogy made by Richard Wollheim between the speaker of a language who could, but contingently does not, express
himself and the speaker who, through the lack of an outward language, cannot express
himself. See Richard Wollheim, *Art and Its Objects*, 2d ed. (Cambridge: Cambridge
University Press, 1980), pp. 105–17.

stands parallel to the speaker who has the thought or feeling before he has the word or sign that attaches to it. The meaning of the word must, to make this view good, come first, just as the meaning of the work must precede its expression. With these theoretical requirements in mind, requirements which themselves secure the immediate relevance of linguistic to aesthetic considerations, we may at last turn to the case of Wittgenstein's private diary keeper and the argument housed within it.

"S" AND THE DIARY ARGUMENT

We now have very good reason to believe that the logic of the expression theorist of art parallels exactly that of the linguistic privacy theorist. The privacy theorist claims that our emotion words, e.g. "anger," get their meaning through reference to inner private experiences, and that words only serve as signs for prior inner objects signified by them. On this view, the emotion word is connected in a merely contingent way with the actual inward emotion. Thus the person who is angry hooks together the sign or name and its correlated inner object by introspection, focusing inward attention on the experience we call "anger" and then associating it with that outward label, the actual word "anger."[15] On this linguistic theory such an act of inner ostensive definition should be the way out of solipsism, serving to bridge the gap between oneself and the external physical world, but at this theoretical juncture the way is actually opened into solipsism. To be precise, the first step toward metaphysical solipsism is to reflect that, because sign-meaning correlations are contingent, we cannot really tell if A's red is not B's blue, A's sweet is not B's sour, and A's anger is not B's delight.[16] The second step is to generalize this skepticism, concluding that we can never authentically know the contents of the mind of another, and the third and final step is to conclude from this that we cannot really know *if* there is a mind of another. Aesthetic solipsism, as an

15. See Wittgenstein, *Philosophical Investigations*, sec. 256.
16. See also Wittgenstein's earlier discussion of this issue in *The Blue and Brown Books* (Oxford: Basil Blackwell, 1958), p. 60.

analogue to this metaphysical-linguistic variety, should then be
clear enough. We begin by reflecting that we cannot authentically
determine what the emotive content of a particular work of art is
(as this is inviolably private to the mind of the artist); we then go
on to generalize this into the critical dictum that we can never
know that a description of a work of art involving emotive predicates is true; and finally we arrive via an explicit rational progression at precisely the critical-metaphysical priority granted the
artist with which we began this chapter, namely, that only the
artist, as the sole possessor of the inner object, knows with certainty what the contingent emotion-work association is. With
these often-suppressed conceptual maneuvers brought to the surface, it is now clear how we arrived at our central claims, only supported intuitively at the outset: (1) the artwork functions as an
outward physical sign, (2) artistic meaning is ultimately mental
and hence private, and (3) the fundamental task of criticism is to
lead us from sign to meaning.

The fundamental tenet of the linguistic theory behind the foregoing aesthetic solipsism is that when I say the word "anger" what
I mean is the inner emotion I have felt. It is at this point that we
may begin to fill in some details and review, if only in a cursory
fashion, Wittgenstein's argument as it applies to the linguistic side
of the art-language analogy. It should, if the linguistic privacy theory is correct, be possible for someone—a genius[17]—while showing
no outward signs of emotion, to invent a language in which inner
emotional experiences are recorded. For a particular sensation, let's
say the emotion of anger, he decides to write down an "S" in his
diary every time the inner sensation makes an appearance on his
private mental stage. Wittgenstein remarks at even this very early
point that we are already bound up with conceptual impossibilities,
for "a definition of the sign cannot be formulated."[18] In short, we
cannot let ourselves too quickly presume that we possess a full
comprehension of this case, because a definition of the sign would

17. See Wittgenstein, *Philosophical Investigations*, sec. 257.
18. Ibid., sec. 258. For the purposes of this discussion I have brought together the
genius who invents a name for a sensation of sec. 257 with the diarist who marks an
"S" for every occurrence of the sensation in sec. 258.

refer to the genius's emotion—which is by definition private. We could never know the referent of the word and thus, within the narrow referential confines of this theory, never know the meaning of the "sign" "S."[19] Thus we already find ourselves in the impossible theoretical position of having subtracted the general schema of object-and-designation with one hand while retaining it with the other. The privacy theorist, however, will insist that this is nevertheless fully intelligible. The genius-diarist is giving *himself* a definition by looking at the "S" on his page and focusing his inner attention on the anger; nothing more complicated than that is happening, and we, as outside observers or as, indeed, other minds, have nothing to do with the issue. We should here remind ourselves that the activity of the genius-diarist is nothing like dwelling on anger, or thinking to oneself how angry one is, or holding a grudge, or trying to put aside one's anger; it is not like anything that may normally come to mind as turning our attention to our anger. This is, as an introspective act of definition, different, and uniquely so. Any descriptive formulation of the act of inner definition of the linguistic sign involving any part of the life and language in which we are communally resident is necessarily wrong; indeed these more familiar mental-emotive acts *cannot* constitute, in whole or in part, what our genius is doing. He is allegedly carrying out the ghostly equivalent of pointing to a chair and saying, "chair," except that he does so in utter isolation from others who use this word and in isolation from any history of the word's public use. This definition of the linguistic sign, however, not only is in the present context beyond understanding, but it in fact cannot in any case be understood, as the following problems—which worsen as they progress—will make clear. We are told that the genius impresses on himself "the connexion between the sign and the sensation." Here Wittgenstein points out that this curious ceremony—

---

19. We are not discussing a *contingently* private language, i.e., one that no one else happens to speak, but rather a *necessarily* private one, i.e., one which no one else, because of its private referent, could understand. See Wittgenstein, *Philosophical Investigations*, sec. 243, and Robert Fogelin, *Wittgenstein* (London: Routledge & Kegan Paul, 1986), p. 155, where it is made entirely clear that it is not merely a private use of a public language that is at issue.

"for that is all it seems to be"—could only amount to one thing, which is that the genius will remember the connection correctly in the future. In the private interior world, however, utterly devoid of a larger language or linguistic community into which this new sign "S" falls, there could be no "criterion of correctness. One would like to say: whatever is going to seem right to me is right. And that only means that here we can't talk about 'right.' "[20]

This passage is severely damaging for the linguistic privacy theorist. The genius-diarist may not be able to remember accurately what the inner object was; he may mistake the sensation to which we allegedly attach the sign "melancholy" for the sensation he thinks he remembers, the one actually corresponding to "anger." If the genius cannot remember or cannot be sure of the connections, which are already defined as contingent, then the meaning of the sign "S" cannot be ascertained in any particular case, which is to say that it cannot be ascertained at all, thus irreparably wrecking the operative conception of a "language." There is a corresponding impact on any conception of creativity in art whereby the artist alone, in his exclusively private emotional world, determines and then fixes upon the emotive content of the contingently associated artwork to follow. This part of Wittgenstein's argument can, however, be read in a perhaps more accurate and certainly deeper way. The problem is not merely that the private speaker cannot *remember*, but more strongly that the very issue of linguistic consistency, of performing the inner ostensive definition correctly, is vacuous because, in the absence of any possibility of verification, the idea of consistency has no discernible content and thus no linguistic sense.[21]

20. The three quotations at the end of the paragraph are from Wittgenstein, *Philosophical Investigations*, sec. 258.

21. See in this connection Edward Craig's insightful "Meaning, Use, and Privacy," *Mind* 91 (1982): 541–62, especially pp. 561–62, in which this part of Wittgenstein's argument is identified, through its association of sense and testability, as a new employment of the verification principle that was central to positivism. Craig here identifies the consistency of practice as the crux of the private language issue, and this of course connects to the issue of consistently following a rule. In *Philosophical Investigations*, sec. 202, Wittgenstein says that " 'obeying a rule' is a practice. And to *think* one is obeying a rule is not to obey a rule. Hence it is not possible to obey a rule 'privately': otherwise thinking one was obeying a rule would be the same thing as obey-

The problems of memory and consistency require for their intelligibility the existence of two things, each in its proper category of mind or matter. The inner sensation or emotion has to be phenomenologically present, as the inner object around which all other considerations, i.e. attending to, identifying, or naming, revolve. Secondly—and here the argument takes another step—there has to be the mental act of comparison, specifically the placing of the currently felt emotion against a memory image of the emotion from its previous occurrence, when "S" was outwardly connected then to its sign as it is to be again connected now.

The serious problem with the very idea of mental comparison within this private context is introduced by imagining "a table (something like a dictionary) that exists only in our imagination."[22] An authentic table of this sort, we are reminded, "can be used to justify the translation of a word X by a word Y."[23] Now a question arises as to the similarities and differences between the employment of any such real table and the consultation of an imaginary table existing only in the mind of the genius-diarist. The privacy theorist might assert that the imaginary table is to be used in precisely the same way as the real one, just as one might, in wondering whether one knows the departure time of a train, call to mind how the appropriate page in the timetable looked. This, however, as Wittgenstein reminds us, is wholly unlike consulting a real table, because for this to stand equivalent to an actual consultation, the memory of the table and of the way it looked would have to be

---

ing it." This is clearly closely related to the claim that if we cannot distinguish between a case of correct private ostensive definition and the *impression* of correct private ostensive definition, then there can be no such thing as a correct case. Christopher Peacocke has made the point that by "practice [Wittgenstein] means the practice of a community," in *Wittgenstein: To Follow a Rule*, ed. S. Holtzman and C. Leich (London: Routledge & Kegan Paul, 1981), p. 72, indicating that what it is to follow a rule cannot be explained without reference to a community, and this is, I would argue, directly analogous to the necessarily *public* nature of art, directly analogous to the *possibility* of artistic meaning. In the same collection G. P. Baker makes the welcome point that the gaining of an overview of all the different kinds of things which constitute rule-following would prevent the illusion of a need for a *theory* of rule-following to take hold; see pp. 57–58.

22. Wittgenstein, *Philosophical Investigations*, sec. 265.

23. Ibid.

correct. This correctness, here again, would have to be capable of being put to the test, and not merely for practical purposes but here too in order to give contextual meaning, to give a functional utility, to the word "correct."[24] This cannot be done with the mental table, for, as Wittgenstein says, here too there is no distinction between seeming right and being right. Because we possess no independent criterion of correctness, we cannot know whether even the *identification* of the emotion, yet to be contingently associated with its sign, is correct. In this way, the "mental table" case cuts more deeply than the memory argument. The alleged act of inner ostensive definition requires for its coherence this table-checking notion of comparison, but the genius-diarist's prelinguistic activities, within the strict confines of his own private language, cannot reach out to a public confirmation of sensation-identification or emotion-naming that would ensure intelligibility. Indeed, if we rely uncritically on such a notion, as Wittgenstein warns generally, we construct our idea of the inner on the model of the outer, or construe the mental on the model of the physical. This error is, of course, perfectly analogous to a number of problems we have encountered in our consideration of expressionistic, idealistic, and intentionalistic conceptions of artistic meaning.

THE INCONCEIVABILITY OF ART
AS A PRIVATE LANGUAGE

Further problems concerning the internal coherence of the privacy theory as the linguistic forebear to aesthetic solipsism remain, and these problems concern not the issue of connecting the inner object to a sign, but rather the possible relevance of the inner object itself. The central relevance of the inner object is, of course, assumed by both the linguistic privacy theory and the artistic expression theory; in the former it determines the meaning of a word and in the latter it determines the meaning of a

---

24. For a full discussion of the necessity of context to meaning, see my *Meaning and Interpretation* (Ithaca: Cornell University Press, 1994), pp. 9–83.

work. This brings us to the well-known problem of the "beetle in the box."[25]

Wittgenstein invites us to think of a group of people, each of whom has a box with something in it, an object which each calls "beetle." Each person can only see his private beetle, but they all share the common word, the meaning of which they learn from consulting the contents of their own boxes. Now it is "quite possible for everyone to have something different in his box." The point here is that the supposed relation between the object and its sign, i.e. referent and sign, could not be that which is envisaged by the privacy theorist, because all of these people do in fact have the word in common. Of course, we cannot object by skeptically saying that they do not really know what it means, because each learns it from his own case, which, as a perfect specimen of immediate ostensive definition, allegedly guarantees referential certainty. Wittgenstein further suggests that the object in the box could be a sort of chameleon object, constantly changing, and curiously, this fact would have no effect whatsoever on this word, "beetle," which has "a use in these people's language." For the aesthetic parallel, we might imagine a group of painters in a studio, all of whom agree to use a bright red stroke on their canvases as the sign for a particular feeling; the inward feeling could constantly change without the change being detected and yet the red stroke would continue to operate within the "language" defined by the studio's practices. "If [the word "beetle" had such as use] it would not be used as the name of a thing. The thing in the box has no place in the language-game at all; not even as a *something*; for the box might even be empty." Similarly, although publicly used in the studio, the red stroke would not be used as the "name" or sign of an emotion. Thus, although it would undeniably have a meaning—or a range of meanings—within the studio, it would *not* acquire this meaning through reference to an inner object.[26]

Wittgenstein's last point is the final blow to the account of inward emotion-naming. The problem is not only that the "beetle"

25. Wittgenstein, *Philosophical Investigations*, sec. 293.
26. All quotations in this paragraph are from ibid.

users all have *something* there, which may differ and change but to which the word "beetle" still refers and in virtue of which it still possesses meaning as a sign. Nor is the problem merely that they may indeed have *nothing* there and yet still use the sign. The deeper problem is that the categories in terms of which the entire explanation is constructed are misleading and insufficient; the sign is not what the privacy theorist presumed it to be—a dead linguistic sign given life by the inner object to which it refers—precisely because the inner object is not relevant as the sole determinant of meaning in the way predicted. It may have, in fact, as we have seen in the "beetle" case, no position at all; thus it becomes clear that the supposition concerning the central relevance for meaning of the private object was erroneous. "No, one can 'divide through' by the thing in the box; it cancels out, whatever it is." One may similarly "divide through" by the emotive significance believed to be private to each of the artists in our imaginary studio. Clearly, the categories of inner object and outward designation within which this explanation of emotive-linguistic meaning is given are indeed insufficient. Thus the starting point of this theory, the inner emotion whose occurrence the genius is to record by inscribing an "S" in his diary, misleads from the beginning by forcing any subsequent conception of linguistic significance to conform to the categories of the inner object and its contingently attached outward sign. Indeed, these categories *must* be theoretically otiose if not pernicious, for "if we construe the grammar of the expression of sensation on the model of 'object and designation' the object drops out of consideration as irrelevant."[27]

27. Quotations in this paragraph are from ibid. The object drops out *if*, as John Cook has pointed out, we construe the case on the model of object and name, or object and designation; thus the point is not that of the crude behaviorist, i.e., that the inner life as here discussed does not *exist*, but rather that the picture of object and designation, applied to this case, is itself the result of a misleading grammatical analogy. See John Cook, "Wittgenstein on Privacy," *The Philosophical Review* 74 (1965): 281–314, reprinted in *Wittgenstein: The Philosophical Investigations*, ed. G. Pitcher (Notre Dame: University of Notre Dame Press, 1968), pp. 286–323, especially pp. 321–22. Compare Wittgenstein's remark in *Zettel*, (Oxford: Basil Blackwell, 1967), sec. 487: " 'Joy' designates nothing at all. Neither any inward nor any outward thing." The crucial word in this remark is not "nothing," but rather "designates." This remark is interconnected with Wittgenstein's refutation of the Augustinian picture of meaning,

We know, then, that the privacy theorist regards as unproblematic the notion of the naming of an object, and we now know that this cannot be taken for granted, and moreover cannot be a part of the explanation of what the genius-diarist is doing in his prelinguistic silence. After all, what *could* it mean, in the absence of everything except the genius-diarist and his emotion, to say: He named it by concentrating on the emotion and connecting it with the sign "S"? These words, along with the very concept of naming, must remain incoherent in isolation from a public language. Here, of course, the "stage-setting" that Wittgenstein reminds us is so easily assumed is brought more clearly into focus; the stage-setting is, of course, the conceptual apparatus of object and designation.[28] Without this stage-setting, nothing that gives the privacy theory of meaning its initial plausibility—the assumption of a language into which the new sign S fits—can be taken for granted or presumed as given at a preexplanatory stage. For this would mark "the post where the new word is stationed," and if this account of meaning is to be made good, where the meaning of the word is given *solely* by

i.e., that all words function as names and derive their meaning through reference, as discussed in the opening sections of the *Philosophical Investigations*, sec. 1–9. It should also be noted here that the "dropping out" of the inner sensation within the model of object and designation does not for a moment suggest that inward experience without linguistic formulation is inconceivable, for example that we could not experience what we call a headache without knowing the word "headache," or that any inner event is ruled outside the bounds of possibility (by a curious variety of psychological nominalism) if we do not first have a name for that event. This implausible interpretive direction would turn Wittgenstein's argument here into an argument for behaviorism of the most extreme kind. But on the other hand it hardly follows from the fact that prelinguistic sensations are conceivable that we can also then have or make non-linguistic beliefs, knowledge claims, assertions, explanatory hypotheses, or definitions. In this connection see Richard Rorty, *Philosophy and the Mirror of Nature* (Princeton: Princeton University Press, 1979), pp. 182–92. On the issue of knowing our sensations, for example the genius-diarist's "S" sensation, or our possibly non-linguistic headache, or Picasso's rage at Franco's saturation bombing of Guernica, see Wittgenstein, *Philosophical Investigations*, sec. 246, where we are reminded that the claim "[O]nly I can know whether I am really in pain" is in one sense false, and in another (interesting) nonsense. The ease of misplacing doubt in the context is also epistemologically significant; on this matter see Robert Fogelin's remark that "if there were such a word, we might say that here it is easy to confuse the *a*dubitable with the *in*dubitable," in his *Wittgenstein* (London: Routledge & Kegan Paul, 1976), p. 158.

28. Wittgenstein, *Philosophical Investigations*, sec. 257.

the inner object to which it refers, then such a post, comprehensible only within a larger linguistic context, cannot be put to any explanatory use. Thus we cannot, in the end, explain what the genius-diarist is supposed to have done. We cannot say that he named his sensation, because the public words "naming" and "sensation," already situated within a linguistic context, cannot enter into the account. Wittgenstein takes this to the argumentative end by pointing out that the privacy theorist cannot even resort to explanations as vague as Well, he *has something*, and he affixes a *sign* to it—and that's all, because "has," and "something," and again the idea of "affixing the sign" are part of our public usage, they "belong to our common language."[29] In the same way, we must now go back to our imaginary studio with its "language" of red strokes and subtract the concept of object (or emotion) and designation, leaving only incoherence and an utter inability to explain the communal meaning of even that single artistic-expressive gesture. Of course, if this theory lacks the explanatory force to account for the expressive power of the first gesture within an expressive-interpretive community, it cannot begin to explain the vastly more complex meanings of its actual artistic practices, its visual language.[30]

29. Ibid., sec. 261. For a particularly helpful presentation of Wittgenstein's argument concerning sensation and naming, or the problem of the meaning of "S," see Malcolm Budd, *Wittgenstein's Philosophy of Psychology* (London: Routledge, 1989), pp. 46–76.

30. Further, if works of art were the visual, literary, musical, poetic, or sculptural, recordings of "S" in artwork diaries, the fact that some works of art are deeper or more resonant than others would remain forever inexplicable, and if artistic communication were analogous to private language, we could not explain our desire to reread, e.g., *The Brothers Karamazov* or listen again to *The Rite of Spring*. Also, to construe a work of art as an analogue to a linguistic sign given content through inner ostensive definition is to adopt a narrow critical monism, as there would be only one correct critical identification of the inner object behind the work. By contrast, to see an artwork as an analogue to a meaningful word or phrase in a spoken communal language is to reserve interpretive space for the multiple meanings of critical pluralism. See in this connection Wittgenstein's remark that "Schubert's *Wiegenlied* is clearly deeper than Brahms's *Wiegenlied*, but . . . it can be deeper only in the whole of our musical language," in Rush Rhees, *Without Answers* (New York: Schocken, 1969), p. 136. Of course, there is a great deal more to be said in explanation of this contextual or communal conception (I resist the word "theory" here) of meaning, but it can certainly be said here that artistic meaning will not be successfully explicated in terms of

The privacy theorist has nowhere to turn at this point—nothing more can be said to explain the theory or give it content. Linguistic solipsism is, in the end, profoundly vacuous; there remains no means with which to give it an intelligible formulation. Thus Wittgenstein says, "So in the end when one is doing philosophy one gets to the point where one would like just to emit an inarticulate sound."[31] In precisely the same way and for the same reasons, aesthetic solipsism—the theory that the meaning of a work of art is ultimately private to the mind of the artist and thus categorically and ontologically beyond our reach—is utterly vacuous. Picasso's rage is, I believe, perfectly visible in *Guernica*, and it would be deeply misguided to deny that brute aesthetic fact. To claim, however, that the emotion is metaphysically private, that it is only contingently associated as the mental meaning behind a physical artwork, and that the proper function of criticism is to provide guidance from the visible artifact to an hypothesis concerning the immaterial emotional state hidden behind it, is to revert to the dualistic categories from which Wittgenstein's arguments provide a much needed escape. Indeed, we might claim—with something of a sense of relief—that in a curiously literal sense aesthetic solipsism, along with its correlated conceptions of the ontology of art and the task of criticism, are theories for which nothing can be said. The metaphysical priority or interpretive privilege we are inclined to grant the artist and its consequent intentionalistic critical theories may well be deeply embedded in an intuitive substrate. As we have seen, however, they are in fact the aesthetic vestiges of a linguistic mythology. Our task in the final two chapters will be to reconsider the linguistic issues resident in, or embedded beneath, three of the most influential recent aesthetic theories.

---

analogues to the "S" entries considered above, be they red strokes in painting studios, or chords, chordal passages, or melodic and rhythmic motifs in musical composition, or Corinthian columns or fluted pilasters in architectural design, or cubes, pyramids, and spheres in sculptural composition, and so forth. These elements are indeed meaningful in artistic compositions, but not as "S"-analogues in an ultimately private artistic language.

31. Wittgenstein, *Philosophical Investigations*, sec. 261.

7 The Aesthetics of Indiscernibles

Philosophy itself was transfigured by Wittgenstein's reflections on the nature of linguistic meaning, and these reflections had, insofar as they were intertwined with problems of perception, an epistemological aspect. With characteristic insight and lucidity Arthur Danto, as one small part of his larger project of developing a comprehensive aesthetic theory, has encapsulated that intellectual revolution.[1] As I shall argue, however, it appears that he has, perhaps unwittingly, both concealed and preserved within his own aesthetic methodology a good deal of the old ways of thinking beneath the more attractive surface of the new, and this implicit theoretical preservation is symptomatic of the powerful grip of those old ways. Wittgenstein himself did not, in the later philosophy of the *Philosophical Investigations*,[2] merely decide to change his mind on conceptually fundamental questions and answers, as they were formulated in the *Tractatus Logico-Philosophicus*.[3] He *struggled* against those earlier, and more theoretically accessible, views.

1. See Arthur Danto, "Description and the Phenomenology of Perception," in *Visual Theory*, ed. Norman Bryson, Michael Ann Holly, and Keith Moxey (New York: HarperCollins, 1990), pp. 201–15. The phrases quoted in the following discussion are from this paper unless otherwise indicated.

2. *Philosophical Investigations*, 3d ed., trans. G. E. M. Anscombe (New York: Macmillan, 1958).

3. *Tractatus Logico-Philosophicus* (1922), trans. D. F. Pears and B. F. McGuinness (Atlantic Highlands, N.J.: Humanities Press, 1974).

DANTO AND AESTHETIC ATOMISM

Danto's fundamental strategy, in aesthetic theory, is that of assembling imaginative collections of works that are separate and distinct in identity but indistinguishable from each other perceptually.[4] Thus a set of square canvases painted red might be variously entitled "Kierkegaard's Mood," "Nirvana," "The Israelites Crossing the Red Sea," "Red Square," "Untitled," or any of a number of other possible identity-determining titles. One of the many achievements of this strategy is that it brings to the surface and very finely focuses the central question of aesthetic perception: What is the *difference* between our perception of an artwork and of a non-art object (a "mere real thing") that is, on a perceptual level, indistinguishable from it? I would suggest that this is indeed a new and improved version of the question common to much work in aesthetics predating Danto's contributions: What is (if any) the distinctively *aesthetic* mode of perception, and how does it differ (if it does) from nonaesthetic perception? Danto has shown us that until the mid-century conceptual turmoil, perception was regarded as epistemologically

---

4. It should be mentioned here that Danto's larger project in aesthetics runs vastly beyond my present concerns in this section; what appears here is thus not in any sense intended as a complete or full treatment of his larger contribution, which would require a book unto itself. What I have concerned myself with here is a single point of convergence between Danto's method and Wittgenstein's philosophy—although I do believe that this convergence is the foundation of Danto's project. It should also be said here that Danto's work is of course a large part of the "return to theory" mentioned in the Introduction above. See Mary Mothersill, *Beauty Restored* (Oxford: Oxford University Press, 1984), pp. 33–73. It is true that the preceding antitheoretical movement took its impetus from Wittgenstein's work, although it concerned itself primarily with the very limited issue of artistic definition, arguing that the concept "Art" does not behave as one whose members are included on the grounds of fixed necessary and sufficient conditions. As I have argued elsewhere, the notion of "family resemblance," and of overlapping characteristics that constitute varying criteria for inclusion in the class "Art," is in fact only one of the many Wittgensteinian concepts that hold deep and direct significance for our understanding of art. I have explored some of these, e.g., language-games, forms of life, linguistic and artistic practice, a gesture-language, aspect perception, antiessentialism, expressive tone and context, and philosophical method, in my *Meaning and Interpretation: Wittgenstein, Henry James, and Literary Knowledge* (Ithaca: Cornell University Press, 1994); on the antitheorists' narrow sense of the significance of Wittgenstein for aesthetics, see particularly *Meaning and Interpretation*, pp. 1–8.

fundamental or *basic*, and that language was regarded as only an acoustical adjunct, an ex post facto representation, of the primary perceptual event. One *sees* first, one *says*—if at all—only later. Given this perceptual primacy, it is only natural to then identify the essential function of language as that of naming, where a word gets its meaning through direct reference to a simple or basic perception, i.e., a perception that is unanalyzable and thus, as Danto succinctly puts it, "capable of being named but not defined" (202). With this perceptual atomism, one would recognize any familiar object as a composite of basic perceived data collected through the five sensory modalities, and if required, one could (although this would be in almost any context unusual) list the basic perceptions out of which the object is, on this model, constructed. Thus the apple is "round," "red," "tart," and so on through what would be, in toto, a very long list of basic perceptions.

Of course, linguistic atomism closely follows perceptual atomism; just as one is led to the conception of language as naming, one is led to the idea of correspondence, where a given word stands for a given perception and the truth of any utterance is then a function of the match between word and world. As Locke and his twentieth-century successors believed, we generally trouble ourselves to name only composites in actual spoken language. Thus, if I hold up an apple, study it, and say "avocado," I have uttered a falsehood; the language following the perception does not refer to the composite "round, red, tart . . ." Now, having glimpsed only this one example in which truth is construed as a function of correspondence, one can already see that spoken, or natural, language is a rather messy affair. Although atomistic in structure, it is systematically imprecise, because the linguistic name, the word, does not refer, through referentially clean one-to-one correspondences, to perceptions. Words refer, imprecisely, to clusters. At this point one can both feel the motivation for the *Tractatus* and at least minimally appreciate its modernistic elegance. It describes, not a makeshift and even chaotic natural language, but a logically perfect language, inside which there are no such things as ambiguity, vagueness, metaphorical undertones, allegorical overtones, or even simple misunderstandings. In the *Tractatus*, as we saw in Chapter

1, a proposition is a picture of a state of affairs in the world, and at the most fundamental level of significance, basic perceptual atoms are directly and precisely represented by basic linguistic atoms. The only possibility is that of absolute clarity; owing to the presence of corresponding atomistic basics, confusion and interpretative disagreement cannot arise. Thus in the prerevolutionary philosophy of science we arrived, as Danto reminds us, at the idea of "observation sentences," i.e., those sentences "which could be verified or falsified through some isolated single perception" (203). Analogously, prerevolutionary philosophy of art would insist on the possibility of aesthetic "observation sentences"; these would be *post factum* descriptions of properties exhibited in works of art which could be verified or falsified through a single perception, or through checking the correspondence between word and work. Although the problem of verifying criticism ranges considerably beyond the specific concerns of this discussion, it seems clear that contemporary discussions of critical objectivity and of its possibility still rest squarely on atomistic foundations. Stated directly, if a critical observation is thought to be a proposition about properties exhibited by the work, where the conception of the meaning of criticism reduces in the final analysis to naming, atomism is still exerting a powerful influence, and its full manifestation is seen in the often employed but rarely stated definition of critical truth as a verified description of a prior perception. These are, in summary, the old ways of thinking.

Wittgenstein's search for a new philosophical method was carried out in large part as a struggle against himself, against the ways of thinking expressed in the *Tractatus*. This exorcism of atomism is what Danto has referred to as Wittgenstein's chief thesis, the claim that "we cannot as easily separate perception and description as had been taken for granted by philosophers" (204). On the earlier view, the claim that a proposition is a picture of the world itself implies that perception and description are wholly separable and only contingently related—when in fact they are related. Reminding us of the *Tractatus*'s historical affinities with the views of Schopenhauer, who solipsistically asserted that "the world is my representation," and with Nietzsche, who made the related claim that if we change languages (meaning here a radical exchange of the structure of language) we change worlds, Danto characterizes Wittgenstein's later view as a repudiation of the distinction thought to exist between "the world on the one side and language on the other" (204). Indeed, as our epistemological access to the world runs exclusively through representation, we can never, as a logico-epistemological impossibility, arrive at an independent position from which to assess the accuracy of the representation against its original, or the description against the perception. Nor can we take the first step toward such a position, because it is a departure from the linguistic that is not only impossible but inconceivable.[5] Of course, it is crucial to any elucidation of the later Wittgenstein to distinguish between an assertion that is false and one that is unintelligible. Danto accurately identifies Wittgenstein's repudiation not as concerning the falsity of a specific theory regarding the distinction between perception and description, but rather as concerning the very intelligibility of that distinction. If perception does not precede description, and if perception within any sensory modality or combination of modalities (as in synaesthetic perception) is ineluctably linguistic, then any discussion of the *relation* between perception and description is as otiose as it is misleading. If the new way of thinking is a repudiation, then it is, at bottom, a repudiation of the explanatory function of the *basic*. Atomism, in both its perceptual and subsequent linguistic forms, is the theoretical consequence of an illusory epistemological distinction. Here too a full elaboration of this point would take us far beyond present purposes, but a few passages from Wittgenstein will suffice to suggest the general direction of the newer thought as it opposes the old.

5. The separability that I here refer to as inconceivable is not only beyond our imaginative grasp, in the way that a one-hundred-sided figure is inconceivable but still, of course, possible, but rather inconceivable in the sense that, once we have departed from the linguistic there could be no *content* to the conception. With the first sense of inconceivability, this utter separation of perception from description would be possible, but only contingently beyond our imaginative bounds. The point, on the second sense of inconceivability, is that the very idea of this separation, as a *conceptual* impossibility, is incoherent.

Very early in the *Philosophical Investigations*, among preliminary reflections on the old conception of meaning, Wittgenstein
writes, "When we say: 'Every word in language signifies something'
we have so far said *nothing whatever;* softening this categorical
statement only slightly by adding "unless we have explained
exactly *what* distinction we wish to make."[6] Slightly later he adds
to that repudiation of naming as the origin of meaning the well-
known remark, "To imagine a language means to imagine a form of
life."[7] To imagine a language is not, presumably, to imagine a net-
work of correlated basic objects or an assemblage of perceptions and
names. A bit later he is at a position from which the oddity or
remoteness of the naming model can be sensed, and says, "And you
really get such a queer connexion [of a word with an object] when
the philosopher tries to bring out *the* relation between name and
thing by staring at an object in front of him and repeating a name or
even the word "this" innumerable times."[8] Indeed, even from the
very beginnings of an overview of the multiple functions of language, achieved early in the *Philosophical Investigations*, the dream
of the ideal or logically perfect language and its method of reduction
to basics seems impossibly alien to actual linguistic practice. Much
later in the same work he makes a pointed inquiry: "Can I not say:
a cry, a laugh, are full of meaning?"[9] Such utterances are, at least in
certain contexts, both intensely meaningful and beyond the
explanatory reach of the naming theory of meaning.[10]

These few passages serve to illustrate Wittgenstein's attack on
the conception of language as a system of names that signify basic
perceptions or clusters of basic perceptions. The second site of battle with the old way of thinking is the collection of remarks on

6. Wittgenstein, *Philosophical Investigations*, sec. 13.

7. Ibid., sec. 19. I discuss the fuller ramifications of this claim for aesthetics in
Meaning and Interpretation, pp. 45–83.

8. Wittgenstein, *Philosophical Investigations*, sec. 38.

9. Ibid., sec. 543.

10. This of course connects to the private-language argument discussed above; for
an elucidation of the significance of this argument specifically for the naming theory,
see John Cook, "Wittgenstein on Privacy," *Philosophical Review* 74 (1965): 281–314,
reprinted in *Wittgenstein: The Philosophical Investigations*, ed. G. Pitcher (Notre
Dame: University of Notre Dame Press, 1968), pp. 286–323.

aspect perception or "seeing as."[11] Danto reminds us of both the irrepressible duck-rabbit[12] and the reversing Necker cube (208); if one comes to the first of those visually ambiguous figures with the concept—or perhaps more accurately, the context—of a duck, then that is what one sees, and if one comes with, say, Beatrix Potter rather than Walt Disney in mind, one sees not Donald but Peter. Of course, this variety of visual ambiguity, an ambiguity resolved by a description seeming to reach into and transform a perception, has more than trivial consequences.[13] These consequences, identified by Danto (205), can in the philosophy of science generate the idea of radically incommensurable world views, each carrying its own internally generated criteria for verification and certainty. In the philosophy of art, one could develop the analogous theory of radically incommensurable interpretations, where it would be not only inappropriate but in fact impossible to argue against one interpretative scheme employing the discourse of another. But these consequences, which are the scientific and aesthetic implications of a deeper philosophy of language[14] and perception,[15] were as Danto says (205) not drawn by Wittgenstein himself but by some of those directly influenced by his work, and I believe this is more than an incidental fact.

11. *Philosophical Investigations*, Part II, sec. xi.

12. A few of the discussions of this visually ambiguous figure in connection with artistic perception are: E. H. Gombrich, *Art and Illusion*, 5th ed. (Oxford: Phaidon, 1977), pp. 4–5; Roger Scruton, *Art and Imagination* (London: Methuen, 1974), pp. 107–20; Richard Wollheim, *Art and Its Objects*, 2d ed. (Cambridge: Cambridge University Press, 1980), pp. 205–26; and for an employment of this type of visual ambiguity within discussions of the "period eye" and a cognitive style, Michael Baxandall, *Painting and Experience in Fifteenth-Century Italy* (Oxford: Oxford University Press, 1972), pp. 29–108.

13. One of these consequences, although beyond the range of what is being discussed here, is that positivism, or positivistic epistemology, is severely threatened by the duck-rabbit case. While Wittgenstein did not put the matter in this way, cases of this sort of visual-descriptive ambiguity were clearly antipositivistic, because the relation between what is perceivably the case and that case's accurate description is severed by them. To put the matter in positivism's own language, a *single* visual object is the means of verifying *two* mutually incompatible assertions.

14. The "deeper philosophy of language" here referred to is the argument against the *possibility* of a private language, discussed in Chapter 6.

15. For an elucidation of the scientific view here alluded to, see Thomas Kuhn, *The Structure of Scientific Revolutions* (Chicago: University of Chicago Press, 1962).

The result of the above reflections was, as Danto explains, the widespread belief in analytic philosophy that "a given thing has a given identity 'only under a description' " (205). Anscombe's[16] assertion that a bodily movement is an action only under a description was, as part of a thorough analysis of the concept of intention, the most focused of these post-Wittgensteinian claims. To hold this view, one must hold a number of prerequisite beliefs, beliefs which are often left unspecified. These prerequisite beliefs, in my view, both underwrite Danto's aesthetic methodology of juxtaposed indiscernibles[17] and preserve (as well as conceal) those elements of the old ways of thinking that Wittgenstein opposed in his work.

If one claims that a human action is a bodily movement under a description, one implies that the bodily movement is constitutive of that action. In other words, the bodily movement is present as the physical component of a more complex ontological entity, i.e., an entity possessing both physical and psychological or intentional aspects. This is, of course, perfectly analogous to the potentially misleading construal of the duck-rabbit case, where the drawn figure is taken as the physical—and constant—constituent to which the interpretative or intentional constituent is added. It is helpful, in seeing the central relevance of this analytical scheme to Danto's aesthetic methodology, to underscore the extent to which this approach is a dualistic (or, as the post-Wittgensteinians called it, "Cartesian") theoretical enterprise. Physical events in the external world are classified either as bodily movements or as human actions according to whether they correspond to mental events, where these mental events are encompassed by the descriptions under which the movements fall. This, then, is the first prerequisite belief, viz., that bodily movements are components of human actions, or more generally that the intentional will include a component of, or in a sense rest just above, the physical.

16. G. E. M. Anscombe, *Intention* (Ithaca: Cornell University Press, 1969).

17. This method is of course primarily developed in Arthur Danto, *The Transfiguration of the Commonplace* (Cambridge.: Harvard University Press, 1981), and extends through many of the essays in his *The Philosophical Disenfranchisement of Art* (New York: Columbia University Press, 1986).

Although one can see at this juncture the method of indiscernible counterparts waiting to present itself as a corollary to these views, let us first state directly the second prerequisite belief. Closely allied to the first, it is that there are, beneath the human action and behind the perception of the duck and of the rabbit, *uninterpreted* constants upon which or over which the concept, context, or description is placed.[18] There are movements behind actions,[19] events behind causes,[20] perceptions behind descriptions, and—here we arrive at the aesthetics of indiscernibles—objects behind artworks.[21] That this is a natural way of thinking, especially after the philosophy of perception developed in the first half of this century, is beyond dispute.[22] Its truth, however, is another matter,[23] and here one is reminded of a remark from Wittgenstein's *Zettel*, "It is very difficult to describe paths of thought where there are

18. In this connection see Wittgenstein's discussion of what one *really* sees, in Norman Malcolm, *Ludwig Wittgenstein: A Memoir* (Oxford: Oxford University Press, 1958), pp. 49–50.

19. See Arthur Danto, *Analytical Philosophy of Action* (Cambridge: Cambridge University Press, 1973), for this analytical scheme applied to deliberate human action.

20. See Danto's *Analytical Philosophy of History* (Cambridge: Cambridge University Press, 1965).

21. See Danto, *Transfiguration of the Commonplace*, pp. 1–32.

22. It must also be said here that this natural way of philosophical thinking prevents or obscures a view of the *power* of language, in that language is, within this schema, kept "neat," so that *all* contradictions, apparent or authentic, are regarded as unacceptable. Simply put, they are not. *Seeming* contradictions, once understood for what they are, are not rationally unacceptable. Many claims, torn out of context and placed side-by-side, are explicitly inconsistent, but they *both* can be, nevertheless, perfectly acceptable. See Renford Bambrough, "Ethics and the Limits of Consistency," *Proceedings of the Aristotelian Society* 90 (1989–90): 1–15; and Renford Bambrough, "Discipline and Discipleship," in *Philosophy and Literature: Essays on John Wisdom*, ed. Ilham Dilman (The Hague: Nijhoff, 1984). To bring this point in language down to the theory of action, one could admit that, in a certain kind of case, a human action could be *one* thing, it could be *described* differently, and those divergent descriptions could be both acceptable and contradictory, where no one description provides the "canonical" interpretation.

23. I should point out that it certainly does not follow that this dualistic way of thinking is true from the fact that interpretative ambiguity can exist, e.g., in not knowing whether the appearance on a blackboard of the word "TIMES" indicates a discussion of Latin, of newspapers, of history, of theoretical physics, or of something else. (I owe this example and its placement in this context to Renford Bambrough.) Such ambiguities encourage the action-body and meaning-word distinctions as discussed here, but they do not necessitate them.

already many lines of thought laid down,—your own or other people's—and not get into one of the grooves."[24] On the old way of thinking, the search for the basic in both perceptual and linguistic form was a manifestation of the desire to originate an epistemology at a point of absolute and indubitable certainty, a point immune to Cartesian doubt. Perceptually, those basic atoms were uninterpreted givens of experience; in language, they were corresponding linguistic simples that could be named but not, under the delimitation of atomistic simplicity, described; and in art, they are not *interpreted* works, but rather, to employ Danto's phrase, mere real things.[25] They are the objects behind the works, the basics over which an interpretative scheme is superimposed.

There are, I believe, serious problems with post-Wittgensteinian analyses of basic actions that range into philosophical logic; to abbreviate them one might simply point to some of the extremely odd conclusions resulting from such an analytical program. Among countless such examples one finds the unembraceable conclusions that what takes place as a knee jerk in a medical examination is part of what a soccer player does under the description of kicking a goal, that acting the part of a participant in a ritual is, at least in part, what the authentic participant does, and, moving to the linguistic case, that the sounds a parrot makes in "saying hello" are, in part, identical to what a person does under the description of saying, "Hello."[26] These are, again, problems internal to this method of analysis;[27] more important

24. Ludwig Wittgenstein, *Zettel*, ed. G. E. M. Anscombe and G. H. von Wright, trans. G. E. M. Anscombe (Oxford: Basil Blackwell, 1967), sec. 349, p. 64e.

25. Danto, *Transfiguration of the Commonplace*, pp. 1–32.

26. Another way of casting the problems into which we are led within this basic-action-plus-intention analytical program is that of descriptive contradiction. If a knee jerk in a medical examination, a reflex action that does not involve nerve impulses from the cerebrum, is a basic constituent of what a soccer player is doing in kicking a goal, which obviously must involve such cerebral impulses, then we arrive at the absurd conclusion—a direct contradiction—that a voluntary action is composed of involuntary movements, i.e., that part of what we mean by "voluntary" is "involuntary." My point above is that if this is our point of arrival, then there is sufficient warrant to reconsider our point of departure—which is the additive analytical program.

27. Further problems intrinsic to this kind of analysis are shown in detail in Frank B. Ebersole, *Language and Perception: Essays in the Philosophy of Language* (Washington, D.C.: University Press of America, 1979), pp. 199–222.

in the present case is to suggest, first, that such an analytical program is alien to Wittgenstein's later thought and, second, that the program, as a method in aesthetics, unwittingly reiterates the old ways.

Consider then this remark: "Nothing could be more mistaken than to say: seeing and forming an image are different activities. That is as if one were to say that moving and losing in chess were different activities."[28] In fact, if actions are basic movements performed under descriptions, then precisely such a claim *is* being made. In the parallel visual case, if one insists on the existence of the uninterpreted basic as the perception behind the description, then one is saying precisely that seeing and forming an image *are* different activities. The affinity between this and the strategy of assembling indiscernible counterparts is clear. First identify the perceived entity common to both a mere real thing and an artwork, and this yields, through an act of conceptual subtraction, the isolated descriptive or interpretative essence of an artwork, an essence which exists, as an ontological intangible, above and beyond the physical object and its uninterpreted perception.

From this vantage point one can well understand Danto's admiration—his *theoretical* admiration[29]—for snow shovels, porcelain fixtures, and Brillo boxes. They satisfy the requirements of this analytical program perfectly. We have already seen, however, the deeper affinities of this theoretical program with the old ways against which the revolutionary thought concerning perception and description was opposed, and hence its actual distance from Wittgenstein's later thought. To state the matter bluntly, this aesthetic method perfectly exemplifies the very atomistic analytic strategy against which the later Wittgenstein was struggling.[30]

28. Wittgenstein, *Zettel*, sec. 645, p. 112e.

29. That this admiration is a function of the theoretical fittingness of readymades is made explicit in Danto, *Philosophical Disenfranchisement*, p. 35, where Danto writes of Duchamp's *Fountain*, "I confess that much as I admire it philosophically, I should, were it given me, exchange it as quickly as I could for more or less any Chardin or Morandi."

30. For Danto's reading of Wittgenstein as an atomistic analyst of human action, see *Transfiguration of the Commonplace*, pp. 4–6. For a competing interpretation, where Wittgenstein is seen as disputing the very possibility of the atomistic analysis of action, see B. R. Tilghman, *But Is It Art?* (Oxford: Basil Blackwell, 1984), pp. 96–98.

There are two questions remaining. The first concerns the applicability of the method of indiscernible counterparts to central or noncontroversial cases in art, quite apart from the question of its affinities with an earlier stage of analytic philosophy; the second task is that of sketching more fully the later Wittgensteinian view as it applies to the relation between description and perception.

It is clear that the method of juxtaposed indiscernibles fits "found" art as well as any conceptual apparatus could; Duchamp's bottle rack is not identical to a non-Duchampian bottle rack. This fittingness, however, allegedly extends far beyond such specific cases, and it is, as Danto claims, the achievement of Duchamp and Warhol to have brought the question concerning the essence of art to this focal point. Their achievement is not, then, to have drawn our attention to the otherwise unnoticed formal features[31] of commonplace objects, but to have bought the history of art to a stage of development[32] from which it can itself engender acts of conceptual subtraction among its percipients; i.e., it provokes the focused question, "What is left over when we subtract the object from the artwork?" Now, in order for the method to apply generally, as Danto clearly believes it does, we must, as a contextual necessity, have a kind of ambiguity present. We must have, in a way closer to the spirit of the later Wittgenstein, a contextual *occasion* for the asking of this focused question. Such an occasion is, in the noncontroversial cases, precisely what we are quite clearly lacking. It is true that, as a way of insisting on the implicit applicability of the question, Danto invites us to engage in the *gedankenexperiment* in which an accident involving paints and canvas produces an object phenomenally indistinguishable from the *Polish Rider*.[33] Such an imaginative act, he believes, will secure the relevance of the Duchampian question because we are, through the side-by-side comparison of these indiscernibles, provoked to search for an ontologically less solid

---

31. See Danto's discussion of George Dickie's institutionalist conception of Duchamp's *Fountain* as a candidate for appreciation, an object exhibiting a "gleaming white surface" and a "pleasing oval shape," in *Philosophical Disenfranchisement*, p. 33.

32. For a concise expression of this philosophy of art history see ibid., pp. ix–xv.

33. Danto, *Transfiguration of the Commonplace*, pp. 31–32.

item, such as a description or an interpretation, which explains the difference. Danto admits that such para-aesthetic accidents are unlikely—one might feel compelled to say *very* unlikely—but any such reaction is beside the point; it is, Danto insists, logically possible, and that is enough, i.e., it is not a *gedankenexperiment* that refutes itself in self-contradiction or internal incoherence. But the function of any theory is, presumably, to *explain*, and the method of indiscernibles can demonstrate an explanatory force only within the context of a problem or set of problematic particulars which that theory covers. Again, what we lack in central, or more specifically "non-readymade," art is the very visual ambiguity that obtains between a mere object and an artwork.[34] Whatever the answer to the question posed by those specific indiscernibles, that answer cannot illuminate until its contextual necessity, in the form of the Duchampian question, is first established.

PERCEPTION IN DESCRIPTION

The foregoing remarks concerning context lead to a related but separate task, that of discussing the late-Wittgensteinian view of perception and description. Surely the most widely known project in Wittgenstein's later philosophy is the repudiation of linguistic atomism as a viable theory of meaning. This is related, however, to a parallel repudiation of visual atomism or an epistemology based on sense data, and this relation can now be explicitly stated. To say of the duck-rabbit that we *first* see an unanalyzed basic and *then* give it one descriptive interpretation or the other is still to insist on the distinction—in both logical and psychological terms—between perception and description. To say then that the "rabbit" description can reach into or "suffuse" (as a Kantian might put the matter) the unanalyzed basic figure, is in this way

34. To see more clearly the lack of contextual necessity for this method, and its consequent restricted explanatory capacity, one might try to imagine the formulation of questions concerning non-readymade indiscernibles: "Is that an actual Kandinsky portrait or is it rained-on Pollock leftovers?" "Is that Klee's geometric design or a blotter for small sponge pads?"

also to remain within the very categories from which the later Wittgenstein was trying to escape. Indeed, we would be developing a theory of the relationship between perception and description rather than, in a manner consistent with the new ways of thinking, denying that distinction's intelligibility. In the repudiation of linguistic atomism Wittgenstein shows at great length and in a way deeply resistant to summarization the significance of context as a determinant of, and occasion for, meaning. The assertion that a bodily movement is an action when it is performed under a description only superficially acknowledges the significance of context; as we have seen, this way of putting the matter pretends that "bodily movement" is not *itself* a description that has its use within rather specific meaning-generating contexts. It pretends, as we have seen, that the brute perception of the movement comes first and that its descriptive interpretation follows. In the parallel aesthetic case we are presented with an ingeniously developed conceptual template of indiscernible counterparts, and to put this template to explanatory use we must presume that we see the mere thing first and that its descriptive interpretation follows. But "mere thing" is no more descriptively inert a phrase than "bodily movement," and to believe that it is interpretively vacuous is to conceal within the aesthetics of indiscernibles precisely the conservative epistemological categories against which the struggle was carried out. Conversely, to insist on the significance of context is to deny the intelligibility of a fundamentally misleading distinction, to insist on a view which seems at once radically untraditional and, insofar as it delivers us from reductionistic atomism, theoretically liberating.[35]

Danto has quoted Nietzsche to the effect that there are no facts, only interpretations, and it is clear that Wittgenstein's remarks on aspect perception fundamentally concern the multifarious relations between sight and thought, seeing and interpretation. Taken together, these remarks illustrate the antireductionist affinities between Nietzsche and Wittgenstein, as well as their shared antipa-

35. A clear demonstration of the significance of context for elucidating artistic intention is found in Michael Baxandall, *Patterns of Intention* (New Haven: Yale University Press, 1985), pp. 41–73.

thy to the perceptual and linguistic foundationalism at the core of the old ways. In any case, it is clear that atomistic analysis—in perception, in language, and in their intersection in aesthetics—is a theoretical program, or as Wittgenstein characterizes it, a "picture," not easily left behind. One might still insist that there *must* be a way of separating perception from description and of theoretically capturing their complex interrelations.[36] Against such insistence, such theoretical captivity, one might place Wittgenstein's remark about his own earlier philosophy, "A *picture* held us captive. And we could not get outside it, for it lay in our language and language seemed to repeat it to us inexorably"[37]

DICKIE, STATUS-CONFERRAL, AND THE LIMITS OF AESTHETIC DOUBT

Following the direction set out by Danto,[38] George Dickie[39] has elaborated and systematically defended one answer to the question

36. I emphasize here that what I am opposing is the attempt to generally, theoretically, capture once and for all in a general theory *the* distinction between description and perception. But in opposing this philosophical "picture" resident in our language, I do not want to fall into another error frequently diagnosed in Wittgensteinian investigations, i.e., asserting a negative version of the positive general and abstract doctrine being opposed, or accepting the formulation of the problem but denying its solution. We do, of course, frequently make distinctions between perception and description, and between description and interpretation, in particularized, ordinary, contextualized ways. The problem arises when we proceed beyond, as Wittgenstein puts it, saying what we know and no more, and presume that there must be some absolute, decontextualized version of these distinctions which can serve as the basis for a philosophical theory.

37. Wittgenstein, *Philosophical Investigations*, sec. 115.

38. This is true even if, as Danto puts it, he must do Oedipal battle with the theory that has resulted from this aesthetic direction having been followed. See Danto, *Transfiguration of the Commonplace*, p. viii. A further remark Danto makes in this preface is significant for the present and the previous discussion: "More important, if anything I write fails to apply throughout the world of art, I shall consider that a refutation: for this aims at being an analytical philosophy of *art*, even if it may also be read as a sustained philosophical reflection on the painting-and-sculpture of the present time" p. viii.

39. For this elaboration, see George Dickie, *Art and the Aesthetic* (Ithaca: Cornell University Press, 1974). Helpful discussions of both Danto and Dickie can be found in L. Aagaard-Mogensen, ed., *Culture and Art* (Atlantic Highlands, N.J.: Humanities Press, 1976); see especially the contribution by Colin Lyas, "Danto and Dickie on Art," pp. 170–93.

how it is we can coherently account for the classification[40] of some artifacts as works of art. The institutional theory boldly brought about a return to a search for essence in aesthetic theory; this was made all the more bold, of course, by the fairly widespread acceptance of a general skepticism about the possibility of ever locating a defining essence.[41] It was not thought possible to accommodate the multifariousness of the arts up to the present, incorporate a conceptual flexibility to allow for the future development of art, and reveal the inner coherence, indeed the defining feature, of the concept of art. Dickie's answer, however, was formulated *not* in reference to an intrinsic property of an object where its automatic and prereflective inclusion within the class of artworks was assumed, but rather in reference to an extrinsic act of conferral, so that, once the conferral was performed, the object was allowed entry, in what must be a postreflective way, into the category of art.

This attempt to capture the hidden unity of art, through focusing on the "non-exhibited characteristic"[42] of conferred status, is clearly close in spirit to Danto's position, because it is here too the non-exhibited, the reliance on a characteristic that, in Danto's felicitous phrase, the eye cannot descry, that allows the project of the search for unity to go forward. For its very reliance on the conceptual instead of on the perceptual, the institutional theory was seen by many to have assimilated whatever lesson the Wittgensteinian position had to offer, in that it no longer looked for a defining essence both intrinsically contained and perceptually locatable, and it was seen to have returned the subject of aesthetics very generally to its higher calling of conceptual analysis. Both of these

40. That this theory is developed in the interest of *classification* renders it fundamentally different from a variant of the institutional position that does not seem to embody the precise problems discussed here; see, e.g., T. J. Diffey, "The Republic of Art," *British Journal of Aesthetics* 9 (1969): 145–56.

41. For a densely packed article exhibiting the artistic diversity that seriously impedes the traditional search for essence, see Marshall Cohen, "Aesthetic Essence," in *Philosophy in America*, ed. Max Black (Ithaca: Cornell University Press, 1962), reprinted in *Aesthetics: A Critical Anthology*, ed. George Dickie and Richard J. Sclafani (New York: St. Martin's Press, 1977).

42. See Maurice Mandelbaum, "Family Resemblances and Generalization Concerning the Arts," *American Philosophical Quarterly* 2 (1965): 219–28, reprinted in *Aesthetics: A Critical Anthology*, ed. Dickie and Sclafani, pp. 500–515.

beliefs, it seems to me, have far more to do with appearance than with reality, but to argue this I must return first to the institutional theorist's starting point, and then, later, to the presuppositions within that misleadingly auspicious beginning.

Heavily weighed-down by the multitudes of aesthetic *differentiae* collected in the interest of applying the idea of family resemblance to the problem of artistic definition,[43] aestheticians were offered the possibility of tossing the hard-won overview of diversity aside for the simplifying and much lighter conception of conferral. For all the waywardness of the art world's artifacts, they would still have one thing—a thing available not to the senses but to the intellect—in common. They would have the status of candidacy for appreciation conferred upon a collection of their aspects by a spokesperson acting on behalf of the social institution of the art world.[44] As a start, this does seem refreshingly straightforward after the multitudinous distinctions offered as illustrations of family resemblance, but indeed *only* as a start, for as the theory attempts to progress beyond this initial stage it turns back on itself in an ever-more-confining circularity.[45] The question directly facing this theoretical start is, naturally, "Why is one artifact and not another put forward as a candidate?" Or, "Why is *this* [pointing to the *Polish Rider*] an object with conferred candidacy and *these* [pointing to thumb tacks and plastic forks][46] not?" It is here that we are led around the first curve of circularity, for the answer must be put forward: "Because that is a masterpiece painting, a true work of art, and those squalid objects are not." This distinction, of course, is not available as an explanation of the institutional position, since it presupposes an understanding of the very subject the theory set out to explain. From this point, indeed a disappointingly early point, the circularity accelerates: the

43. See Mothersill, *Beauty Restored*, pp. 33–73, for an unusually helpful overview of the state of play just before Dickie's return to theory.

44. See George Dickie, "What is Art?" in *Culture and Art*, ed. Aagaard-Mogensen, p. 23.

45. On these grounds Richard Wollheim has offered what seems the decisive refutation of institutionalism in "The Institutional Theory of Art," in *Art and Its Objects*, 2d ed. (Cambridge: Cambridge University Press, 1980), pp. 157–66.

46. See Ted Cohen, "A Critique of the Institutional Theory of Art: The Possibility of Art," in *Aesthetics: A Critical Anthology*, Dickie and Sclafani, pp. 183–95.

difference between art and non-art must be explained by reference back to what is appropriate as a candidate, and the appropriateness will then be employed to justify the conferral which was the non-exhibited reason for our selection of the example in the first place. Vicious circularity can be escaped only at the higher conceptual cost of vacuity, since to answer the question concerning the justification of conferral with any such vague locution as, "Some objects just are justifiable candidates and some are not," is simply to restate the question with diminished clarity. Works of Ovid and Kafka are works of literature, and works of compulsive list makers (e.g., shopping lists, laundry lists, and lists of texts for the core curriculum) are not. To offer an explanation of this difference is to offer justification for the inclusion of the former and the exclusion of the latter from the very category of art; to say *that* one possesses conferred status and the other not is not of course to say *why*. It is only to reiterate a diffusion of the initial question. These, however, are problems near the starting point of the institutional theory; less often discussed are the darker problems lurking within that starting point's presuppositions.

At the core of this aesthetic strategy is the search, albeit in an attenuated form, for a necessary and sufficient condition for arthood. This strategy, familiar to philosophy since at least the time of Plato's early dialogues,[47] implies a conception of the perception of particulars which, at a prereflective stage, are only *candidates* for inclusion in general classes or universal categories. This is to say that the presumed utility of such a category-determining condition itself enforces the belief, otherwise unaddressed, that the perception of the particular object, as yet or at this early metaphysical stage unclassified, is invariably and fundamentally problematic. Problems, of course, call for solutions; on this picture of the perception of the particulars, i.e., within the framework of the presumed utility of a necessary and sufficient condition, the solution will take the form of a *decision*. In schematic form, in the perception of object O we ask, on encountering it, "Is O a member of S?" (where S is a

47. In *Euthyphro*, for example, the definition of piety proceeds in terms of a search for its essence; the process of definition and counter-example is characteristically more instructive than the definitional essentialism that motivates it.

larger class, set, or category, such as the class of all artworks), and
the solution to this problem is then sought through the employment of the subsequent question, "Does O exhibit (or, in the attenuated institutional theorist's sense of non-exhibited characteristics,
possess) necessary and sufficient condition C, such that O's categorical inclusion is explicitly justified?" If the answer is affirmative,
our problem, allegedly intrinsic to the perception of particulars, is
solved: O is a member of S. Obviously, the problem is solved in a
negative case as well; O, in the absence of C, is not a member of S.
This strategy of searching for the determining attribute is clear; it
offers a simplification of unwieldy diversity; and it promises judgmental certainty about aesthetic controversy. But in a way (not
surprisingly) like Danto's method of indiscernibles, it rests on a misconstrual of the experience of art; moreover, the misconstrual in the
case of the institutional theory is more severe.

In the method employed by Danto, what is described as the
"Duchampian question," i.e., asking whether we are justified to
include what appears to be a mere real thing within the larger category of art, was generalized—where this generalization constitutes
the misconstrual—to all art. The institutional theory encourages a
similar misconstrual, but one of greater severity, because it does not
begin with a context-specific[48] question and then generalize; rather
it superimposes the schema, "Is O a member of S through the presence of C?" over all cases of art from the outset. The presupposition
that would justify this superimposition is precisely that the perception of all works of art, despite all the vicissitudes and variances of
differing sectors of the larger institution of art—the art world—is *in
this sense* uniform. Simply stated, it is not. Less simply stated, the
strategy of determining a necessary and sufficient condition presupposes that far more is in question, and thus that far more objects are
precariously situated on the controversial edge of art, than is actually the case. For this strategy to have more than merely apparent
utility, two conditions would need to be satisfied. First, it would

---

48. The significance of this context specificity for our comprehension of artistic
meaning and for the avoidance of a "haunted" critical condition (as depicted in Henry
James's "The Figure in the Carpet") is discussed in my *Meaning and Interpretation*,
pp. 139–48.

have to be necessary for us to answer the following question in all cases: Does every given art object have the non-exhibited characteristic of possessing aspects[49] put forward as candidates for appreciation by an aesthetic "spokesperson" or, since this is aesthetics and not linguistics, by an institutionally empowered artist? And second, the question of artistic definition would have to be the best situated of aesthetic questions[50] vis-à-vis its solution's power to illuminate. As it stands, we have been given a tool to perform a task for which there is no conceptual need. It must be explained, however, why this task—the definitional process of question and answer as schematized above and as presumed by any institutionalist—is one we are not called to perform. In providing this explanation it will help to focus on some observations made by Wittgenstein on the experience of certainty—the aesthetic relevance of which will become increasingly clear as we progress through them.

In a discussion of certainty of the sort that precedes justification, Wittgenstein remarks, "Giving grounds, however, justifying the evidence, comes to an end;—but the end is not certain propositions striking us immediately as true, i.e. it is not a kind of *seeing* on our part; it is our *acting*, which lies at the bottom of the language-game."[51] The ways in which language-games are relevant to an understanding of the arts is a topic I have pursued elsewhere; for the present we can consider all but the concluding line of this remark. The giving of grounds in the aesthetic case would of course be the giving of grounds for, or explicitly justifying, the inclusion of any particular artifact within the larger class of artworks. So far, this is compatible with the project envisioned by the institutional theory,

49. There is a serious problem here as well for the institutional theory concerning the distinction between aesthetic and nonaesthetic properties; see again Wollheim, "The Institutional Theory of Art," in *Art and Its Objects*, pp. 157–66, and Colin Lyas, "Aesthetic and Personal Qualities," *Proceedings of the Aristotelian Society* 72 (1971–72): 171–93.

50. I believe the question of artistic definition is in fact not only not the best situated question in this sense; it is among the worst. The unfortunately appropriate accusation of dryness or aridity made of much twentieth-century aesthetics is a function of an excessive concern with this question to the exclusion of questions of meaning, style, depth, resonance, ethical significance, and so forth.

51. Wittgenstein, *On Certainty*, ed. G. E. M. Anscombe and G. H. von Wright, trans. Dennis Paul and G. E. M. Anscombe (Oxford: Basil Blackwell, 1969), sec. 204.

in that it seeks a finality—indeed a certainty—about the categorical classification of the artifact. But the compatibility of Wittgenstein's insight into the nature of certainty and the institutional conception stops here—for the end of giving grounds is *not* that a proposition strikes us as immediately true. The proposition, in the aesthetic case, would be formed in something like this way: "Every work of art that we unproblematically include as the member of a larger class of all artworks has had status conferred upon it by an appropriately empowered representative." This proposition, indeed, captures the very essence of the institutional theory, as it gives clear expression to the postreflective conferral that must have occurred, according to the question template considered above. For those who have accepted the applicability of the template, this proposition would strike them as immediately true: the *Pieta* in St. Peter's, the *Fifth Symphony, Divine Comedy*, and *Flowers of Evil* all have this feature of conferred status in common. As with Danto's method of indiscernibles, the institutionalist will claim that we come on our part to *see* that this is the case, where what we "see" is the nonexhibited characteristic C that justifies the inclusion of O in S. It is clear at this stage that the institutional theory is utterly incompatible with Wittgenstein's insight into the nature of certainty, and I would want to include our knowledge of these artworks—and the way we *take* them to be artworks—as examples of the variety of certainty Wittgenstein is examining. Indeed, as exemplars of such certainty, they embody the same logic. It is our taking them, in a way far deeper than the reflective institutional template can reach, that constitutes the "acting which lies at the bottom." The proposition above which captures the essence of the institutional theory also captures the essence of the falsification, or the postreflective misconstrual, of this variety of aesthetic knowledge.

The institutional template, like the strategy of indiscernibles, has its place; i.e., there are cases where the proposition has uses. Thus if it is true that a piece of driftwood, or a remnant of a bicycle, or a woven textile, or a bottle rack, has had status conferred upon it— explicitly in response to a contextually situated *need* to do so—the misconstrual is *grounded* in the rest of our regular, nonproblematic cases. This does not mean—against the central tenet of the institutional theory—that those grounds, those multiform practices, are justified in the same explicit way. Wittgenstein continues, "If the true is what is grounded, then the ground is not *true*, nor yet false."[52]

We might well imagine someone listening, for the first time, to the music Schönberg composed after *Transfigured Night*, and asking "But is it *true* that you count that along with Bach and Brahms as *music*?" Depending on exactly what is being asked, we might say "Yes," and if asked for grounds for this inclusion, we might say, "I can't give you any grounds, but if you listen more—and come to hear more—you will think the same." Wittgenstein's next remark is, "If someone asked us 'but is that *true*?' we might say 'yes' to him; and if he demanded grounds we might say 'I can't give you any grounds, but if you learn more you too will think the same.' " Wittgenstein then adds "If this didn't come about, that would mean that he couldn't for example learn history."[53] To complete the analogy to the aesthetic case, if, in listening again and again to Schönberg, our auditor did not come to agree with us, then it would indeed mean that the listener could not learn the music history of the twentieth century.

The operation of the problematic particular case against the ground that itself is neither true nor false is brought out strikingly in a subsequent example from Wittgenstein. He writes, "I have a telephone conversation with New York. My friend tells me that his young trees have buds of such and such a kind. I am now convinced that his tree is. . . . Am I also convinced that the earth exists?"[54] If we are in the position of the listener above, and are then told that Schönberg's harmonic language has some previously unknown forms of structural coherence of such and such a kind, and we thus become convinced that composition after *Transfigured Night* is what I will for now call simply rather serious business,[55] are we then also convinced that music exists as an art? The ludicrous generality of this remark is born of the conflation of what *is* called into

---

52. Ibid., sec. 205.
53. Ibid., sec. 206.
54. Ibid., sec. 208.
55. I discuss this case of musical seriousness as a development and gradual expansion of a circumscribed set of musical possibilities—a musical language-game—in *Meaning and Interpretation*, pp. 36–39.

question—the problematic particular—and what is *not*—the ground that is, not beyond, but *beneath*, justification. This is the conflation, in aesthetic form, that the institutional theory forces upon us. In fact, the existence of music as an art, and, even beyond this, the place of the arts in our lives, is part of the whole picture that forms the starting point of our belief that the late works of Schönberg are indeed *musical* works. As Wittgenstein writes, "The existence of the earth is rather part of the whole *picture* which forms the starting-point of belief for me."[56] In the next remark, we encounter again the question, "Does my telephone call to New York strengthen my conviction that the earth exists?"[57] Ludicrous in the same way, for the same reasons, is the claim, "My inclusion of a bottle rack or a gigantic clothespin in the class 'artworks' strengthens my conviction that the entire art world has existed from its inception to the present day, and that it has existed because of the status conferred upon its included particulars." This is the claim, a claim falsifying the epistemology at the foundations of aesthetics, that the institutional theory must insist upon. Much, as Wittgenstein puts it within the context of this discussion, is "fixed," and it "gives our way of looking at things, and our researches, their form."[58] Just as, I would suggest, what is fixed in the art world gives our way of looking at the problematic cases in aesthetics, and indeed the researches, i.e. the theories that ensue, their form. Wittgenstein adds, "Perhaps it was once disputed. But perhaps, for unthinkable ages, it has belonged to the *scaffolding* of our thoughts."[59] We do not have to derive, through the application of a general rule to a particular human being, the conclusion that that human being has parents. Nor do we have to derive, through the application of the institutionalist's central proposition above, the conclusion that Titian's canvases are works of art. Wittgenstein asks how it is we regard a mathematical calculation as sufficiently checked, and what gives us the right to declare it checked. "Somewhere," he says, "we must be finished with justification, and then

56. Wittgenstein, *On Certainty*, sec. 209.
57. Ibid., sec. 210.
58. Ibid., sec. 211.
59. Ibid., sec. 211.

there remains the proposition that *this* is how we calculate."[60] What if someone, an aesthetic skeptic in the extreme, were to ask what gives us the right to count Titian's *The Three Ages of Man* as a work of art?[61] We ought not to say here that our justification for this claim rests on the conferral of status conducted in Titian's time. This is, rather, aesthetic scaffolding, and as such is *fixed*; we answer best—if we answer at all—by saying, like saying *this* is how we calculate, *this* is a work of art.

At this precise juncture many have thought that a way is open for the skeptic to continue in a way that in fact is not. The skeptic, who tries to relieve his skepticism with the institutional theory, wants to say that our response just shows that the aesthetic ground, i.e., what is fixed, *is* a matter of truth and falsehood, and that indeed everything calls for justification. Wittgenstein asks, "Can I believe for one moment that I have ever been in the stratosphere? No. So do I *know* the contrary, like Moore?"[62] The suspiciousness of this Mooreian conclusion, that we know this *because* we cannot seriously entertain the contrary, is indicated by the emphasis placed on the word *know*, and it is followed by the answer "There cannot be any doubt about it for me as a reasonable person.—That's it.—"[63] Nor can we, without lapsing into an irrationality bordering on madness, *seriously* doubt the Titian in the way encouraged by the aesthetic skeptic.[64]

---

60. Ibid., sec. 212.

61. I do not mean here the case in which such a question can arise, viz., when a connoisseur is called into service to scrutinize brush-strokes for the verification of an attribution under suspicion of forgery. That is honest doubt, not philosophical skepticism, and it is thus clear how to proceed in pursuit of certainty.

62. Wittgenstein, *On Certainty*, sec. 218. Naturally much of *On Certainty* can be read as a commentary on Moore; this way of putting it also clearly brings out the mistake of making all of epistemology a matter of postreflective knowledge. As I am attempting to show, this is also the fatal weakness endemic to the institutional theory.

63. Ibid., sec. 219.

64. If the skeptic claims at this point that we are thus holding fast to one proposition, i.e., that the Titian is a work of art, we should then respond, as does Wittgenstein to a parallel claim, "What I hold fast to is not *one* proposition but a nest of propositions." Ibid., sec. 225. Moreover, the "nest" we hold to will not uniformly relate to one concept only—in this case the concept "work of art"—but to a number of interrelated concepts; this fact further erodes the credibility of the definitional project of aesthetic essentialism. I discuss this issue in connection with literary aesthetics in *Meaning and Interpretation*, pp. 149–78.

In a last-ditch attempt to keep this way into doubt open, the
skeptic might say, "Well, just suppose that you really *do* doubt the
inclusion of the following one hundred works in the category
'Works of Art' " and he then lists the Titian and ninety-nine others.
If the skeptic says, in the nagging style characteristic of epistemologically indiscriminate aesthetic skeptics, "What would you say
then?" it is surely a temptation—but a mistake—to answer in
terms of conferred status. To justify scaffolding is to collaborate
with skepticism, and at the end of our explanations we will find,
not our multiform aesthetic practices, but the institutional theory.
It is *not* a mistake to resist this temptation, to close off this avenue
into skepticism, and to say, as Wittgenstein does, "The reasonable
man does *not have* certain doubts."[65] The skeptic will insist, "But
I said *suppose* you doubt these one hundred works," and we should
then answer, "Can I be in doubt at *will?*"[66] Doubt, as the pragma-
tist tradition has demonstrated in opposition to the Cartesian
method in epistemology, is not subject to the will—that is to say,
not *really*.[67] If attempts to understand the arts, to cast light on the
place they have in life, and to locate them within a nexus of cultural and social practices, are not concerned with what are in reality the facts of the case, then—insofar as they house within their
seemingly auspicious beginnings[68] a requirement to take a kind of
doubt seriously that in point of fact *cannot* be so taken—those
attempts ought to be regarded, if for rather complex reasons, as

65. Wittgenstein, *On Certainty*, sec. 220.

66. Ibid., sec. 221.

67. See for example C. S. Peirce, "Some Consequences of Four Incapacities," *Journal of Speculative Philosophy* 2 (1868): pp. 140–141, reprinted in *Classical American
Philosophy*, ed. John Stuhr (New York: Oxford University Press, 1987), pp. 32–33.
Peirce provides here a particularly useful maxim: "Let us not pretend to doubt in philosophy what we do not doubt in our hearts" (32). More pointedly, he writes, "Many
and many a philosopher seems to think that taking a piece of paper and writing down
'I doubt that' is doubting it, or that it is a thing he can do in a minute as soon as he
decides what he wants to doubt" (p. 88).

68. It is true that in his most recent formulation of what he still regards as the institutional theory, Dickie has removed any discussion of the explicit conferral of status, and
thus has obscured the central role of the aesthetic doubt to which conferral is a response.
See George Dickie, *The Art Circle* (New York: Haven Press, 1985). But in fact this
removal seems to eradicate the *institutional* character of the theory. See Richard Wollheim, *Painting as an Art* (London: Thames and Hudson, 1987), pp. 13–17 and p. 358, n.1.

engaging only with appearance instead of working with reality. In his influential contributions to aesthetics, Joseph Margolis has attempted to describe, through a theory of aesthetic ontology, that very reality, and it is thus to an examination of his position, and of where his position leads us, that we shall turn in Chapter 8.

8   Art and Cultural Emergence

Providing a succinct encapsulation of his own position in regard to the nature and definition of art, Joseph Margolis has stated confidently, "Works of art, then, are culturally emergent entities, tokens-of-a-type that exist embodied in physical objects."[1] This definition warrants very serious consideration, and I begin by following the path of reason he has taken to arrive at it.

MARGOLIS AND AESTHETIC DUALISM

In his initial remarks setting out the strategy for a philosophy of art, Margolis cites P. F. Strawson's *Individuals*, where, with respect to a larger but perhaps not fundamentally dissimilar problem from that of the nature of art, it is argued that both persons and bodies are ontologically basic, and that while both P and M (personal and material) attributes can be properly ascribed to persons, only M attributes can be properly ascribed to bodies. Therefore, persons are not identical with, and thus cannot be reduced to, physical bodies.[2] In reminding us of Strawson's contribution, Margolis explicitly says that "Strawson refused to countenance a Cartesian dualism regarding persons,"[3] yet he quickly adds an acknowledgment of some of

1. Joseph Margolis, *Art and Philosophy* (Atlantic Highlands: Humanities Press, 1980), p. 24.
2. P. F. Strawson, *Individuals* (London: Methuen, 1959).
3. Margolis, *Art and Philosophy*, p. 2.

the most salient limitations of Strawson's position, namely, that the *relationship* between persons and bodies has never been explained in acceptably nondualistic terms and that a respectably consistent Strawsonian would have to admit that, even on this allegedly nondualistic ontological scheme, two distinct entities, different in kind at a basic level (as one is the subject of P and the other of M ascriptions), must occupy the same place at the same time.[4] The diffidence that these rather dark ontological problems might engender is quickly replaced by optimism within the context of aesthetics, with Margolis identifying the important lesson from Strawson's work as contained in the claim that "persons and physical bodies cannot be distinguished from one another in any purely perceptual way."[5] It would be a short step to the analogous claim that works of art and physical objects cannot, mutatis mutandis, be distinguished from one another in any purely perceptual way either, but instead of rushing to this analogous aesthetic assertion Margolis first tells us that persons and bodies can be explained (although Strawson did not do so) as being "(nondualistically) 'affiliated.' "[6] Moreover, once we grasp this point, there awaits an analogous assertion in the philosophy of language, i.e., that words and sentences cannot be reduced to, or exhaustively identified with, the sounds and marks with which they are "affiliated," where here too the distinction between these categorical types cannot be made by purely perceptual means. Having thus enriched the postponed aesthetic assertion by showing first its interrelations to the ontology of persons and second its interrelations, in the post-Wittgensteinian philosophical world, to a particularly resonant formulation of the problem of linguistic meaning (i.e., how the "sign" gets its "life"), Margolis suggests that perhaps *all* cultural phenomena exhibit the characteristic of being nondualistically and nonreductively affili-

4. I emphasize that this problem of two entities occupying the same place arises on *this* ontological scheme. In fact, whether one is perceiving "one thing" or "two things" depends on the needs of the context. One person may see a face of a familiar figure in a mosaic, or in an arrangement of beads, while another does not; the methods of counting perceived entities, objects, or patterns, or the recognition of internal relations, will be context-specific.

5. Ibid., p. 3.

6. Ibid.

ated with physical bodies or material entities. Thus works of art, as cultural phenomena and as analogues to the person-body connection and the sound-meaning connection, are similarly affiliated with physical objects. We have, in short, begun to piece together an understanding of Margolis's own definition of art with which we began, or at least of the last phrase of that definition, an artwork existing "in physical objects."

Strawson is by no means the only philosopher concerned with ontological questions discussed by Margolis in the delineation of his strategy for a philosophy of art. Danto, we are reminded, has claimed that, through the employment of the "is" of artistic identification, we distinguish works of art from physical objects, and that this difference prevents us from identifying, or exhaustively reducing, the artwork to the object.[7] Of course particularly problematic works, or works that provoke among their percipients the question "Why is this not *just* a Brillo box, plumbing fixture, bottle rack?" can indeed be "easily mistaken for real objects,"[8] but the mistake in such cases would be precisely that of failing to recognize (which is not the same as refusing to acknowledge) that the art object enjoys a "double citizenship," holding passports, as it were, for two-way commerce between the real world and the art world. At this point the Strawsonian ring to this aesthetic assertion is undeniably clear, and Margolis is surely right to place these views pertaining to Art on the one hand and Persons on the other in such close conceptual proximity. Danto, however, has two claims here: first, that it would be possible to identify two distinct artworks,[9] each possessing different kinds of properties, that are in fact indistinguishable by unaided perception alone, and second, that to identify an object as an artwork is to transcend mere perception, i.e., to invoke historical, intentional, causal, or conceptual-theoretical (all allegedly nonperceptual) reasons in justification. Danto is reiterat-

7. Arthur Danto, "The Artworld," *Journal of Philosophy* 61, no. 19 (1964): 571–84.
8. Margolis, *Art and Philosophy*, p. 4.
9. This is the visual analogue to the competing senses of, e.g., the word "TIMES" referred to above, or the multiple meanings of the word "bank" (i.e., financial, river, billiards, and so on) hovering as possibilities until the word is dropped into context. In Danto's case, of course, the visual ambiguity would need to outlive contextual placement.

ing the claims, albeit the aesthetically analogous claims, that generated the trouble for Strawson, and at this point conceptual proximity is escalated to guilt by association. Margolis claims that, with regard to both Strawson's and Danto's positions, "to the extent that each contradicts the very distinction on which it rests"[10] it must fall, Strawson having two numerically distinct and mutually irreducible entities occupying the same place, where the occupation of place is the criterion of identity, and Danto facing the incompatible claims that a given work of art both is and is not a physical object. Whether or not these are the best possible succinct formulations of these views, and thus whether they really capture the heart of the problem or the deeper tensions housed within each position, is debatable. It is at least clear, however, that Margolis has identified strategies that in outward appearance look very much like his own, but from which he wants to disentangle himself, having seen that, in those positions, the crucial relationships with which they are concerned have been left unspecified. We have heard of *basic* P and M ontological entities and of entities enjoying double citizenship, and in both cases we have had repudiations, but not convincing refutations, of the dualism implicit in these analogous views. This is the dualism that Margolis sees must be obviated, and to pursue his contribution to this problem we must turn to another phrase of his own encapsulated definition, the "token-of-a-type."

Beginning with the more general and less tangible side of this distinction, Margolis explains that by "types" he means "abstract particulars of a kind that can be instantiated."[11] For example, prints pulled from Dürer's engraving *Melancholia I* instantiate the *Melancholia I* type. A captivating way to put the matter generally is to say, as Margolis goes on to do, that artists make tokens of the type they have created, and that they *cannot* create the type unless they instantiate that type in a made token. Thus, just as on Margolis's version of the Strawsonian account, we cannot on purely perceptual grounds distinguish a person from a body, and just as in

10. Ibid., p. 7.
11. Ibid., p. 18.

Danto's description we are relying on a distinction between artworks and physical objects that the "eye cannot descry," so in Margolis's employment of the type-token distinction an artist like
Duchamp creates the type "bottle rack" by making (or, rather, in
this case, "making") an instance of that type, where the manufac-
turers of the actual bottle rack did *not* make a token-of-a-type.
They did of course make *something*, namely, the material out of
which Duchamp made the instantiated type; they did *not*, however, make the token. Margolis encapsulates this part of his position by saying that in the use of the notion of embodiment, "My
own suggestion is that token works of art are embodied in physical
objects, not identical with them."[12] Thus he explicitly draws on
the analogy with the perception of persons that has been implicitly
relied upon from the outset, adding that "persons, similarly, are
embodied in physical bodies but not identical with them." With
this last phrase we can now see how the term "embodiment" found
its way into the encapsulated definition with which we began, and
with the larger Strawsonian model applied to aesthetics, we can see
how it is allegedly the token-of-a-type that is embodied. If we look
at these conjoined ideas more closely, however, I think the magnitude of the task of overcoming or escaping dualism within this type
of aesthetic theory will appear larger than Margolis has heretofore
allowed.

Let us first look at the features of the type-token distinction as
Margolis wants to use it. He says, first, that "types and tokens are
individuated as particulars." The startling assertion here, I take it, is
that *types* are being defined as particulars. Types are, however, as we
have already been told, embodied *in* particulars. It would seem a reasonable condition of intelligibility that they be separable from those
particulars; were such separability not available the very idea of
embodiment, as we normally understand the word, would remain
impenetrably mysterious. Nevertheless, the next feature of types
and tokens is, indeed, that they "are not separable and cannot exist
separately from one another." Thus, it would appear, tokens *and*
types are both particulars and yet intertwined or commingled in

12. Ibid., p. 21.

such a way that neither eye nor mind can identify one in isolation from the other. We are, it seems, already in rather deep trouble, because again the concept of embodiment is central to the definition and its cogency is thus crucial; yet at this point types and tokens, although in every customary philosophical employment categorically distinct, are here *not* distinct, and while they traditionally stand in a relation of general-to-particular, here they stand as particular-to-particular. Moreover, this last relationship eludes our intellective grasp, because type and token stand in this rather idiosyncratic use as particular-to-particular-yet-inseparable. This pull toward strings of hyphens seems endemic to this territory, and I think this is symptomatic of a deeper problem. The next feature of the type-token distinction as Margolis wants to use it is that "types are instantiated by tokens," which is clear, as we have seen, from what he has said earlier, where "embodiment" is the operative concept. He then goes on to explain this by adding that "token" is an ellipsis for "token-of-a-type," with the hyphens symptomatic of a desire to obviate the very kind of dualism enforced by the type-token apparatus. Yet Margolis would not, I suspect, accept the phrase "Person-in-a-body" as a philosophical *solution* to the Strawsonian problem, nor would he accept "Artwork-in-an-Object" as a solution to the ontological question raised by Duchamp and Warhol and articulated by Danto.[13]

The deep trouble we are in here is further manifested by the statement, "Types are actual abstract particulars only in the sense that a set of actual entities may be individuated as tokens of a particular type."[14] Beginning with the first part of this quotation, let us consider, if only briefly, the phrase "actual abstract particular," which is a densely packed amalgam of extremely counterintuitive combinations. If actual, then is it *abstract*? If abstract, then is it *particular*? Of course, "actual" and "particular" are conceptually harmonious, but they are the two components here *not* together. If we are to take these features as giving the real content to the phrase "token-of-a-type" as it appears in the encapsulated definition, then

13. Quotations in this paragraph are from ibid., p. 20.
14. Ibid.

it seems that we are owed substantial further elucidation. Directly stated, what we are given so far simply is not helping. The second part of the quotation given above is, I believe, far clearer, but it implicitly signals a change of subject from types and tokens. The qualifying line "only in the sense that a set of entities may be individuated as tokens of a particular type," brings to mind the familiar process of individuation according to a type; an artistic example would be that of identifying a particular Madonna and Child painting as one instance of the genre. This familiar variety of aesthetic individuation, however, is not the type-token distinction as Margolis wants to employ it; it in fact rather indicates how far his use of this distinction is from the familiar cases. His usage is rather more like ascertaining that rows of production-line vehicles are the end products of long labors expended on a *prototype*, or that a series of machine-made violins are tooled to the dimensions of their hand-carved prototype. Prototypes, as a change of subject, would appear to help, because they are *particular*, they are *made*, and they are not reducible to their production-line progeny. The help is only illusory, however, and the implicit change of subject is itself a further manifestation of conceptual difficulty, because prototypes are decidedly not embodied in their progeny. They are, in and of themselves, their own particulars. Thus to move to a discussion of prototypes could help relieve conceptual tensions in Margolis's account, but it would not help the aesthetic project of explaining what Duchamp does in creating *Bottlerack*, Warhol in producing *Brillo Box*, Rauschenberg in erasing de Kooning, or for that matter what any other artist is doing. It might help explain what printmakers do with engraved plates, but that, again, is too far down the production line to contribute to the central aesthetic question of definition.

These problems are only exacerbated when Margolis says that "it is incoherent to speak of comparing the properties of actual token- and type-particulars as opposed to comparing the properties of actual particular tokens-of-a-type."[15] Given what Margolis has already said, the attempt to compare a token-particular with a type-

15. Ibid.

particular should yield incoherence, because the one, being embodied in the other, is inseparable from it. But then, again, nothing is left of the concept of embodiment other than identity, i.e., the one *is* the other, and that is of course the very reduction to identity Margolis is most centrally concerned to avoid. We can compare, according to this feature of the type-token distinction, one "actual particular" with another, but then we are comparing the group of cars manufactured today with those from yesterday, the group of violins made this week with those from last week, and, in the artistic case, this Dali print with that one, or this run of a thousand with that run of a thousand. Although interesting aesthetic questions arise, in connection with such comparisons of existent particulars, concerning mechanical reproduction, forgery, unintended duplication, qualitative erosion through excessive printing, and the like, the issue of the *definition* of art and the explanation of what takes place, ontologically speaking, at its creation, remains untouched. Recalling Margolis's claim that artworks are *"embodied in physical objects, not identical with them,"* we arrive, in summary form, at this: If the claims that elucidate Margolis's use of the type-token distinction are coherent, then they are reductively physicalistic (and thus not really about *types* and tokens at all, but about prototypes and production models, or about tokens and tokens) and the concepts of "embodiment" and of "token-of-a-type" as they appear in the encapsulated definition are empty. And if they are not empty, they are—insofar as they refer to the embodiment of one kind of thing within another and the presence of an intangible entity within a physical object that transcends unaided sensory perception—dualistic.

PERCEIVING ARTWORKS AND SEEING PERSONS

It takes neither argument nor subtlety to see that persons exhibit an enormously broad range of properties that bodies do not, thus reserving linguistic space for each and every one of the Strawsonian P predicates or ascriptions that are quite clearly not ascribable to a material body. To see that this is the case, we need only imagine

the profoundly deep shock, or perhaps terror, that a coroner would
feel if, after a lifetime of contact with a good number of bodies, one
day the bodies were all suddenly to start exhibiting person-properties. It seems beyond dispute that persons and bodies[16] fall into separate, i.e., ontologically distinct, categories. We have seen that
Margolis has imported this categorical distinction between persons
and bodies from metaphysics into aesthetics and employed it as the
model for the closely analogous distinction between artworks and
physical objects; we have also seen him remark on a similarly perceived distinction between meaning and marks or sounds in the
philosophy of language. The prevalence of all of these distinctions
in recent philosophy is beyond doubt, and, as I hope to show in
more positive terms below, the understanding of art can only be
enriched by placing it next to our understanding of persons and our
understanding of language. Moreover, the potential illuminating
power of these analogies between persons, language, and art, is
nourished by our knowing the transformative difference it makes
to our perception when, for example, a seemingly lifeless accident
victim suddenly moves, or we are told that a set of seemingly
meaningless marks in the sand is a message encoded in obscure
symbols, or we suddenly realize that the LeCorbusier chair we are
about to sit on in the gallery is in fact part of the exhibition. For the
perceiver in such cases, a body becomes a person, marks become
language, and an object becomes an artwork. But these intuitions,
categories, and analogies can mislead as well as illuminate. Among
modern philosophers Wittgenstein was perhaps most aware of the
conceptual dangers here, and in the *Philosophical Investigations* he
discussed in detail the nature of the distinction between persons
and bodies that Margolis has employed as his model. Wittgenstein
also showed that, out of that distinction, there quietly emanates a
dense conceptual fog.

   As the issue is shaped at this point, Margolis construes his definitional problem in aesthetics—the problem of what an artwork is,

---

16. To take an initial example, one might think of the response to war photography,
where one rightly describes the scene as one in which there are "bodies everywhere."
On the view under discussion, *this* kind of perception would constitute a physical
constituent in the perception of persons—which it obviously does not.

given that it invites ascriptions of properties above and beyond those allowed by the physical object in which it is (nondualistically) embodied—on the model of the following question: What is a person such that it invites (or in this case demands) ascriptions of properties above and beyond those allowed by physical bodies? This formulation of the question in metaphysics concerning persons is structured in such a way that, to put it strongly, in seeing persons we see bodies first, i.e., it is the body we first see, identify it with M ascriptions, and then transcend what it intrinsically allows, moving up to P ascriptions. A weaker variant would be that part of our seeing a person involves the seeing of a body, such that in seeing a person we see a synthesis of M and P properties. Either formulation suggests that, on this view, the perception of persons involves, either as a prerequisite or contemporaneously, the perception of bodies. To make the aesthetic analogy explicit, the perception of artworks would involve the prerequisite or contemporaneous perception of physical objects.

Regarding the perception of bodies, Wittgenstein's reliably errant interlocutor (here appearing in the guise of a behaviorist), asks, "But doesn't what you say come to this: that there is no pain, for example, without *pain-behavior*?" Resisting this kind of reduction, Wittgenstein responds immediately with the well-known passage "It comes to this: only of a living human being and what resembles (behaves like) a living human being can one say: it has sensations; it sees; is blind; hears; is deaf; is conscious or unconscious."[17] The important contrast for our present purposes is that we do not say these things, or rather make these ascriptions of sensation, of sight, of consciousness, and so forth, all of which lie beyond the kinds of ascriptions allowed by physical bodies, of anything *other* than living human beings. More directly, we do not make such ascriptions to *bodies*. This becomes even clearer in the following discussion, which turns next to the fairy tale in which the pot can see and hear. (This is of course again the interlocutor's suggestion.) Is this not a clear refutation? A pot is not a human being, yet, at least within the

17. Both quotations from Ludwig Wittgenstein, *Philosophical Investigations*, 3d ed., trans. G. E. M. Anscombe (New York: Macmillan, 1958), sec. 281.

imaginary world of the child's tale, we make the allegedly pro-
scribed ascription. Wittgenstein responds this time with the paren-
thetical remark, "Certainly; but it *can* also talk,"[18] and this
imputed capacity shows that this is in fact, within the context of
this charming fairy tale, something like the limiting case of anthro-
pomorphism, i.e., the entire concept of personhood is first established (through the capacity of speech and all that that implies) and
then we ascribe this humanity to a previously inanimate object, the
pot. In a following passage, the point is amplified through the case
of children saying of an inanimate object that it is in pain. Is this a
refutation? Again, it is an exception that further proves the rule,
because the inanimate object is a doll, so again the initial imputa-
tion of humanity precedes the ascription of sentience, thus again
showing that we do *not* in fact make such ascriptions to inanimate
objects. Reiterating the initial point, Wittgenstein says, "Only of
what behaves like a human being can one say that it *has* pains."[19]

Recall that the formulation of the metaphysical question that
we have considered thus far leads us to explain how it is that we
transcend what it is we "really" see at the level of unaided perception, that is, bodies, and proceed to a perception of persons above
and beyond those perceptual preliminaries. Consider then
Wittgenstein's next remark: "Look at a stone and imagine it having sensations." At first glance, this would seem a strikingly curious remark to make in this discussion. If the perceptual theory of
persons we are entertaining as a basis for work in aesthetics is correct, however, then this ought not to be so odd, because the perceptual theory holds that we ascribe person-attributes above and
beyond the material attributes we ascribe to a perceived body. But
Wittgenstein, responding to this suggestion, adds, "One says to
oneself: How could one so much as get the idea of ascribing a *sensation* to a *thing*? One might as well ascribe it to a number!" That
is to say, this is extraordinarily odd, as odd as ascribing sentience
to an abstract entity, as odd as reporting to a theorem that the
number "2" cannot participate in the calculation because it has a

18. Ibid., sec. 282.
19. Ibid., sec. 283.

terrible headache. Wittgenstein's next step is to restore us to intellectual sobriety with the remark, "And now look at a wriggling fly and at once these difficulties vanish and pain seems able to get a foothold here, where before everything was, so to speak, too smooth for it." The metaphor of smoothness is appropriate, because it makes salient the "hardness" of the conceptual surface of inanimate objects, i.e., far from being an essential component or basis of our ascriptions of human features like sentience, such objects are rather antithetical to such ascriptions. But then what of the *body*? Wittgenstein next remark is, "And so, too, a corpse seems to us quite inaccessible to pain." Here again such dark tones are inescapable, because bodies are not what constitute persons, they constitute corpses, and thus while persons are animate, sentient, conscious, unconscious, and so forth, bodies, in and of themselves or as constituents of some larger metaphysical construction, are not. Indeed, on the distinction between bodies and persons, Wittgenstein says, "All our reactions are different.—If anyone says: 'That cannot simply come from the fact that a living thing moves about in such-and-such a way and a dead one not,' then I want to intimate to him that this is a case of the transition 'from quantity to quality.' " This last phrase, an expression with which Wittgenstein is obviously not entirely happy, is for our present purposes perhaps the most significant. A change in *quantity* would be the change of proceeding, up the ascriptive scale, from M predicates to P predicates, from the initial recognition of a body to the recognition of a person. By contrast, to characterize this distinction, surely more accurately, as a change in quality strongly suggests that such an ascriptive *ascent* is not made, but that we have a change of a more fundamental order.[20]

Still, one might feel compelled to insist, putting it linguistically, that there simply must be such an ascriptive ascent or, to put it metaphysically, that the material simply must be a component of

20. All quotations in this paragraph are from ibid., sec. 284. The final point is, it must be said, probably compatible with Strawson's theory, because after all he was arguing for the *basic* nature of both categories. My present concern, of course, is with Margolis's employment of the Strawsonian distinction in aesthetics, with which this is clearly not compatible.

the personal. But does the material, the physical, play the role it should if this were true?[21] This insistence is met by Wittgenstein's next section: "Think of the recognition of *facial expressions*. Or of the description of facial expressions—which does not consist in giving the measurements of the face! Think, too, how one can imitate a man's face without seeing one's own in a mirror."[22] Measurements of the face, a minute description of its material state of being, do not enter into the recognition of and response to facial expressions; it would be extremely odd if they did. Nor need we examine our own facial-material state of being in a mirror when adopting another's expression; if it were true that the facial-material is relevant in the way that the theory implies, then it would be odd that we in fact do *not* need to do this—which is in fact not odd in the least. In summary, the more we look for the bodily component in the perception and ascription of human features the more remote that component becomes, which is Wittgenstein's meaning, with revealing italicized emphasis, in the question "But isn't it absurd to say of a *body* that it has pain?"[23] But *not* to say such a thing now seems enormously difficult—precisely because of the pervasive misleading influence of this dualistic conception of the self.[24]

Let us return from the prototype in metaphysics to its progeny in aesthetics. Margolis sees the understanding of persons as being closely related to the understanding of artworks, and has identified

21. To say that this dualistic conception of the self is misleading is not to say that every utterance tending toward the mental, or toward the physical, is confused. This, incidentally, is why Ryle's diagnosis in terms of the Cartesian "Myth" is too stark. See Gilbert Ryle, *The Concept of Mind* (New York: Barnes and Noble, 1949), pp. 11–24. Any account of the self must accommodate the facts, as John Wisdom has identified them, "which lead people to say that a person has a way of knowing how he feels which no one else has, has a right to say what he does about how he feels which no one else has ever had or ever will have." See John Wisdom, *Other Minds* (Oxford: Basil Blackwell, 1952), pp. 238–44. The recognition of such facts *need* not, however, give rise to a skepticism about other minds, just as, in our case, the analogous aesthetic dualism is not *necessitated*.

22. Wittgenstein, *Philosophical Investigations*, sec. 285.

23. Ibid., sec. 286.

24. See ibid., sec. 286; see also sec. 417, where a parallel point of philosophical logic is made about the oddity of observing, or perceiving on the basis of evidence, that we are ourselves conscious.

the central puzzle as that of getting beyond the body or physical object to the person or work of art. We have seen that the encapsulated definition promises a solution to this problem, but we have also seen that the phrase "tokens-of-a-type" as it appears in that definition is problematic. Equally problematic is the employment of the related concept of embodiment; as we have seen, the metaphysical origins of the idea of "physical object" are uncertain. The role of that idea in the perception of artworks will, by conceptual parity, remain as dubious as the role of bodies in the perception of persons.

There is, however, a component of Margolis's definition we have not yet considered. This is the notion of cultural emergence, and it is this idea which lies at the center of Margolis's attempt to obviate dualism. He says, "But particular works of art cannot exist except as embodied in physical objects. This is simply another way of saying that works of art are culturally emergent entities; that is, they exhibit properties that physical objects cannot, but do not depend on the presence of any substance other than what may be ascribed to purely physical objects."[25] We are here again given with the right hand the now-familiar idea of an object exhibiting properties which transcend the limits of that object, but as we are given it, the left hand takes away the traditionally associated Cartesian idea of the presence of another substance in which those exhibited properties inhere. This maneuver, as we have seen, strains coherence, but the strain is allegedly relieved by cultural emergence. We have here a denial of dualism through the denial of the existence of another substance, but what we are here given is blunt repudiation, and not, I think, obviation. How, apart from the Cartesian categories we have already considered, have we arrived at this position?

From empiricism we are familiar, perhaps overly familiar, with the distinction between primary and secondary qualities. The primary qualities, of course, were thought to be actually in the object perceived, such that a relation of resemblance obtained between the idea of the object and the object itself; the secondary qualities, by contrast, were thought to depend, for their existence as percep-

25. Margolis, *Art and Philosophy*, p. 23.

tual qualities, on human perception. Culturally emergent properties, such as "design, expressiveness, symbolism, representation,
meaning, style, and the like,"[26] are apparently dependent upon aesthetic perception for their existence, and exist beyond what the
physical object just is. From ethics we are familiar with the conception of evaluation hovering above description, with the facts of
the matter being fixed and the values floating around them. Culturally emergent aesthetic properties apparently "float" in the
same way above the fixed objects below. From aesthetics proper,
Margolis himself says that the point of admitting the issue of interpretation into any discussion in aesthetics is "simply that it entails
that artworks must be entities quite distinct from mere physical
objects, or objects accessible merely through sensory perception."[27]
Yet an interpretation is not "something *added* to an artwork—
intact, so to say, without an interpretation; we are speaking, rather,
of what often must be supplied in order to be able to speak of a
work of art at all, that is, to give a reasonably adequate account of
its properties."[28] Thus emergent properties are the aesthetic properties "carried" within the interpretation of the work, where this
interpretation is not added to an object but the presence of the
interpretation is a prerequisite for speaking of the object as art.
Taken one way, this is again a move made against aesthetic dualism, because, even with its affinities to the Cartesian categories,
empiricist epistemology, and moral relativism, the interpretation is
not superadded to the object. Can this move take us beyond the
mere repudiation we already encountered? I do not believe that it
can, and this is borne out in the further elucidation of Margolis's
conception of interpretation.

Aesthetic realism holds that, if we encounter two competing
interpretations of a given work, and those interpretations are
incompatible, then at least one of them is false, a consequence of
aesthetic illusion, misperception, misapprehension, judgmental
error, and the like. On such realist grounds it could (whether or not
it should) be argued that the interpretation is in some way emergent

26. Ibid.
27. Ibid., p. 31.
28. Ibid.

from the object, and that the emergent properties are contained within this interpretation. Margolis explicitly rejects this view, however, claiming instead that "it is logically possible to identify one and the same work under alternative and incompatible interpretations (each interpretation compatible with the minimally describable features of the work in question), where the truth value of further characteristics and appraisals of given works will be affected by such intensional identification."[29] It follows that the interpretation can be severed from the object and replaced by another equally plausible, where the equal plausibility will be determined by a prior minimal description. To illustrate this return to the traditional and irremediably dualistic distinction between description and interpretation, let me bring up once again that line drawing with the notoriously uncertain identity. If I say, "Look, those are rather elongated ears on that rabbit, aren't they?" and you say, in surprise, "What?! Do ducks have protruding ears, really?" then it is clear that my criticism of the drawing as having excessively long ears is both irrelevant and false on your interpretation,

29. The simultaneity of properties is here crucial, since this is why they are incompatible. In many cases the incompatibility of descriptions is only apparently problematic, since the competing descriptions arise out of separate contexts and thus do not in fact collide; this is a fact often missed by philosophers—or art critics—with minimal tolerances for seeming or apparent contradiction. It might also be remarked here that such cases never in fact endorse a perceptual relativism in the way they are taken to do, since it is, in such cases as the duck-rabbit, objectively true that a case of visual ambiguity is before us, and *that* fact is not open to interpretation. See Renford Bambrough, "Literature and Philosophy," in *Wisdom: Twelve Essays*, ed. Renford Bambrough (Oxford: Basil Blackwell, 1974), p. 289. In this connection consider as well the passage in Wittgenstein, *Philosophical Investigations*, p. 205: " 'Her picture smiles down on me from the wall.' It need not always do so, whenever my glance lights on it." Indeed, when a multitude of aspects, of associations, of thoughts and feelings, surround the picture in such a way that we are "enveloped" within it, then it "smiles." This is an experience exactly like, as we say, being "reached" by a person. The fact that we are sometimes beyond the reach of a person, or that the person fails to reach us, is not by any means an argument for the position that they *never* so reach us, or do not *really* do so; here again we arrive at the parallel process of perceiving persons and perceiving works of art, which I have discussed more fully in *Meaning and Interpretation: Wittgenstein, Henry James, and Literary Knowledge* (Ithaca: Cornell University Press, 1994), pp. 84–148. See also pp. 209–10 of *Philosophical Investigations*, where Wittgenstein discusses the competing claims, made in response to hearing the plaint in a plaintive melodic passage, "I hear it" *versus* "I don't really *hear* it," and the case of coming to "feel the seriousness of a tune."

and your remarks about the elongated bill will be similarly irrelevant for me. Moreover, if I say that the duck is drawn as a strong
and confident member of the species, and you say that the rabbit
looks shy and diffident, then these properties emerge from the
drawing at high speed and collide head-on. They are after all equally
plausible, both determined by (competing) minimal descriptions,
and absolutely incompatible as properties held simultaneously[30] by
an object. On Margolis's view, the object beneath the emergent
properties stays fixed, and the emergent properties themselves—
well—hover. Just as secondaries are detachable from primaries on
empirical grounds, and as evaluations are detachable from descriptions on moral-relativistic grounds, so emergent properties are
detachable from underlying physical objects on these aesthetic
grounds. This is, in short, a perfect example of aesthetic dualism,
and it seems to proceed from the idea of emergence.

An interpretation, on this view, is a repository of emergent properties, and as such is not unlike what one might call the soul of an
object of art. In this connection I want to consider a few further
remarks of Wittgenstein. In a discussion well beyond the passages
we considered above, the interlocutor asks, expressing precisely the
sort of persistent dualism we are considering, "But can't I imagine
that the people around me are automata, lack consciousness, even
though they behave in the same way as usual?" That is, can't I see
people just for what they are *physically*, or as mobile clusters of M
ascriptions, without the emergent person-properties? Wittgenstein
answers, "If I imagine it now—alone in my room—I see people
with fixed looks (as in a trance) going about their business—the
idea is perhaps a little uncanny. But just try to keep hold of this
idea in the midst of your ordinary intercourse with others, in the
street, say!" That is, as a fleeting—and uncannily inhuman—
thought-experiment this state can be momentarily sustained, but it
is in any case quite obviously alien to our regular, theoretically
uninterrupted perception of persons. He continues, "Say to yourself, for example: 'The children over there are mere automata; all
their liveliness is mere automatism.' And you will either find these

30. Margolis, *Art and Philosophy*, p. 43.

words becoming quite meaningless; or you will produce in yourself some kind of uncanny feeling, or something of the sort."[31] The feeling, if sustained, *is* uncanny and, again, inhuman and obviously alien to our actual perception of persons.[32] Yet, if the perceptual model Margolis is employing were correct, this should be among the most familiar of human perceptual experiences, because we would see the emergent humanity in a person just as we would the emergent aesthetic properties, or the "soul," of an artwork. The attraction of dualism is strong, however, and its employment is habitual. Thus, as Wittgenstein says, "It seems paradoxical to us that we should make such a medley, mixing physical states and states of consciousness up together in a *single* report: 'He suffered great torments and tossed about restlessly.' It is quite usual; so why do we find it paradoxical? Because we want to say that the sentence deals with both tangibles and intangibles at once." Indeed, it *seems* paradoxical to mix up in a single report of an artwork both tangibles and intangibles, simultaneously, and it *seems* that we stand in need of a theory to explain how it is we so readily accomplish this metaphysical merger. But is the reality of such mergers really so odd? Wittgenstein continues, "But does it worry you if I say: 'these three struts give the building stability'? Are three and stability tangible?—Look at the sentence as an instrument, and at its sense as its employment."[33]

To look at the sentences we use, with mixed intangibles, in the art world or the large and multifarious language-games attending to it, would of course lead well beyond the reach of present purposes. To show the analogies between that language and the language we use in connection with our multifarious perception of persons would constitute still a further project. For the present, it is clear that Margolis's theory does accomplish the large task of bringing these issues together, so that language, persons, and artworks each

31. This quotation, and all previous ones in this paragraph, are from Wittgenstein, *Philosophical Investigations*, sec. 420. See also John Cook, "Human Beings," in *Studies in the Philosophy of Wittgenstein*, ed. Peter Winch (London: Routledge & Kegan Paul, 1969), pp. 117–51, where these passages are discussed in connection with the problem of other minds.

32. See also Wittgenstein, *Philosophical Investigations*, Part II, sec. iv, p. 178.

33. This quotation and the previous one are from ibid., sec. 421.

inform and shape our conception of the others. But he states, again confidently, that within his scheme, "In admitting entities of different kinds we implicitly admit the possibility of entities of one kind being embodied in entities of another—persons in sentient bodies, or works of art in physical objects and movements. So embodiment is essentially a question of reference and attribution, ontologically construed. Consequently it raises no question whatsoever of dualistic substances."[34] If, however, investigations of the phrase "tokens-of-a-type," of the conception of physical objects as analogues to material bodies, of the conception of embodiment itself, and of the conception of cultural emergence all lead to dualism in his definition of art, should we not believe that, while it explicitly avoids raising any direct questions of dualism, it avoids raising them only by concealing them, and that this concealment is the source of the initial plausibility of the definition? Margolis has indeed clearly shown that the nature of an understanding of persons will be very much like our understanding of works of art, and one can only applaud an achievement of that magnitude. If, however, the conception of persons with which we begin is, unlike a very different conception of persons suggested by Wittgenstein, fundamentally dualistic, then the resultant conception of art simply could not obviate dualism; indeed, it would be compelled, even if only covertly, to embrace it.

ARTWORKS AND HUMAN BEINGS

Given the analogical bridge now standing between the work of art and the person, we should look briefly, into some of the specific conceptual similarities supporting it. One approach would be to examine some salient aspects of artworks and of our critical language, and then to identify parallels in persons. Another tactic would look at some of the aspects of a human being as they have been identified by philosophers and then seek parallels in the arts. Here I will take the latter approach.

34. Margolis, *Art and Philosophy*, p. 44.

Charles Taylor provides a convenient list of such human aspects.[35] First, the concept of personhood "figures primarily in moral and legal discourse."[36] So does the concept of an artwork, both as a vehicle for moral discourse (see, for example, the works of Hogarth and David, and even less initially plausible cases like architecture)[37] and as an object of legal discourse (see, for instance, the Rothko legal disputes)[38] Second, a "person is a being with a certain moral status, or a bearer of rights." An artwork has, indeed, a kind of moral status, because its integrity, as we appropriately call it, can be violated by popularizations, film versions of novels, and inappropriate stylistic mergers, e.g., of classical and popular music. An artwork is without question a bearer of rights,[39] as is registered in our shocked and defensive reaction to its abuse in the phrase, "But that is a work of *art!*" Taylor continues, "But underlying the moral status, as its condition, are certain capacities. A person is a being who has a sense of self, has a notion of the future and the past, can hold values, makes choices; in short, can adopt life-plans." It would, of course, be going too far— too far beyond analogy toward identity—to claim that a work of art possesses a sense of self, but if we are speaking *analogically*, it would be difficult to find a better way of succinctly capturing the kind of internally generated coherence many artworks exhibit. Any sprawling, disjointed, architectural facade (or, indeed, "face"), standing in contrast to, say, the *Petit Trianon*, illustrates the quality: a quietly dignified and truly elegant *composure* and self-containedness, that simply is best described—and perhaps only

35. Charles Taylor, "The Concept of a Person," in *Human Agency and Language: Philosophical Papers*, vol. 1 (Cambridge: Cambridge University Press, 1985), pp. 97–144.

36. Ibid., p. 97, and the following brief quotations.

37. See, e.g., David Watkin, *Morality and Architecture* (Oxford: Oxford University Press, 1977).

38. Although the detailed sorting out of such cases is well beyond my concern here, such a project would prove of considerable conceptual value in showing how integrated—against claims for the morally-severed autonomy of the work of art—aesthetic and ethical issues in fact are; it would also show that the rights of a work can in fact be strong enough to compete with the rights of a person.

39. For the debate about film colorization, see Jerrold Levinson, "Colourization Ill-Defended," *British Journal of Aesthetics* 30 (1990): 62–67.

describable—in these terms. Nor, of course, do artworks themselves possess notions of the future and the past, but they do
exhibit many varieties of historical relation, both to past and to
future works. Any archetypal work, any stylistically definitional
work, any work that becomes much imitated, or any work that is
"strong" enough to reorient the history of its genre behind it,[40]
exhibits such relations. "Can hold values" is Taylor's next feature
of personhood, which is quite clearly in evidence throughout the
arts, as are debates about that value,[41] and this feature is followed
by the slightly more difficult "makes choices." Again, the *work*
does not choose, but it indisputably serves as the embodiment of
a multitude of choices made on the part of its author. The sym-
metry of cantos in *The Divine Comedy* is an embodiment of a formal choice, just as the choice to pursue the inwardly revelatory is
embodied in Petrarch's sonnets, the choice to conflate sonic identities is embodied in Ives's work, and the choice to make no
choices is exemplified in Cage's aleatory composition. In a deeper
sense, however, artworks *can* "make choices." A collection of
quietly profound Rothko panels can, when put side to side with a
few bombastic sculpture-paintings of Stella, condemn them for
being visually cacaphonous. *Rothko*, of course, does not condemn;
he is absent. The works themselves can do this. Last on Taylor's
list, it would seem to range well beyond coherence to say that a
work of art adopts a "life-plan." But again, within the context of a
developing artistic style—and there are countless such cases—one
trajectory of development seems appropriate or fitting[42] within
the larger context from which the work emerges, whereas another
trajectory seems alien, remote, or ill-fitting. This is, of course, not
a life-plan, and is perhaps far from it, but it is no farther than anal-

---

40. I allude here to Harold Bloom's Oedipal view of the development of poetry; see
A Map of Misreading (Oxford: Oxford University Press, 1975), especially pp. 63–105.
   41. See, e.g., Barbara Herrnstein Smith, *Contingencies of Value: Alternative Per-
spectives for Critical Theory* (Cambridge: Harvard University Press, 1988), and, for a
brief discussion of this direction, my review of her work in *British Journal of Aesthetics* 30 (1990): 287–88.
   42. For a detailed discussion of this sense of fittingness see E. H. Gombrich, *The
Sense of Order* (Oxford: Phaidon, 1984), and Roger Scruton, *The Aesthetics of Architecture* (London: Methuen, 1979), pp. 206–36.

ogy is from identity: developmental trajectory is indisputably something *like* a life-plan.

Taylor next identifies the capacity to respond, and the appropriateness of being addressed in the first place, as salient human traits. These too find their direct parallels in the arts, and again at this preliminary level of generality there are countless cases. Among the more obvious ones are the processes of refinement to an emotional concept upon reading—or, indeed, "consulting," as we in some contexts put it—poetry or verse. Moreover, there is the familiar experience of finding a comparatively vague experience given specificity when we locate its mimetic depiction in poetry; this is a variety of aesthetic experience strikingly close to "addressing" a poet and getting a response. Taylor also mentions the feature of consciousness, where "consciousness is seen as a power to frame representations of things."[43] Quite apart from the accuracy of this definition of consciousness, it is vividly clear that the arts, at least the representational arts, very often shape, or indeed frame, our views or conceptions of the objects depicted. Again, this impression is almost too general to illustrate, but one need only imagine seventeenth-century Holland, and then ask oneself for the sources of those images, to see the point of the analogy. At a deeper level, however, Taylor identifies as essentially human the capacity to become engaged within a particular *situation*, where emotional descriptions of ourselves arise, and within which those descriptions are rendered appropriate, accurate, in need of revision, in need of further specification, and so on. Thus he says that "formulating how we feel, or coming to adopt a new formulation, can frequently change how we feel."[44] Of course, as humans, we can have this emotionally transformative effect on ourselves and on each other. But such "new formulations" can also be, and often are, the consequence not of human interaction, or self-reflection, but of aesthetic experience.

"Emotion terms," Taylor recognizes, are linked to "situation-descriptions," and some of the "significances a situation can have"

43. Taylor, "The Concept of a Person," p. 98.
44. Ibid., p. 100.

include " 'humiliating,' 'exciting,' 'dismaying,' 'exhilarating,' 'intriguing,' 'fascinating,' 'frightening,' 'provoking,' 'awe-inspiring,' 'joyful,' and so on."[45] Artworks are, invariably, placed in contexts and, within those situations, these emotively descriptive terms are rendered appropriate, accurate, in need of revision or further specification, and so on. The need for such descriptions often arises in aesthetics when comparisons are made within particular contexts, just as moral questions come up in human affairs. In fiction, for example, one often encounters full situation-descriptions which show—without directly saying—which "significance-terms" are accurate. Taylor summarizes this aspect of persons by saying that they exhibit an "openness to certain matters of significance," and the arts surely exhibit a parallel openness. Beyond these, one could easily imagine many further parallels between the perception of persons and the perception of artworks,[46] between ethics and aesthetics; these might include artistic integrity, internal coherence, developmental patterns, expansions and trajectories, the "break-

45. "The Concept of a Person," p. 107.
46. There is a closely related issue, beyond my present concerns, that would extend the analogy between artworks and persons that arises in relation to the human "I." Anscombe claims that " 'I am this thing here' is, then, a real proposition, but not a proposition of identity. It means: this thing here is the thing, the person . . . of whose action *this* idea of action is an idea, of whose movements *these* ideas of movements are ideas, of whose posture *this* idea of posture is the idea. And also, of which *these* intended actions, if carried out, will be the actions." G. E. M. Anscombe, "The First Person," in *Mind and Language*, ed. Samuel Guttenplan (Oxford: Oxford University Press, 1975) pp. 45–66. This claim, transmuted to aesthetics, would hold considerable significance. The artwork would be the object in which *this* aesthetic idea is situated, *this* movement (of line, of melody, of acting, of stylistic trajectory) is situated, *this* aesthetic "posture," and so forth. This way of putting the matter would obviate the need for Margolis's question, which stands as the artistic analogue to the question Anscombe's formulation obviates, namely, "But what is the self *apart* from all those things, to what *identity* does 'I' refer?" Anthony Kenny, in discussing Anscombe's claim, says, rather extremely, "For myself, I am wholly persuaded that 'I' is not a referring expression. . . . I accept that the 'self' is a piece of philosopher's nonsense produced by misunderstanding of the reflexive pronoun—to ask what kind of substance my *self* is is like asking what the characteristic of *ownness* is which my own property has in addition to its being *mine*." Anthony Kenny, *The Legacy of Wittgenstein* (Oxford: Basil Blackwell, 1984), pp. 77–87, quotation from p. 81. Thus to cast the matter one way, asking here for the substance of the self quite apart from the locus of these relational properties, is the metaphysical variant of the ontological question Margolis and those in his tradition ask.

ing" of a style or a set of expectations, and so on through what would be, in toto, an extraordinarily lengthy list.[47] The assemblage of such a survey would of course itself constitute a rather full philosophical investigation of a kind that would remain, against the various misleading influences of aesthetic theory, honest to our actual aesthetic practices.

In all of the preceding attempts to unsettle and rethink the sources and formulations of traditional aesthetic questions, as in this final brief sketch of the analogy between persons and artworks, it has been language, the richly multifarious capacities for description and for linguistic expression, that has been fundamental. One conception of language served as a foundation for aesthetic atomism in Langer's theory, where the forms embodied in works of art were thought to bear a logical resemblance to the forms of human feeling. But Langer's synthesis of formalism and linguistic atomism, insofar as that synthesis led us to expect the meaning of a work of art to be one metaphysical *kind* of thing and the physical outward symbol of that meaning another, generates the need for an escape from those very categories. Wittgenstein discovered that the picture-theory of meaning in the *Tractatus*—the view that a meaningful proposition bears a logical resemblance to a state of affairs in the world—could not be intelligibly stated even if it were true, and Langer's Tractarian aesthetics were found to lead to the same discovery.

47. Another way of extending the analogy between artworks and persons is taken by Eva Schaper, who has made clear the remarkable parallel that exists between the emotional attachments ensuing from our perception of people and works: "Perhaps the closest analogue to the regard for an object of aesthetic preference is that of the love in which one person can hold another. . . . And as the value attached to the object of love is not additional to what is already contained in the act of loving, so the values we place on the objects of our taste do not go beyond or outside what is grasped in the act of appraising them. Nevertheless, the emotion of love permeates the entire life of the person who loves. And so it is also with the pleasures of taste." Eva Schaper, "The Pleasures of Taste," in *Pleasure, Preference, and Value*, ed. Eva Schaper (Cambridge: Cambridge University Press, 1983), p. 51. See also in this connection Wollheim's closing remark in his review of Ashbery's and Updike's art criticism: "A sense of what is special about art depends on our recognizing that art is, strangely enough, something that we humans can love." Richard Wollheim, "Objects of Love," *Times Literary Supplement* (May 25–31, 1990): 553. See also Mary Mothersill, *Beauty Restored* (Oxford: Oxford University Press, 1984) pp. 405–8.

A somewhat different linguistic foundation was uncovered beneath Collingwood's aesthetic theory: here the idealist's belief that, in order to have meaning at all, there must be one-to-one correlations between thinking and speaking, or meaning and saying, was found to obscure more than it illuminates. Indeed, the idealistic sense in which Collingwood intended his compact assertion "Art must be language" led to absurd conclusions. If the raw emotive content of either language or art is first imaginatively specified or refined, and only later—and contingently—expressed in a linguistic or artistic manifestation, then the materials of art—the *medium*—are relegated to an undeservedly subordinate position vis-à-vis meaning. By reconsidering some of Wittgenstein's remarks on the complex relations between thought and speech—vastly more intricate than the simplified one-to-one correlation model would either suggest or allow—we gained a perspective from which to appreciate the aesthetic significance of Wittgenstein's remark: "When I think in language, there aren't 'meanings' going through my mind in addition to the verbal expressions; the language is itself the vehicle of thought."

In making the assertion, "Art is the language of the emotions," Ducasse was relying on a familiar conception of linguistic meaning best expressed by Locke; here again a prior conception of language generated a corresponding conception of art. If thoughts are initially "hidden from others," and only later linked to "sensible signs," i.e. words that stand for those hidden ideas, then we understand each other when the sign excites the same idea in the hearer that the speaker has linked to the sign. Ducasse contends that, if art is the language of the emotions, we understand an artist if we aesthetically experience a corresponding emotion, where this is excited by the "sign" of the work. Through an investigation into some particular cases, we saw that this linguistically generated model of artistic meaning is also too simple and theoretically neat to fit the facts. A brief inquiry into Wittgenstein's complicating remarks on the many kinds of things that actually occur (and that do *not* occur) in experiencing meaning—like the meaning of the name "Schubert"—revealed the irreparable unsoundness of the Lockeian distinction between idea and sign employed as a foundation for this way of construing artistic meaning.

Beginning with Wittgenstein's remark that we can want to speak without speaking, just as we can want to dance without dancing, and that thinking about wanting in this fashion leads us naturally to grasp at the *image* of speaking or dancing as a way to specify the content of the want, we turned directly to intentional considerations in art that are shaped by assumptions concerning linguistic intention. The dualistic criticism that these assumptions generated was found to falsify the facts of a number of individual cases of artistic creation and interpretation. Transferring Wittgenstein's advice—not to guess at how a word functions but to look at its use and to learn from that—from linguistics to aesthetics, we looked into cases where particularized questions of artistic intention actually arise. We found that the very sense of the general question of artistic intention—especially in music, where it seems to have ready application—was called very much into question. Indeed, "a misleading picture of 'intending,' " as Wittgenstein put it, also generates an initially plausible but ultimately misleading picture of artistic creativity, to which we turned in Chapter 5.

The translation model is obviously an aesthetic consequence of a linguistic position: here creativity is viewed as a process of rendering a preexistent meaning in a way directly analogous to linguistic translation. After sorting out a conflation of transitive and intransitive usage, however, and reconsidering aesthetic descriptions both of artworks and of facial expressions in such a way that nothing *apart* from the expressive phenomenon under consideration was available as a subject for description, we found that the concepts of creation and translation, commingled, mystify far more than they explain. Still, the phenomenon of searching for the right expression in writing seems almost to require the translation model. A look at cases, however, strongly suggested that the most relevant Wittgensteinian question here, "Do you have the thought before finding the expression?" does not have the unitary, affirmative answer it should have, if the translation model in fact applied even to the apparently most amenable cases. Indeed, the antiunitary acceptance of contextual complexity proved on reflection more enlightening than the unitary conception of creativity derived from a similarly strait-jacketed conception of linguistic meaning. Nevertheless, we are strongly inclined to privilege the artist with regard to any question of meaning, and even if the work of the artist is not accurately cast in terms of translation, still it seems that there must be some meaning-content to which the artist has *immediate* access.

Thus we turned to the significance of the private-language argument for aesthetics, beginning with the curious sense that artistic expression is impossible, insofar as it entails crossing the ontological divide from the animate and phenomenologically private to the inanimate and physically public. With this ontological divide in place, we are naturally led to the notion of an artist working from an "inner model," the inner private emotive content of the work that Langer called the "envisagement of feeling," Collingwood the "given emotion," and Ducasse "the feeling-image." These notions, it emerged, are the aesthetic analogues to the "private objects" under investigation in Wittgenstein's argument; if the meaning of the sign of a sensation "S" in a private-linguist's diary is not given by the inner object (which, as Wittgenstein shows, drops out as irrelevant), then the artistic version of "S"—a red stroke of oil on canvas—cannot, by parity, be given by an aesthetic inner object. Problems of consistency of use, of memory of the referent of "S," of inner-object identification, of the very possibility of being "right" about the sign-sensation relation, and the impossibility of there existing an inner table or chart to ascertain such relations, together called into question the entire underlying apparatus of object and designation, and of the very ontological divide with which this larger construction of the parallel problems of inner linguistic meaning and inner artistic meaning began.

Submerged but powerfully influential conceptions of language have not been absent in post-Wittgensteinian aesthetic theory. In reconsidering one foundational element of Danto's method—that of employing collections of perceptually indistinguishable counterparts with separate identities to focus on questions of aesthetic perception—we uncovered an atomistic analytical program that, in its distinctive way, harked back to the *Tractatus*. It also recalled notions of artistic perception shaped by deeper conceptions of linguistic meaning, specifically of basic word-world relations. Indeed, in art as in language we found that the uninterpreted constants over which descriptions and interpretations are placed, according to this analytical strategy, are not *basic* in the interpretively inert way they need to be if this analytical program is to prove viable not just for cases of genuine indistinguishables, e.g. Brillo boxes, snow shovels, bottle racks, and so forth, but for all art. Here, too, the very distinction at the base of the theory, between perception and description, does not on investigation prove as clear, or as structurally sound, as it should if it is to serve as a linguistic-perceptual foundation for an aesthetic theory.

Because Wittgenstein's remarks on certainty concern the giving of grounds in epistemology and the legitimacy of questions about those epistemic grounds, those remarks concern truth in language. Certainty and truth are certainly not foreign topics to aesthetics, and a reconsideration of Dickie's explicit institutionalism provided the occasion for bringing these subjects together here. It was a *general* skeptical question concerning artistic identity prerequisite to the institutional theory that proved most problematic; genuine doubt is not subject to the will, so what we need, what is truly prerequisite, is a genuine *particularized* question given life within an aesthetic context; otherwise we find ourselves, knowingly or not, attempting to "justify our scaffolding." Margolis's theory of culturally emergent artifacts provided an occasion to reconsider the logical behavior of the type-token distinction, itself drawn from the ontological sectors of the philosophy of language, and to encounter some of the illuminating interrelations between perceiving works of arts and perceiving persons. This in turn led us to a consideration of some of Wittgenstein's observations concerning the language we in fact use to speak of our perceptions of, and interactions with, human beings, and this, lastly, led us to a brief consideration of the striking similarities between our language about persons and our language about art.

One eminent aesthetician has said that "Wittgenstein would seem always to have remained of the opinion that, whereas the various false views of language can be stated or lend themselves to assertion, the true view is something that has to be seen—it remains a *view*."[48] This remark captures something of vital importance not only for an understanding of Wittgenstein's philosophy of language, but also for an understanding of the various asserted views of the arts that have been shaped by views of language. The remark may also help us understand what it means to move into a position of conceptual clarity that is itself an antidote to philosophical perplexity, leaving those false views in aesthetics and the linguistic misconceptions that engendered them behind. All of the foregoing has been, of course, an attempt to take a step in that direction. Because language has been fundamental to aesthetics in the many ways we have seen, it seems fair to say that, so long as we remain mindful of the many and various intricacies, difficulties, and dangers of art-language analogies, an investigation into language is among the best strategies at our disposal for achieving an understanding of artistic meaning and, indeed, of achieving a clear and perspicuous view of the vast range of visual, aural, and conceptual engagements that we call aesthetic experience.

48. Richard Wollheim, "The Art Lesson," in *On Art and the Mind* (Cambridge: Harvard University Press, 1974), p. 131. On the analogy between Wittgenstein's view of language and of art, consider his own statement: "What we call 'understanding a sentence' has, in many cases, a much greater similarity to understanding a musical theme than we might be inclined to think. But I don't mean that understanding a musical theme is more like the picture which one tends to make oneself of understanding a sentence; but rather that this picture is wrong, and that understanding a sentence is much more like what really happens when we understand a tune than at first sight appears." *The Blue and Brown Books* (Oxford: Basil Blackwell, 1958), p. 167. In discussing our compulsion to make such pictures of understanding, Wittgenstein memorably refers to the insistence to posit "something private," "the intangible *something*," as "a dream of our language," in *Philosophical Investigations*, sec. 358. Aesthetics also dreams.

INDEX